THE
ISLAMISTS
A CONTEXTUAL HISTORY OF POLITICAL ISLAM

BASHEER M NAFI

TRANSLATED BY ASLAM FAROUK-ALLI

First published in Arabic as *al-Islamiyun* in 2010 by Al Jazeera Centre for Studies, Doha. The second Arabic edition was published in 2014.

ALJAZEERA CENTRE FOR STUDIES

AMEC

First published in English in 2017 by the Afro-Middle East Centre (AMEC), PO Box 411494, Craighall 2024, Johannesburg, South Africa.
http://www.amec.org.za

ISBN: 978-0-9946825-3-6

Cover photograph by Aslam Farouk-Alli: Tinmel Mosque in Morocco, built by the Caliph 'Abd al-Mu'min ibn 'Ali in 1153, in honour of Ibn Tumart, the spiritual father of the Muwwahid Dynasty.

Copy edited by Mary Ralphs
Cover design by Karen Graphics
Text design and layout by Karen Graphics
Printed in South Africa by Impress Printers.

Contents

Acronyms and abbreviations

AKP	Justice and Development Party (Turkey)
AQI	al-Qa'ida in Iraq
EU	European Union
FIS	Islamic Salvation Front
IRGC	Islamic Revolutionary Guard Corps
PJD	Justice and Development Party (Morocco)
PAS	Pan-Malay Islamic Party
PLO	Palestine Liberation Organization
SAVAK	Organization of Intelligence and National Security
SPLM	Sudan People's Liberation Movement
US/USA	United States of America
YMMA	Young Muslim Men's Association

Introduction to the English edition

Work on the manuscript for this book was completed in 2006. Minor additions and corrections were made before the first Arabic edition was published in 2010. In 2012, a Turkish edition went to the press in Istanbul, and in 2014, the second Arabic edition was published. I am pleased that the book is reaching a broad range of interested readers. This introduction has given me an opportunity to test the veracity of my arguments in light of the subsequent Arab revolutions and counter-revolutions, which have incited profound and comprehensive political and intellectual change in most Arab countries.

It is important to note that this work was never intended to offer a history of Islam or the Islamic world in the modern era. It is a limited attempt to understand a single aspect of Muslim history, namely the emergence and development of political Islam in the mid-twentieth and early twenty-first centuries. Furthermore, since it was written with the objective of reaching a broad audience, the book does not target academics and specialists, although I am hopeful that colleagues in the fields of modern history, politics and Islamic studies may find it useful for undergraduate students. I have avoided elaborate referencing of sources and have tried to keep the footnoting as sparse as possible. However, a detailed bibliography is provided for those interested in further reading.

I write this introduction as the initial effects of the major political transformations initiated in the Arab world at the onset of 2011 are coming into view. In the immediate aftermath of the Arab revolutions,

Islamist political forces made significant gains in parliamentary elections in Tunisia, Egypt, Libya, Morocco, and Yemen. However, the wave of counter-revolution that has swept through the Arab world since 2013 has led to the ousting of Islamist movements in a number of Arab countries while others have descended into civil war. Not surprisingly, many who initially saw the Arab revolutions as signalling the rise of political Islam have since become more circumspect. Some have even described the reversal in the fortunes of the Muslim Brotherhood in Egypt and Ennahda in Tunisia as the decline and fall of political Islam.

Such an analysis is not without precedent. In 1994, against the backdrop of the bloody internecine conflict in Afghanistan after the Soviet occupation and the degeneration of the Algerian transition into a civil war, the eminent French political scientist Olivier Roy published a book entitled *The Failure of Political Islam*. Since Islamist groups had played a significant role in the events that engulfed Afghanistan and Algeria in the early 1990s, the collapse of post-Soviet Afghanistan and Algeria's short-lived democracy were regarded as the failure of the Islamist movement.

Although political Islam has existed in one form or another since the 1920s, it was not until the 1970s that it was seen as a force to be reckoned with in Muslim-majority societies. This era witnessed the triumph of Iran's Islamic revolution, the spearheading of resistance to Soviet occupation by the Afghan mujahidin, and the re-emergence of the Muslim Brotherhood in Egypt as a mass movement. The sometimes-violent backlash against political Islam in the 1980s and 1990s, combined with the Islamists' inability to grasp the nature of the modern state, has made it difficult to predict the trajectory of the Islamist phenomenon. However, the truth is that there is no 'ideal type' against which to measure its progress – political Islam was, and still is, an incomplete project and it is still far too early to write it off as a failure.

With the onset of the twenty-first century, it was clear that the Islamists were making a comeback. In Turkey, threats posed by the corrupt and inefficient ruling elite to the livelihoods of the middle classes and the integrity of the country propelled the newly founded Justice and Development Party (AKP) – with its mildly secular and Islamic views – to power. In most other Arab countries, brutal ruling elites compensated for their legitimacy deficit by monopolising political authority and national wealth, while turning state apparatuses into instruments of oppression.

In this context, the political power of the middle classes largely disintegrated. None of the nationalist, Arab nationalist or liberal political parties were able to provide credible opposition to the alliance between state institutions and the ruling elites. Only the Islamists, who now began to make their presence felt across the social spectrum, could claim to speak on behalf of the people.

In 2005, the Muslim Brotherhood made huge gains in Egypt's parliamentary elections despite flagrant manipulation of the electoral process by Hosni Mubarak's state security services. In the following year, Hamas won an undisputed majority in the Palestinian elections for the West Bank and Gaza. In the next few years, Islamists made significant gains in almost every Arab country where relatively fair elections were held. Nevertheless, the confusion surrounding mainstream expressions of political Islam and what this means for Muslims searching for freedom and justice in the modern world persisted. The outbreak of the Arab revolutions in 2011 thus represented a turning point in terms of the status of the Islamist movement in Muslim societies.

In political terms, there is no doubt that the Islamists were the main beneficiaries of the Arab revolutions. However, this was not because they were the sole initiators of these revolutions. In reality, the Arab revolutions were neither the product of a specific social group nor the outcome of any organisation's plans. They were mass uprisings in every sense of the term, reflecting widespread concern over the failure of the state and the persistence of corrupt and inept ruling elites. Yet, the Islamists emerged at this critical juncture as the only force capable of challenging the state and shaking loose the authoritarian grip of its rulers. The Arab revolutions thus paved the way for the ascendance of Islamic political parties.

Revolution swept through a number of Arab countries in the few months between December 2010 and the spring of 2011, affirming the shared political experience and close ties that continue to bind the Arab peoples. The old regimes collapsed in Tunisia, Egypt, Libya and Yemen. In Morocco, a prudent king met his people halfway, implementing crucial constitutional changes and inaugurating an era of free and fair elections. However, by 2013, the achievements of the Arab revolutionary movements seemed to have been almost completely reversed.

One of the reasons for the rapid advance of the counter-revolution was the pan-Arab nature of the revolutions. Since the movement for change was a pan-Arab phenomenon, it was – in a cruel twist of irony – confronted on a pan-Arab level. States that had not yet felt the stirring of revolution in 2011, especially Saudi Arabia and the United Arab Emirates, mobilised their influence and resources to defeat the forces of change sweeping across the Arab region. The revolutionary movement was stopped in its tracks in most of the countries where the old regimes had fallen. In almost all cases, the revolutions did not manage to topple the traditional ruling elites or fundamentally reform the structures of governance. Essentially, the few reactionary and powerful Arab regimes that had not been exposed to revolutionary uprisings formed alliances with the traditional ruling classes and state apparatuses in the countries that had. This unholy alliance led to the counter-revolutionary coup in Egypt in July 2013, the containment of the movement for democratic change in Yemen, further political fragmentation and internal conflict in Libya, and the fall of the Islamist-led coalition government in Tunisia.

In Syria, Iraq, and Yemen, Iran played the counter-revolutionary role. Rooted in its sectarian vision of the region, Iran adopted a policy of maximum support for its Shiite allies in Baghdad, Damascus, and

Sana'a. As a result, the conflict in these three countries spiralled into bloody civil wars, turning the struggles of the Syrian, Iraqi, and Yemeni people against despotism and minority-rule into crises with major international ramifications.

Since the Arab revolutions marked the ascendance of Islamic political forces, the counter-revolutionary wave in many respects became a war against the Islamists. The August 2013 massacre in Cairo's Rabi'a Square of supporters of deposed president Mohamed Morsi – who had been democratically elected – was praised by several Arab regimes and celebrated in anti-Islamist Arab circles. A witch-hunt against the Islamists was launched in some Arab countries and the Saudi and Emirati governments issued lists of terrorist organisations in which democratic, mainstream Islamic organisations were lumped together with the Islamic State group (IS). Western governments were pressured to declare the Muslim Brotherhood a terrorist organisation.

Clearly, there have been limits to what the counter-revolutionary forces could achieve. In terms of terminating transitions towards democracy and restoring the *status-quo ante*, the counter-revolution succeeded in only a few countries. In others, the democratic process is proceeding – without major hurdles, as in Morocco, or in an environment of uncertainty, as in Tunisia. Attempts to bring down the government of the AKP in Turkey, whether by mobilising opposition groupings in street protests, or through the electoral process, or even by military coup, have failed completely. In complexity-ridden Yemen, the Saudis and the Emiratis sided with the government of Abd Rabbu Mansur Hadi (who was legitimately elected after 2011), after Yemen's former ruler 'Ali 'Abdullah Saleh secured the support of the Iranian-backed Houthis and toppled Hadi. Thus, in Egypt, Yemen, Syria and Iraq, the counter-revolution has failed to offer a successful and convincing alternative, or a political order capable of responding to people's hopes and demands.

Nevertheless, the counter-revolution not only managed to violently disrupt the democratic process, it also dealt a heavy blow to the largest and most influential of all Islamist groups: Egypt's Muslim Brother-hood. The impact of their drastic reversal in Egypt – the biggest of the Arab countries – was felt throughout the Middle East, where the Mus-lim Brotherhood has a strong presence. It was in Egypt that the crisis of the wider Arab movement for change became most apparent, and where the position of the Islamists was most affected.

What these developments powerfully affirm is that the historical context within which political Islam – and the modern social groups that led it – was born has made the movement extremely sensitive to the political and social transformations that Islamic societies are experienc-ing. Groups that were initially established as charitable organisations quickly entered the political sphere. Organisations that were inspired by the idea of forming a community of believers ultimately developed into democratic political groups. Those that started out as flag bearers for an Islamic League of Nations ended up accepting the modern nation-state. Along the way, some became more radical than they had been; some chose to bear arms like their peers in Marxist revolutionary groups; yet others embraced the idea of democracy without necessarily being aware of its origins, implications or consequences.

The forces of political Islam are not trying to replicate an ancient Islamic legacy; they are modern political entities in terms of their social backgrounds and their visions of the major social and political issues that inform their discourse, from governance to economics and law. Consequently, the differences between them are no fewer than their agreements. Moroccan Islamists for example, are very different from Jordanian Islamists – at least from the perspective of their relationships with the monarchy and the royal families in their countries, and espe-cially since the start of mass mobilisation in Jordan.

Similarly, because the cultural and political climate in Tunisia is dif-ferent from that in Algeria and Egypt, we should not be surprised that Ennahda was one of the first Islamist organisations to adopt a demo-cratic vision. And, although most Islamists ultimately followed their example, it is not difficult to see multifaceted differences of opinion, not only between Islamists and others, but also between Islamist groups themselves. Issues such as secularism and its relationship to the state, the limits of nation-states, and what it means to be an Islamist in this post-Arab-revolution era are all open to question and debate.

A large number of Muslim countries are either in, or approaching what Antonio Gramsci called a 'crisis of authority'. With their mass following, Islamic political movements have played, and might continue to play, a considerable role in re-establishing order and bringing about stability. This is not to ignore the divisions and lack of consensus already mentioned. It is precisely because the contemporary Islamists have expressed strong commitments to political pluralism, that they have the potential to contribute significantly to achieving a new consensus as well as to consolidating democratic practices and the rule of law in Muslim-majority countries.

Some regard the Islamic sprint towards democracy, and the inspiration that Islamists draw from both liberalism and conservatism as evidence of political expediency and of their willingness to say whatever is necessary for them to attain power by the quickest means possible. This might be true in some cases. How else are we to understand the sudden change of direction in the discourse of the new Salafi groups? However, it is equally true that actual political and economic realities, not arguments or debates, are the most effective crucibles for producing agents of change and for developing concepts in ways that cast new light on how they may be put into practice. Those who try to respond to changing realities in order to achieve effective and tangible goals find that they themselves are transformed, whether they like it or not. The power of reality is far more illuminating than any preconceived idea.

Students of modern Islam, as well as political leaders in the Muslim and the Western worlds, have rarely differentiated between mainstream Islamic political organisations, such as the Muslim Brotherhood, and extremist groups, such as al-Qa'ida. The use of violence, extremism,

and international terrorism by fringe groups within political movements is nothing new. Socialist, Marxist, and nationalist movements
have all had, and continue to have, their share of violent extremists.
Yet, the manner in which the margins express themselves cannot be
allowed to invalidate the legitimacy of the mainstream. Violent and extremist Islamic political organisations will be defeated in due course.
Lacking any substantive popular following, they are already isolated
and shunned by the great majority of Muslims. However, the future of
the mainstream and largely democratic Islamic political movement is
another story.

This larger political movement, like nationalism, is a historical development. It is the outcome of the transformational currents within
modern times, not the plotting of ingenious Muslim activists. Political
Islam is a universal phenomenon, influencing life and politics in almost
all Muslim countries. Although its agendas are quite specific to each
country, it is not an isolated phenomenon military or intelligence forces
can eradicate; nor can it be destroyed by propaganda.

Undoubtedly, the rise of the Islamists places political Islam at the
heart of the debates raging among contemporary Muslims about their
very existence, the renewal of their lives and countries, and their struggles to answer questions pertaining to statehood, governance, citizenship, pluralism, unity, revival, truth and obligation. This is essentially
what I wanted to clarify in this book, and this is what I believe the
ongoing changes in an increasing number of Arab and Islamic countries
provide evidence of.

Oxfordshire, 3 July 2016

1

Islam and politics

More than a billion people in the world are Muslim. Islam represents one of the grand narratives of human history, and it has generated countless other narratives. Its influence is evident in the faith, customs, moral values and devotional practices, as well as in the sense of collective identity among its adherents. Political Islam, however, has aroused major contestation. While the twentieth century witnessed the rise and fall of many ideologies including fascism, Nazism, and communism, the influence of political Islam is still growing. Some even see the end of the twentieth and the beginning of the twenty-first centuries as the era of Islamic power. Political Islam is present in every Muslim country from Indonesia to Mauritania. In Egypt and Pakistan, Islamist groups have been a constant force in political life since the mid-1950s, even though they have often been banned from formal participation in the political arena; and in Yemen, Jordan and Morocco, Islamists occupy a central position on the political map.

In the late 1970s, Iran's Ayatollah Ruhollah Khomeini, an eminent religious scholar with a traditional educational background and a revolutionary outlook, led one of the most important revolutions of the twentieth century, establishing the first Islamic Republic in modern times. Despite the series of internal and external challenges and profound problems the Islamic Republic has faced since its inception, Iran seems more stable today than many of its neighbours. However, this does not mean that it succeeded in solving the intractable question of the relationship between the state and religion, or that it has found effective ways of easing the tensions that characterised its relations with the rest of the world.

In June 1989, Sudanese Islamists took control of the state via a military coup – a means of state capture that had long been used by other political forces but, prior to this, never by an Islamist group. However, soon after seizing power, Sudan's Islamist government became embroiled in a ruinous civil war at huge human and financial cost to itself and its people. A few years later, facing strong opposition from both traditional and secular circles – and in accordance with the logic of military coups – the Sudanese Islamists turned against their leader and teacher, Hasan al-Turabi, and flung him into jail.

In Malaysia, the Pan-Malaysian Islamic Party (PAS) plays an instrumental role in maintaining the country's cultural, intellectual and political balance. As the ruling party in the country's northern Kelantan state, PAS has created a strong centre of influence from which it is able to give full expression to its moderate Islamic approach. Since 2007, PAS has also been a major partner in a broad national coalition that seems very close to putting an end to the rule of the United Malays National Organisation (UMNO), which has been in power without interruption since Malaysia's independence in 1957.

In Algeria, an Islamist party was on the verge of ascending to power in the early 1990s, not by a popular revolution or a coup, but by the power of the ballot box. Only the flagrant intervention of the Algerian military and a prolonged civil war was able to block the Algerian Islamists' rise to power. The civil war ended in 2000, when limited democratic reforms were introduced and some sections of the Islamist movement agreed to become minor partners in government, but the political crisis has by no means been resolved.

In 2002, after a series of frustrated attempts, Turkish Islamists, represented by the Justice and Development Party (AKP), managed to break the power monopoly that had been held by secular military and political forces for almost a century. However, the success of the AKP, which was achieved via a democratic election, would have been impossible without a major compromise between strongly held Islamic values and Atatürk's secular legacy – a compromise that reflected the AKP's commitment to the founding values of the Turkish republic, which once seemed to inspire admiration in major Western capitals. Yet, even after granting further electoral victories to the AKP, Turkey has not achieved lasting political stability, and the conflict between its different ideological and political camps shows no sign of ending.

In many ways, the influence of political Islam is equally evident among Muslim minorities in western Europe, the Balkans, and South Asia. Under pressure from non-Muslim majorities and escalating Islamophobia, sections within Muslim minority communities seem to see political Islam as a shield for their identity and a refuge from political and social discrimination. It must be added that massive progress in the field of communications has aided this enormously.

Even non-Islamists see Islamist political parties and groups as highly influential opposition forces. That is, the Islamists' ability to mobilise popular protest against despotic regimes and state corruption is undisputed. Similarly, their objections to foreign intervention in national affairs, their moral challenges to consumerism and the squandering of economic resources, as well as their defence of the grand causes around which Muslims usually rally, both within and without the Muslim world, are universally acknowledged as exerting political pressure.

❧⟨✦⟩❧

The rise of the political power of Islam in the modern world is associated with the emergence of the Islamic revivalist movements. The first of these were born in Egypt in the 1920s; they were the Jam'iyyah al-Shubban al-Muslimin (Young Muslim Men's Association or YMMA) and al-Ikhwan al-Muslimun, better known to English speakers as the Mus-

3

lim Brotherhood. Both organisations captured a growing feeling among Muslims that their country and community were under threat, and that the existence of Islam and its cultural heritage needed to be defended. For the next few decades, the YMMA became increasingly involved in socio-cultural and charitable activities, while the Muslim Brotherhood focused on the political arena. As the twentieth century drew to a close, political Islam emerged as the most effective political actor in the wider Muslim world. In fact, its impact is now reverberating through national and international politics, well beyond the Muslim world.

The primary force driving the emergence of political Islam is the preservation of an embattled identity. Islamic culture is struggling against an invasive modernist movement that uncritically adopts Western values and concepts. However, political Islam was also born in the context of the crumbling consensus within Muslim societies and the steady decline in the influence of the 'ulama (religious scholars), who, for centuries, were the institutional voice of Islam and the guardians of its values.

Furthermore, political Islam came into existence at a time when most of the Muslim world was directly or indirectly in the grip of Western imperialist domination. Christian missionaries were organising gatherings in Islamic and Arab capitals, enforced Jewish immigration to Palestine had begun, and the rise of Hindu nationalism seemed likely to undermine the religious and cultural autonomy of Muslims in India. In response, the emerging forces of political Islam played a role in national independence struggles, and began calling for the Islamisation of modern societies or the establishment of Islamic governments. A few even aspired to reconstitute the Caliphate.

During the British occupation of Egypt, and in various stages of the conflicts in Palestine and occupied Afghanistan, Islamists bore a large share of the burdens of national liberation struggles. In Lebanon, the Shi'ite Islamist group Hizbullah spearheaded a resistance movement against Israeli occupation until almost all of South-Lebanon was liberated. In Kashmir and Chechnya, where relations between the majority and minority are more complex, Islamists called for the secession of the Islamic minority from the non-Muslim majority.

Yet, the greatest and the most profound impact of political Islam in Muslim societies has been in the realms of culture, lifestyle change and politics. Islamists call this the Islamic Awakening while their adversaries describe it as a form of 'anti-modernism' that is attempting to isolate Islamic culture and keep it shackled to the past.

As early as the 1960s, contemporary Islamic discourse had become an arena of contestation, intellectual argumentation and disagreement, and this has since permeated the entire Muslim world. Muslim writers, from Hasan al-Banna, Abu'l A'la al-Mawdudi, Sayyid Qutb, Ali Shariati, Muhammad al-Ghazali, Yusuf al-Qaradawi, Hasan al-Turabi, Rachid Ghannouchi, to Tariq al-Bishri, Mohammad Salim al-'Awa, Fahmi Huwaydi, Munir Shafiq, and Muhammad 'Amarah, have been extremely influential in shaping modern culture in their respective countries. Their writings are undoubtedly highly popular in these countries too.

The Islamic Awakening has also restored interest in older Islamic works. Muslims, perhaps more than most other faith communities, still intimately engage with their traditional texts, treating works that were written hundreds of years ago as an inseparable constituent of contemporary culture.

Modern education, with its twin bastions of school and university, began encroaching upon traditional Islamic educational centres and study circles in the second half of the nineteenth century. However, less than a century later, many schools and universities began reclaiming their Islamic image and content. Private Islamic schools are full to capacity in many parts of the world, and in several countries Islamic educational institutions are playing an invaluable role in girls' education. Without these institutions, millions of Muslim girls in conservative regions would receive no formal education.

Similarly, while modernisation succeeded in altering modes of dress in a great number of Muslim countries in the first half of the twentieth

5

century, the Islamic Awakening has seen the re-introduction of Islamic dress in major centres of modernisation such as Cairo, Beirut and Tunis, as well as in many Western capitals.

One can argue that these developments are not solely related to political Islam. Formal Islamic education in Egypt, traditional learning centres in Pakistan, and the network of Nahdatul 'Ulama Islamic schools in Indonesia are run by institutions and associations that are not necessarily linked to Islamist organisations, and which sometimes question the Islamic credentials of the Islamists. Of course, study circles exist in local mosques in many places throughout the Muslim world, and are rooted in an ancient and deep tradition of mosque education. However, it is equally true that the mercurial rise of the Islamists and Islamic discourse has reasserted the importance of countless Islamic expressions and customs, some of which are novel and innovative, while others remain rooted in tradition. Even some of the great traditional Islamic institutions seem to be on the verge of losing their influence due to the appeal of political Islam.

Not only have the Islamists made headway in modern education and politics, they also use the mass media efficiently to create a presence on radio and television, in books and newspapers, and on the internet. In many respects, the Islamists seem to have assimilated modernity and harnessed its power. At the very least, they seem to have managed to wrap a turban around its head. This should not be surprising; the majority of Islamic activists have few connections with the traditional 'ulama. Apart from a small number of leading Islamists, such as Ayatollah Khomeini, Muhammad Taqi al-Din al-Nabhani and Hasan Nasrallah who were formally trained in Islamic law and theology, most Islamist leaders are graduates of universities in Cairo, Damascus, Karachi and Algiers or have degrees from European institutions. In fact, the robustness of political Islam is nowhere more visible than in the fields of politics and governance. When Islamists call for Islamic rule and the implementation of the shari'ah, they are not really advocating a return to the traditional Islamic system of government with its limited powers, but rather promoting an Islamic form of the modern state, centralised, sovereign and all pervasive.

On the other hand, it is not difficult to see the drastic effects that political Islam has had on modern Islamic societies and on perceptions of Islam. Political Islam emerged in the first half of the twentieth century as a response to deep divisions within Muslim societies. Yet, and without necessarily intending to do so, political Islam has exacerbated these divisions. To understand this, it is important to note that several modern Muslim states and their ruling elites were born amid rapid and intense socio-political transformations, often closely linked to disrupting Western hegemony. In this context, state control has become the Islamists' main goal, and the incumbent elites are certainly not prepared to concede their positions and privileges. In many Muslim countries, confrontation between the Islamists and the ruling elites was thus inevitable and bound to engender bitter conflict and social rupture.

The rise of political Islam has precipitated political instability and uncertainty – albeit for longer or shorter periods – in most Muslim countries. From Egypt and Pakistan in the 1950s and 1960s, to Syria and Iraq in the 1970s and 1980s, Algeria, Saudi Arabia and back to Egypt in the 1990s, and to Indonesia and Morocco in the early 2000s, state authorities have waged a multifaceted war against the Islamists. In other regions this confrontation is ongoing. It seems, however, that modern Muslims, or at least the intelligentsia among them, are deeply divided on almost all of the major issues pertaining to the vitality of nation states and the foundations of their stability. Muslims seem to fundamentally disagree about the role of religion in state and public affairs, on the basic values framing their lives, on their visions of their own history, on their cultural relations with the outside world, and even on their understandings of the essentials of Islam.

As a result of these conflicts and inner divisions, hundreds of thousands of politically active Muslims have been imprisoned or forced into exile. Entire generations have lost the right to determine their futures and families have been destroyed. Leading scholars and intellectuals – on both sides – have been hanged or assassinated. Some of the best specialists and scientists have fled to Western countries as refugees, after being told that their (much-needed) services in their own countries' were no longer required. Against this grim backdrop, official expenditure on state security has risen to unprecedented levels in countries that lag behind in the provision of essential services. Perhaps someday in the not too distant future Muslims will look back on this period of their history as an age in which they waged catastrophic and costly wars upon themselves.

Political confrontation has often escalated into armed violence. For example, Egyptian prime minister Mahmud Fahmi al-Nuqrashi was assassinated by a member of the Muslim Brotherhood's Covert Structure in the late 1940s; a bloody civil war swept through Algeria in the 1990s; and confrontation between armed Islamists and the Pakistani state authorities has been escalating since the early 2000s. Islamist forces have shown that they too are willing and able to resort to violence. And once justified, violence only spreads, often in aimless and meaningless ways.

The radicalisation of the Islamic world has since led to the emergence of the new and shocking phenomenon of transcontinental violence perpetrated in the name of Islam. After launching a series of attacks on American and other civilian targets carried out since the early 2000s, al-Qa'ida, became the torchbearer for such violence, and was placed at the centre of the world's concerns. Within and beyond the Muslim world, al-Qa'ida occupied the top of the list of terror organisations targeted by the international order and an increasing number of Muslim countries. However, because al-Qa'ida's discourse of global violence uses Islamic terminology, Islam itself has been blamed and vilified.

In Washington and in most other Western capitals, the belief has taken hold that Islam as a religion, and not just certain Muslim organisations, needs reforming. At the same time, major Western powers have engaged in a wide-ranging enterprise to reinforce the systems of control and dominance in the Middle East and the rest of the world that were established at the end of the First World War. Since the 9/11 attacks in 2001, the USA has engaged in direct and indirect wars against several Muslim countries and organisations. It is difficult not to see the American occupation of Iraq, and the return of direct imperialism to the Middle East, as related to US attempts to assert its hegemony and outright dominance.

Of course, a large number of Islamists see armed and violent groups – including those that use Islamic discourse – as beyond the bounds of political Islam. They assert that the adoption of violent means is in itself a negation of politics. Nevertheless, Islamic violence has contributed to the exacerbation of inner conflict and division, while profoundly damaging the image of Islam and Muslims across the world, especially those in western Europe and North America. At the beginning of the twenty-first century, when modern means of communication are supposed to be bringing nations and cultures closer together, being Muslim is to be a target of doubt, suspicion and blame.

In addition to deepening the internal conflicts and divisions between Muslims, the Islamists are charged with constructing their own version of Islam. The Islamists are accused of reducing a great monotheistic religion, with its innumerable facets and expressions, to mere political discourse, of turning Islam into an ideology with a neatly defined modern political programme, and of stripping Islam of its long and rich history. In the place of a complex religious tradition, the Islamists have allegedly implanted modern Western concepts, wrapped up in an Islamic guise.

The sharpest charge directed at the Islamists relates to their record in government and their concept of the relationship between state and society. While Islamic political discourse bestows a puritanical sense of sanctity on Islamist political slogans and objectives, the Islamist experience in government has not always been enlightening. From the

9

perspective of their opponents, Islamist rulers in Iran and Sudan have been little different from the ruling elites that preceded them. In both countries, the Islamist regimes sent their opponents to jail, justified the use of torture, and forced thousands of people into exile. Once they secured control of the state, access to power corrupted them just like other despotic rulers.

Throughout the long history of Islam (or at least until the beginning of the modernisation movement in the nineteenth century), the ʻulama were the guardians of the shariʻah and the ummah was the repository of the faith and its values. The state has had no prominent role and no special authority to speak in the name of Islam. Does Islam now suddenly require new spokespersons – Islamic political organisations that deem themselves fit to represent the faith and shariʻah, and act on behalf of the ummah? Piety and learning accorded the ʻulama the authority they held through centuries of Islamic history. We may well ask what authority now gives the Islamists the right to represent the people and the faith. The answer seems to lie in another question: if the Islamists did not to speak on behalf of Islam, who would? Have the ʻulama not been too undermined and too often turned into puppets of various governing regimes? Has the modernisation movement and the power of the state not severely undercut the independence of the ʻulama, undermining their moral authority and ability to influence the collective consciousness of Muslims?

In the chapters that follow, I try to widen the debate and answer some of the questions raised by political Islam. What are the main and most influential forces within political Islam? How were they born, and in what context? Where do their roots lie and what are the sources of their inspiration? Do they all share the same discursive underpinnings and systems of thought, or do they differ and reflect plurality? What impact have these forces had in their respective countries and have they influenced the intellectual edifice of modern Islam? Where have the Islamists succeeded, where have they failed, and how should they be judged in the court of history? Have they reached the end of the road, or do they still have a role to play?

Since every socio-political phenomenon – however complex and multi-dimensional – has to start somewhere, I begin with the Islamic Reformists of the late nineteenth-century, who are generally acknowledged to be the legitimate predecessors of the contemporary political Islamic movements.

2

The early reformists

$\mathcal{I}$slamist reformists have played an important role in informing the outlook and orientation of modern Islamic thought. Reformist Islam is not revolutionary or subversive and takes the Qur'an as its guiding light. Unlike the leaders and cadres of political Islam, many of whom have emerged from modern higher education institutions, most of the early reformists were part of the traditional 'ulama (recognised religious scholars). They did not establish political organisations in the sense that we know them today, but they were actively engaged in civic life as individuals or through associations, institutions, schools and often wrote for, or published their own journals. Various reformists rose to prominence at different times in the late nineteenth and early twentieth centuries all over the Islamic world. Although not linked by any single common thread, there is no doubt that the reformists shared similar concerns and influenced one another.

Calls for reform echoed through many corners of the Islamic world during the eighteenth and early nineteenth centuries. Major scholars and reformists, such as Shah Waliullah Dihlawi (1703–1762), Muhammad ibn 'Abd al-Wahhab (1703–1792), Muhammad ibn 'Ali al-Shawkani (1760–1834) and Abu Thana al-Alusi (1802–1854) called for the liberation of Islam from the shackles of taqlid (blind imitation) and superstition, as well as for a revival of ijtihad (intellectual renewal).[1] A feeling of crisis (that began in the eighteenth century) heightened in the nineteenth century, which can be described as a century of impasse for

Islam. This was when the Ottoman Army was forced to pull back from the Russian and Austrian fronts; Egypt was occupied for some years by a French army led by Napoleon; Britain gained control over India and the area around the port of Aden in Yemen, and then took control of Egypt; France gained control of Algeria and then Tunisia. These military defeats were accompanied by economic penetration of Islamic markets in the Persian Gulf and the Mediterranean coast, as well as on the Indian subcontinent and the Malaysian archipelago.

This drove Muslim leaders in Istanbul, Cairo, Tunis and Tehran to initiate modernisation programmes that emulated European administrative and legislative examples. Meanwhile, in countries such as Algeria, India, Indonesia (and Egypt after British occupation), colonial administrations steered a similar modernisation project. Modernisation strengthened state power and introduced the notion of a central state having dominance over the spheres of education, legislation and economics. New roads were built, railroads were laid, telegraphic communication networks were established, and a programme for the translation and publishing of key European texts was initiated. The objective of the new system was to produce 'ideal civil servants', and to establish nations and societies united by a single vision.

In addition, agricultural reforms changed patterns of land ownership that had prevailed for centuries. In the legislative sphere, a brief attempt was made to codify the shari'ah, but this was soon abandoned, and European legislative systems were imported instead. Modern courts replaced the traditional systems that had long relied on qadis (judges in the shari'ah system) and their established sources of Islamic jurisprudence. States also took control of the religious endowment sector, both in areas under foreign control and in countries still under Islamic rule. This was done either because the endowment sector was seen as a possible support base for the traditional powers who might oppose modernisation, or because states were striving to gain additional sources of revenue for their modernisation programmes.

The 'ulama, who had woven and protected the fabric of Islamic society for centuries, were gradually marginalised as the new systems started producing new elites with new value systems; the traditional moral order began to crumble.

Society, as Edmund Burke observed, 'is joined in perpetuity by a moral bond among the dead, the living, and those yet to be born'.[2] Yet at the beginning of the twentieth century, this bond began to break down in many parts of the Muslim world. Modernisation and Western economic penetration brought about a widespread state of turmoil. The ancient Islamic capitals of the world began to overflow with rural people who had left the countryside and city dwellers who had lost their livelihoods. Sectarian fighting broke out in Mount Lebanon and in Damascus. Popular uprisings rocked Mosul, Nablus, Aleppo and Jeddah, and Muslims all over India rose up against British occupation. This increasing social turmoil and insecurity created deep divisions between the 'ulama, the intellectuals, and the politicians.

Some Islamic voices called for a complete and speedy embrace of Western ideas and Western patterns of society and work, while others rejected change entirely and called for steadfast adherence to inherited practices. Between these two camps, certain 'ulama, professionals and politicians, who were later referred to as Islamist reformists, advocated a middle path, arguing that it is possible to reconcile new social conditions with the foundations of Islamic identity. Key individuals and organisations among these were: Tahir al-Jazairi (1852–1920) and Jamal al-Din al-Qasimi (1866–1924) in Damascus; Mahmud Shakir al-Alusi (1857–1924) in Baghdad; al-Bashir Sifar (d. 1937), 'Abd al-'Aziz al-Thalibi (1875–1944) and Muhammad al-Tahir ibn 'Ashur (1879–1973) in Tunis; 'Abd al-Hamid ibn Badis (1889–1940), al-Tayyib al-'Aqabi (1888–1962) and Muhammad al-Bashir al-Ibrahimi (1889–1965); the New Ottomans in Istanbul; the Muhammadan Association in Indonesia; Muhammad Husayn Na'ini (1860–1936) in Iran; Sayyid Ahmad Khan (1817–1898), Siddiq

Hasan Khan (d. 1888), Shibli Nu'mani (1857–1914) and the Nadwatul 'Ulama in India.

All were preoccupied with protecting Islam and Islamic identity as it confronted the onslaught of modernisation: reconciling the new with the inherited, reforming the Islamic intellectual heritage and liberating it from the shackles of blind imitation. Perhaps the most famous among them were Jamal al-Din al-Afghani (1838–1897), Muhammad 'Abduh (1849–1905) and Rashid Rida (1865–1935).

❦

Jamal al-Din al-Afghani

Jamal al-Din al-Afghani was a remarkable intellectual and political activist who was fiercely opposed to European colonialism and called for internal reform and pan-Islamism. His birthplace, like many details of his life, is uncertain. He reportedly said he was born in Asadabad, near Kabul in Afghanistan. However, some insist that he was born into a Shiite family in Asad Abad, which is a city in the Iranian province of Hamadan and that he was educated for a short period in Najaf, a key centre of Shiism in Iraq. However, nothing about al-Afghani indicates that he had any sectarian allegiances. What is more certain is that he spent his youth in Afghanistan, and after performing the hajj at the age of about twenty, he entered into the service of the Amir Dost Muhammad Khan and accompanied him on his campaign against Herat. The death of the amir in 1863 led to a civil war between his sons that lasted for several years. Al-Afghani threw in his lot with what turned out to be the losing side, and then had to leave Kabul. He travelled to India in 1869, where he was subjected to security surveillance by the British authorities for two months, before being asked to leave the country. He travelled to Cairo, where he met scholars from al-Azhar but after less than two months he again decided to move on, making his way to Istanbul in 1870.

Despite receiving a warm welcome from some quarters in the capital of the Ottoman sultanate, criticism directed at him by Shaykh al-Islam Hasan Fahmi forced al-Afghani to leave Turkey. He returned to Cairo in 1871, where the government, led by Khedive Ismail, offered him a salary and permitted him to move around freely. Al-Afghani's second stay in Cairo was perhaps the most influential period of his life. He remained there for eight years before being expelled. A circle of young people formed around him, gathering in al-Bustatah Coffee Shop. Comprised of scholars and laypersons, Muslims and non-Muslims, from Muhammad 'Abduh to Sa'd Zaghlul and Adib Ishaq, Al-Afghani's young followers were encouraged to consider Islam's intellectual heritage from new and critical perspectives and to familiarise themselves with Western intellectual trends. Al-Afghani also urged his followers to pay attention to the print media, which was new to Islamic life. Beyond engendering an animosity among his supporters towards increasing Western interference in Islamic affairs, he also insisted that Muslims resist and unite to confront this problem.

Al-Afghani's affiliation with the Scottish Freemasons' Lodge in Egypt is perhaps one of the most controversial chapters in his biography. However, he soon left the Scottish lodge and established his own Egyptian one, which affiliated to the French lodge, the Grand Orient de France. At that time, the Freemasons' reputation was very different to what it is today, and al-Afghani's lodge rapidly became a gathering place for around three hundred nationalists who were opposed to European influence in Egypt.

In the 1870s, the policies of Khedive Ismail drove Egypt into debt, and respect for their ambitious leader began to decline among Egyptian nationalists. It is widely believed that al-Afghani encouraged his young student, Muhammad 'Abduh, to assassinate the khedive. The assassination plot was, in any case, abandoned when the khedive's son, Tawfiq, ascended to the throne in Egypt. The new ruler soon restricted al-Afghani's activities, and later expelled him from Egypt. Al-Afghani returned to India once again. This time, the British authorities tolerated his presence out of fear that he may try to return to Egypt, which was then on the cusp of the 'Urabi Revolt. Al-Afghani first settled in Hyderabad but later moved to Calcutta. During this period, he wrote his book, *The Refutation of the Materialists*, defending Islam against those striving to adopt Europe's material culture.

Early in 1883, al-Afghani left India for Europe to begin a new phase in his struggle. In the previous year, Egypt had fallen victim to British occupation and al-Afghani saw it as his duty to intensify his resistance to European imperialism. His first brief stop seems to have been in London, where he met the English writer and activist, Wilfrid Scawen Blunt. (Blunt remembered al-Afghani arriving in London after a short stay in America, but this cannot be confirmed and is one of many obscure periods in al-Afghani's life story.) Al-Afghani soon moved to Paris where he wrote his famous refutation of the French philosopher and sociologist Ernest Renan's claim that Islam does not accord with the spirit of modern science. Al-Afghani then invited Muhammad 'Abduh to join him in Paris. ('Abduh had fled into exile in Beirut after the British occupation of Egypt.) From March 1883 to October 1884, the two men issued their magazine, *al-'Urwatul Wuthqa* (The firm handhold). Although no more than eighteen issues of the magazine were published, and it was banned in most Islamic cities, the publication made a deep impression on Islamic thought at the end of the nineteenth century.

After the publishing of *al-'Urwatul Wuthqa* was suspended, the two men took different paths. 'Abduh returned to Beirut, and, in 1886, al-Afghani was invited to Tehran by its shah, Nasir al-Din al-Qajari. However, neither the shah – who at this point was clearly a dictator – nor his entourage were ready to accept al-Afghani's ideas on reform and constitutionalism or on the necessity of uniting with the Ottomans. Al-Afghani then went to Russia to defend the rights of Russian Muslims from Kaiser Wilhelm II, after which he returned to Iran. In 1891, al-Afghani was captured by a cavalry battalion in southern Iran. He was tied up and dumped in the Iraqi city of Khanaqin, near the Iranian-Ottoman border.

Al-Afghani responded by writing a letter to the Iranian marja' (the highest Shi'a authority) Mirza Hasan al-Shirazi who was resident in Samarra, encouraging him to oppose a trade agreement whereby the shah had granted monopoly rights to a British tobacco company. Al-Shirazi responded by issuing his famous fatwa against the use of tobacco, which kick-started what became known as the Tobacco Revolt and eventually led to the cancellation of the trade agreement.

After a short stay in Basra and another visit to London, al-Afghani made his way to Istanbul at the invitation of Sultan Abdul Hamid II. The sultan had made pan-Islamism the official policy of the Ottoman state, and hoped al-Afghani would prove a strong champion of this policy. Al-Afghani was given an extravagant home on the hilltop of Nishan Tash, close to Yildiz Palace, along with a generous monthly stipend. At first, the relationship between the two men was strong and they met regularly.

During one of their conversations in the Yildiz Palace garden, the sultan reportedly asked his guest if he saw any escape from the conflict with European colonial forces over Islamic lands and the Ottoman state. Al-Afghani responded by advising Abdul Hamid to: withdraw from the Balkans whose many revolts were bleeding the Ottoman Sultanate dry; make Arabic the official language of the state; and move the capital to Baghdad the Arabic heart of Islam, thus slamming shut all doors and windows on Western influence. Al-Afghani's advice was naturally an expression of his bitterness towards the Europeans and his sense of the need for strategic fortification. Abdul Hamid did not heed this advice, but it was not long before the forces of political Islam began to advocate similar steps.

Al-Afghani's relationship with Abdul Hamid was undermined by rumours spread by Abu'l-Huda al-Sayyadi, a well-known Sufi of the

Rifaʻi Order who was close to the sultan and his entourage. Abdul Hamid began to fear his famous guest in 1896, when one of al-Afghani's followers assassinated Shah Nasir al-Din. However, al-Afghani's repeated requests to be allowed to leave Istanbul were refused. He died on 9 March 1897 in Istanbul from throat cancer and was buried in the Nishan Tash district.

He had dedicated his life to defending Islam and the Muslim lands, living a simple life that bordered on poverty. He never married, and left no family or significant assets. Apparently, when the moment of death arrived, he was overcome with bitterness and isolation. His dream of pan-Islamism was no closer, and very few Muslims seemed to be aware of, or willing to resist, European encroachment.

This does not mean that al-Afghani's efforts should be understood as having failed. The nineteenth century created new and unprecedented intellectual challenges. It is reasonable to argue that al-Afghani initiated the Islamic response to this challenge and fuelled the development of Islamist praxis. In December 1944, his remains were moved from Istanbul to Kabul. He was reburied on 2 January 1945 in the district of ʻAli Abad in the Afghani capital Kabul. By then, almost fifty years had passed since al-Afghani's departure from Kabul and his flame, which inspired a new generation of Muslim thinkers, had still not burnt out; nor has it been extinguished since.

Muhammad ʻAbduh

The second great reformer Shaykh Muhammad ʻAbduh was influenced by al-Afghani in the formative period of his life. While al-Afghani's early relationships with political and governing authorities placed him on an eventful and tumultuous path, nothing about ʻAbduh's early life revealed much about what his future would hold.

ʻAbduh was a son of the conservative Egyptian countryside, where Sufi traditions held sway; he was also the product of al-Azhar University, where Islamic traditions were never compromised. However this was the nineteenth century during which, as has been noted, Muslims faced many conflicts and crises. Born into a rural family in 1849, 'Abduh spent his childhood in Mahlah Nasr – a village in Egypt's al-Buhayrah province in the Nile delta. He received his primary education in the village school and then moved to the Azhari Institute in the city of Tanta when he was thirteen years old. The institute's traditional teaching methods did not appeal to the gifted student, and he left the school after eighteen months. One of his father's relatives then convinced him to return to the school, and he spent another year in Tanta before moving to Cairo in 1866, where he continued his studies at the bastion of Islamic Education, al-Azhar University.

Since becoming one of the most important centres of the Islamic Sciences for Sunni Muslims in the sixteenth century, al-Azhar has attracted thousands of students from the Egyptian countryside hoping to join the ranks of the 'ulama. 'Abduh expressed dissatisfaction with the education at al-Azhar from the start of his studies there until he attained his degree. This was not related to his own social background but to al-Azhar's traditions and teaching methods. His dissatisfaction motivated 'Abduh to choose a career path different from that of a traditional scholar, and reforming al-Azhar's educational system remained a pressing concern for him throughout his life.

In 1872, 'Abduh met al-Afghani for the first time and was overwhelmed. With al-Afghani's encouragement, he began working as a journalist even before completing his studies at al-Azhar. In 1879, 'Abduh was appointed as a teacher at the Darul 'Ulum (College of Sciences), a teacher-training college established by 'Ali Mubarak as a new centre for higher education after leaders at al-Azhar University refused to respond to calls from the state to modernise and redevelop the tertiary education system. However, the government of Khedive Tawfiq, who expelled al-Afghani from Egypt, then sent 'Abduh into a kind of exile by forcing him to return to his village. In 1880, under Tawfiq's second government, which was attempting to foster a more liberal orientation, 'Abduh was recalled by the state and appointed as editor-in-chief of *al-Waqa'i al-Misriyyah* (Egyptian encounters). This was the government's official magazine, established by the renowned Egyptian reformer Rifa'a al-Tahtawi.

In 1882, 'Abduh participated in the 'Urabi Revolt. After its suppression and Egypt's subjugation to British occupation, 'Abduh went into exile in Beirut. There he met young Syrian reformists, such as Jamal al-Din al-Qasimi. After spending two years in Beirut, 'Abduh made his way to Paris where he helped al-Afghani with the editing and publishing of *al-'Urwatul Wuthqa*. When the magazine began to collapse, 'Abduh went to Tunis on a short visit, to try to attract the funding necessary for them to continue publishing. Soon thereafter, he left Paris and returned to Beirut.

From then on, while al-Afghani became more radical and belligerent towards Western imperialism, 'Abduh began to lose confidence in direct political action, and focused his attention on intellectual and educational reform. His new orientation was clearly visible in a lecture series he delivered in Beirut, which formed the basis of a book he later published called *Risalah al-Tawhid* (The theology of unity). In this work, 'Abduh departed from the approach taken by traditional Muslim dialectic theologians who mix Salafi and Mu'tazili influences. Instead, he laid the foundations for his central claim, which was that the causes of stagnation in the Muslim world were internal and that self-reformation was the only solution.

In 1889, after corresponding with Evelyn Baring, the Earl of Cromer and Britain's first Consul-General of Egypt, 'Abduh was able to return home. On his arrival in Cairo he was appointed as a judge. He was later promoted to serve as a judge in the Appellate Court, and in 1899 he became mufti (chief jurisconsult) of Egypt. 'Abduh's gradual rise indicates that he enjoyed friendly relations with Baring and other British officials, and that he was able to overcome his resistance to co-operating with the British for the sake of achieving internal reforms, and to use his position to effectively oppose the dictatorships of Khedive 'Abbas II in Egypt and Sultan Abdul Hamid in Istanbul.

However, in recent years, correspondence between 'Abduh and Sultan Abdul Hamid was found in the latter's archives which reveals that exchanges took place between the two men until the last years of 'Abduh's life. It now seems that while 'Abduh's opposition to 'Abbas II in Cairo led to the severing of that relationship, 'Abduh still hoped to influence the sultan and awaken the sultanate.

Rashid Rida

In the winter of 1897 a young scholar arrived in Cairo from Tripoli: this was none other than Muhammad Rashid Rida (1865–1935). His admiration for 'Abduh had motivated his move to Egypt and Rida's first undertaking in Cairo was to visit 'Abduh and pledge his allegiance to him.

Rida was born in the municipal district of al-Qalamun – close to Tripoli, on the Lebanese coast – into a family that descended from the lineage of the Prophet of Islam. He received his primary education at al-Qalamun elementary school and then at the National school that was established and administered by Shaykh Husayn al-Jisr (1845–1909). Despite al-Jisr's reformist tendencies, the relationship between Rida and his first teacher was not always easy. During his youth, Rida was affiliated to the Naqshabandi Sufi Order, which was supported and popularised in the Levant and Iraq by the disciples of Mawlana Khalid al-Naqshabandi, who died in Damascus in 1826. However, Rida soon became critical of the Sufis and the support they received from Sultan Abdul Hamid. The development of Rida's reformist stance and his decision to immigrate to Cairo were strongly influenced by his reading of al-Afghani and 'Abduh's magazine, *al-'Urwatul Wuthqa*. A year after his arrival in Cairo, Rida began publishing *al-Manar* (The Lighthouse) magazine with 'Abduh's blessing, turning his home in al-Insha' Street into an office and publishing house. For the next thirty-seven years – until Rida's death – *al-Manar* represented the voice of 'Abduh and his

23

students. Read by scholars and intellectuals from Fez to Singapore, the magazine became the single most influential propagator of the reformist project in the Islamic world.

In the final years of 'Abduh's life, Rida stayed close to his teacher's side and fought all of 'Abduh's battles with him. When 'Abduh wrote about the reformation of the Islamic courts and called for the establishment of an Islamic legal college that was not associated with al-Azhar, *al-Manar* defended the project in the face of vehement protests from Azhari scholars. When Farah Antoine, a Syrian writer based in Cairo, published a call for the separation of religion from state and society, Rida encouraged 'Abduh to respond. *Al-Manar* published 'Abduh's refutation in a series of articles, defending the role of Islam in promoting the nahdah (awakening). The series of articles was later published as *al-Islam wa al-Nasraniyyah Bayna al-'Ilm wa al-Madaniyyah* (Islam and Christianity between science and civilisation), which became one of 'Abduh's most famous books. *Al-Manar* also defended various controversial fatawa pronounced by 'Abduh, such as when he gave permission to a Muslim from one jurisprudential school to lead Muslims from another school in prayer, and when he permitted Muslims in South Africa to wear European-style hats.

Similarly, Rida's *Tafsir al-Manar* (Qur'anic commentary), which is regarded as the first attempt at a reformist reading of the Qur'anic text, was in fact a transcript of 'Abduh's Qur'anic exegesis. Rida also dedicated several years to writing his teacher's biography, which he published in three volumes under the title *Tarikh al-Ustadh al-Imam* (A history of the learned imam), thereby entrenching the dominant position that 'Abduh occupies in the history of the reformist movement.

After the death of 'Abduh, Rida had more freedom to make his own choices. He improved his relationship with Khedive 'Abbas and his associates, while simultaneously strengthening his association with the forces opposed to the rule of Sultan Abdul Hamid and with individuals who had Arab nationalist leanings. In 1908, when officers from the Committee of Union and Progress initiated a coup to oust Sultan Abdul Hamid, Rida supported their overthrow. He also supported the second coup in the following year, which put an end to the rule of Sultan Abdul Hamid and strengthened the control of the unionists over the administration.

Rida saw the unionists as offering salvation from Abdul Hamid's dictatorship, and as the beginning of the constitutional rule that would awaken the sultanate and its people. As a result, he visited Syria and Iraq, calling on the Arabs to pledge their support to the new authority. However, at around that time, Istanbul's new rulers held strong nationalist sentiments and argued that the Turkification of the state was necessary to strengthen unity in Turkey in the face of the secessionist forces that were then spreading across the sultanate. The intensification of policies of Turkification served only to strengthen Arab nationalism, even among those who, like Rashid Rida, had supported the coup to oust Abdul Hamid.[3]

After the Unionists came to power, several Arab nationalist organisations rose to prominence in the Levant, Iraq and even Istanbul. Along with a group of Muslim and Christian Syrians living in Cairo, Rida took the initiative of establishing the Ottoman Decentralized Party in 1912. The party called for the Ottoman Arab principalities to be granted the right to administer their own affairs within the borders of the Ottoman Empire.

From the time of al-Afghani, Arab nationalism began to develop among Arab Islamist reformists. 'Abduh, too, argued that the decline of Islam started with the rise of the Turks and the marginalisation of Arabs from the leadership of the Islamic movement. In 1902 and 1903, while 'Abduh was still alive, *al-Manar* published 'Abd al-Rahman al-Kawakibi's famous book, *Umm al-Qurra* (The mother of all villages), the foundational text of modern Arab nationalism.

It is important to note that the reformists were not nationalists in any ethnic sense; their ultimate goal was still to bring about an Islamic renaissance. However, the thesis that dominated their thinking is summed up in the view that Islam will never rise up as it did at the dawn of its history until Arabs again lead the ummah. This notion was enough to launch Arab nationalism, especially after the unionists launched their Turkification policies. In the early 1900s, Rida and *al-Manar's* opposition to unionist rule intensified. Thus, although Rida called on the Arabs to defend the sultanate and the caliphate against Western colonial forces during the First World War, he took a decisive position against the Ottoman Empire as a result of Jamal Pasha's execution of Arab leaders in Beirut, Damascus and Jerusalem. In June 1916, when Sharif Husayn announced the Arab Revolt against unionist rule in Mecca – in collusion with the British – Rida supported the revolt wholeheartedly.

The outcomes of the First World War did not favour the Arabs. The British reneged on their promises to Sharif Husayn: the British and the French divided the former Arab-Ottoman provinces between them; the Allies refused Arab requests for the establishment of a united, independent Arab state; and the British began to establish a Jewish state in Palestine. Rida and his generation lost all faith in the West.

After a short stint as head of the General Syrian Congress in Damascus, Rida also lost faith in the Hashemites taking the view that their indecisiveness and submission to the British disqualified them from leading the Arabs. After the collapse of the Arab government in Damascus, Rida returned to Cairo weighed down by bitterness. In his writings, he began to express regret for opposing the Ottoman Empire as well as his increasing animosity towards the West and its policies in the Islamic world.

Amidst his bitterness and regret, Rida found new hope in 'Abd al-'Aziz Al Sa'ud, who united the Arabian Peninsula and maintained his independence from the colonialists. Rida saw himself as a revivalist Salafi, and saw both reformist and doctrinal commonalities between the Sa'udi movement and the teachings of Shaykh Muhammad ibn 'Abd al-Wahhab.

Rida's Salafi inclinations intensified through his strong relationship with the Sa'udis and his contributions to *al-Manar* clearly reflected this. However, the main feature of Rida's final years was his support for Arab and Islamic nationalist movements in their struggle against Western colonialism. He saw the West's professed commitments to freedom, constitutionalism and rationality, from which Rida drew inspiration in the early years of *al-Manar*, fade away only to be replaced with the rampant avariciousness that threatened both the lives of Muslims and their homeland. Rida defended the institution of the caliphate when he saw Atatürk moving to abolish it; in the mid-1920s he supported the Syrian revolt with all his energy; he supported the Moroccan nationalist movement against the French secessionist project that favoured the Berbers; and he stood by the side of his student Amin al-Husayni in Palestine, participating in the General Islamic Conference in Jerusalem in 1931. When he passed away in 1935, there was no doubt that he was the most prominent and influential reformist of his generation.

⬦⬦⬦

With the death of Rida, the reformist movement expanded to make space for a new Islamic force: political Islam. In reality, the roots of the Islamist movements stretch back to the reformist project, which not only provided Islamist forces with much of their vocabulary, but also with justifications for their vision.

Reformist discourse concentrated on four central themes: tawhid (monotheism); the return to the Qur'an and the Sunnah as the primary sources of Islam; an affirmation of the importance of intellectual rigour; and an invitation to ijtihad (dynamic intellectual effort).

There is no doubt that the reformists put forward their central themes from a modernist perspective, and modernity – however it was conceived – was the strongest hidden influence on their vision of Islamic revivalism. Accordingly, reformist thought was never purely a manifestation of jurisprudential and theological concerns; it was always rooted in a specific socio-political and cultural context.

By concentrating on monotheism, and a return to the Qur'an and the prophetic tradition, the reformists launched an open attack on Asharite doctrines; that is, on the influence of Sufism and its dogmatic attachment to specific jurisprudential schools of thought. By calling for a revival of ijtihad (dynamic intellectual effort) and affirming that Muslims could find recourse in intellectual rigour, they sought to liberate believers from the shackles of mystical beliefs and to offer them more freedom of choice. The reformist rejection of fatalism and predestination (as referred to by 'Abduh) was not simply an expression of doctrinal belief, it also encompassed a strong denunciation of political despotism and of surrender to tyranny.

Implicit in the reformists' affirmation of the primacy of the Qur'an was an attempt to go beyond the traditional Islamic heritage, while simultaneously confronting the internal divisions between the various jurisprudential schools of thought and the networks of interests they protected. In addition, the reformists strove to vindicate the hypothesis that Islam's traditional heritage could be reconciled with what they saw as the positive aspects of the modern West. Following an apologist path, the reformists presented the Islamic jurisprudential concepts of al-masalih al-mursalah (public welfare) as equivalent to utilitarianism, shura (consultation) as equivalent to parliamentary representation and ijma (consensus) as equivalent to public opinion.

From the perspective of its genesis, reformist thinking emerged from an impasse, the product of a crisis made extremely burdensome by a sense of internal collapse and an apparent inability to respond to the Western onslaught. The first generation of reformists erred by ignoring the impact of Western colonial troops and armadas, assuming that the strength of the West was the direct and simple result of religious reform, science and rationality.

There are several reasons why it is a gross simplification to explain the revivalist inclinations of the reformists simply as a mask that hides their unconditional embrace of, or complete subjugation to, Western modernity. First, the reformists always strove to differentiate between the generally upstanding human values and institutions of the modern West and the total relegation of these values by the colonial project. Second, Islam remained the primary frame of reference for most of the reformists. Third, reformist opposition to the continuously intensifying Western domination over the Islamic world was authentic. This opposition took the form of armed resistance among the third-generation students of the reformist movement, with the likes of 'Abd al-Karim al-Khattabi, 'Izz al-Din al-Qassam and al-Haj Amin al-Husayni. Although, some reformists, such as Lutfi al-Sayyid and Qasim Amin, were more prone to adopting Western values and more willing to reconcile with the colonial administrations, the knot that bound the project of reconciling Islam with the West was undone.

By confronting what they saw as a deviation from the essence of Islam, the reformists helped to reaffirm Islam's eternal values. With their tireless use of modern media, they made sure that Islamic discourse was integrated into the language of the masses. However, their central (albeit perhaps unintentional) achievement was to nurture the idea that Islam has the answers to the questions of any age, including those of modernity.

This has since become the touchstone of political Islam. The central concern of the Islamists was to find an answer to the question of the renaissance. Their search for deliverance from the crisis took them from place to place and from one journey to the next. Their followers have become ever more determined and self-assured. Perhaps the most prominent and influential of these was one of Rashid Rida's most dedicated students and followers: his name was Hasan al-Banna, and he founded the Muslim Brotherhood.

3

Hasan al-Banna
and the Muslim Brotherhood

As the founder of the Muslim Brotherhood, the first major modern Islamic organisation, Hasan al-Banna (1906–1949) was the first Islamist leader, and in the Muslim world, he is still the most famous. During his lifetime, al-Banna was able to enthuse and mobilise the Muslim masses. More than sixty years after his death, he remains a key figure in Egyptian history and in modern Islam.

To members of the Muslim Brotherhood, al-Banna is not only the founder of their organisation, but also their frame of reference. To those who oppose the Islamists, al-Banna is seen as having planted the seeds of all the evils they believe are epitomised in political Islam. The reality is far more complex than either of these two groups would have it. When the Muslim Brotherhood was established, neither al-Banna nor those who worked with him had any clear vision of what the organisation would become. Of course, the group was the product of al-Banna's efforts and his leadership but it was also very much a product of the particular historical conditions that prevailed in Egypt and the Arab region in his time.

Al-Banna was born in 1906 into a family of limited income in Mahmudiyyah, a village in Egypt's governorate of al-Buhayrah. His father was the local watchmaker and because he had studied at al-Azhar, he had various religious responsibilities in the village. Without forcing them to choose specific career paths, al-Banna's father made sure that all his sons were educated. The young Hasan was sent to elementary school in Mahmudiyyah and from there to primary school. The first sign of his deep interest in Islam was his decision to affiliate to the Hasafiyyah Sufi Order that was active in his village. Although his life later took him in another direction, he remained a Sufi until he left for Cairo at the age of sixteen, and the influence of Sufism on his personality and his life should not be underestimated.[1]

At the age of thirteen, Al-Banna made his way to Damanhour, al-Buhayrah's capital and its largest city, to complete his secondary education at the teacher-training college there. Three years later, he arrived in Cairo to register at the Dar al-'Ulum teacher-training college. Cairo in the 1920s was probably the most important city in the Orient and, with all its clamour and novelty, it must have been quite a shock to the young student from the conservative Egyptian countryside.

Al-Banna's vision of Islam, Egypt and the world began to take shape at the Dar al-'Ulum, where he received training in the Arabic and Islamic sciences, as well as in other non-traditional courses taught by modern methods. However, his experiences were not limited to the Dar al-'Ulum. During his four years of study there, al-Banna regularly attended gatherings held by the great reformist Rashid Rida, editor of *al-Manar* magazine. Al-Banna was also often seen at gatherings held by Muhib al-Din al-Khatib, a Syrian journalist and writer who was living in Cairo and who owned both al-Dar al-Salafiyyah publishing house and *al-Fath* (The victory) magazine.[2] Surrounded by scholars and intellectuals such as Rida, al-Khatib and others, al-Banna was introduced to modern Islamic thought, as well as to its sub-categories and its thinkers, Egyptian and non-Egyptian alike. Since Rida and al-Khatib were well known for their Arab nationalist inclinations, Arab identity quickly occupied a special place in al-Banna's own thinking. Just like the earlier Islamist reformers, he became an Arab nationalist, and began calling for an Islamic renaissance and for unity among the Arabs.

In 1923, during al-Banna's first year at the Dar al-'Ulum, Egypt issued its first constitution, provoking much debate about the jurisdiction of the king and the parliament, and establishing the foundations of what is known as Egypt's liberal epoch. By granting Egypt partial independence, the British were able to successfully defuse the after-effects of the 1919 revolution and transfer much of its political fallout onto the Egyptian ruling class. In his first few years in Cairo, al-Banna witnessed the beginnings of this fallout, and observed how internal political divisions began to germinate in the shadows cast by the colonial power.

A year before completing his university education, al-Banna observed the failure of the Islamic Caliphate conference in Cairo. The conference had been convened in an attempt to appoint King Fu'ad as the new caliph after Atatürk had abolished the Ottoman Caliphate. Al-Banna also witnessed the acrimonious debate initiated by the publication of a book by the Azhari scholar and judge, 'Ali 'Abd al-Raziq, titled *al-Islam wa Usul al-Hukm* (Islam and the principles of governance). In the book, 'Abd al-Raziq claimed that upholding the institution of the caliphate was not a religious obligation as it was simply a historical institution of authority. In the coming years, al-Banna always insisted on the necessity of basing all authority on Islamic principles, and he believed in the possibility of Islamic solidarity. However, given the controversy over the caliphate, he avoided including this on his list of priorities.

After graduating, al-Banna was appointed to teach at al-Amiriyyah Primary School in the city of al-Isma'iliyyah, which was the headquarters of the Suez Canal Company and home to Britain's largest military base in Egypt. There he encountered another dimension of the crisis facing both Egypt and Islam. Years later, al-Banna described the impressions the city made on him, saying:

> Isma'iliyyah was an amazing inspiration. The English barracks
> in the west with their might and authority, and their supremacy
> and sway, leave a feeling of jealousy, distress and regret in the
> soul of every nationalist, pushing us to reassess the detestable

33

occupation and the great catastrophe that Egypt has been subjected to: the material and ethical opportunities lost; how the occupation has been the major impediment to Egypt's awakening and progress as well as the primary obstacle to Arab unity and Muslim consensus over the past sixty years. The elegant and luxurious offices of the Suez Canal Company, with all their beauty, splendour, authority and influence, uses Egyptians, treating them like oppressed dependents, and honours foreigners, elevating them to the ranks of masters and rulers. The company has a monopoly over the supply and use of all public amenities, including electricity, water and sanitation. The company undertakes everything that the local municipality should manage. Even the roads and entrances to Isma'iliyyah, an entirely Egyptian city, are in company hands, and no one may enter or leave without their permission.[3]

In essence, the city of Isma'iliyyah epitomised Egypt's continuing occupation by Britain, and while the Suez Canal reminded Egypt of its loss of sovereignty and the country's subjugation to foreign rule, the Suez Canal Company embodied this domination. It is probably no coincidence that the Muslim Brotherhood was born in this very city.

In 1927, in response to intense Christian missionary activity in Egypt and elsewhere in the Islamic world, a group of Egyptian scholars and activists were inspired by the charitable, cultural and sports activities of the Young Men's Christian Association, to establish the Jam'iyyah al-Shubban al-Muslimin (Young Men's Muslim Association or YMMA). Muhib al-Din al-Khatib was by then a close friend of al-Banna. Having helped establish the YMMA, he encouraged al-Banna to join too. However, al-Banna seems to have found little resonance with his own inclinations in the YMMA's liberal Islamic character. From his years in al-Mahmudiyyah, al-Banna had grown accustomed to preaching – speaking in mosques and discussion forums, even in coffee shops. He continued to do this in al-Isma'iliyyah, where a group of local youth gathered around him. This group soon began to discuss forming an Islamic organisation that could be a centre for proselytisation and would support the establishment of Islamic schools and mosques. In this way, the Jam'iyyah al-Ikhwan al-Muslimin (Society of the Muslim Brotherhood) was born and, in March 1928, al-Banna was elected as its president.

In just few years, the Brotherhood blossomed in al-Isma'iliyyah as a result of the loyalty and active participation of its members and their families in a range of activities. Soon, members were able to establish branches in several other cities and villages in Egypt, including in Cairo.

In 1932, al-Banna was transferred to a school in Cairo, and it was then decided to relocate the organisation's headquarters to Egypt's capital city and the centre of the country's political and intellectual life. At this time, neither al-Banna nor the Muslim Brotherhood were nationally well known, but the transfer to Cairo gave al-Banna and the Brotherhood a new platform. A year after their relocation, the Brotherhood launched their first publication, the weekly magazine *al-Ikhwan al-Muslimun*. The organisation flourished, with its increasing activities and growing membership requiring the rapid expansion of its headquarters. The Brotherhood's first offices were located at 13 Nasiriyyah Street in the Sayyidah Zaynab Quarter. They then moved to the Awqaf Ministry Building, in al-'Atabah al-Khadra'a Square, and finally settled in two large houses built alongside each other in al-Hilmiyyah al-Jadidah Square. The activities of the Brotherhood were still confined to preaching and teaching, but as political upheaval swept through Egypt in the 1930s, the Brotherhood was pulled into its sway.

In 1936, the government, then led by the Wafd Party, signed a new treaty with the British that granted Egypt an additional margin of independence. In the following year, the young King Faruq was crowned, succeeding his father King Fu'ad. King Faruq had received a predominantly Egyptian education, making it easier for Egyptians – including members of the Brotherhood – to welcome his ascension. He was also supported by three of Egypt's greatest leaders: 'Ali Mahir (head of the Royal Court), Shaykh Mustafa al-Maraghi (a student of Muhammad 'Abduh's, head of al-Azhar and one of Faruq's former teachers), and 'Aziz 'Ali al-Misri (an Ottoman officer and former Arab nationalist, who had been Faruq's military aide while he was crown prince). These three men were politicians, with all that this implies in terms of strategy and cunning. They were united in their Islamic and Arab nationalist views, a strong belief in Egypt's leadership role in the region, and their desire to be liberated from Britain – especially after the treaty of 1936 granted a wider margin of manoeuvrability to Egypt in terms of its foreign policy. They all saw the young king as a symbol of national liberty, capable of reinstating Egypt as a central power in the region. Since none of these men were too concerned about democratic principles, they strove to undermine the Wafd Party's majority in the government, and worked to reinforce the strength and influence of the palace. In 1939, the king appointed 'Ali Mahir as prime minister; Mahir soon established ties with the new popular organisations, including the Muslim Brotherhood and the strongly nationalist Egyptian Youth Movement, as forces representing a political equivalent to the Wafd Party.

During this time, the Muslim Brotherhood showed their strength by supporting the Palestinian cause rather than engaging the sphere of Egyptian politics. From 1933, the Brotherhood had played a secondary role in garnering popular Egyptian support for the Palestinian struggle. However, they then sent their own delegation to visit Palestine, East Jordan and Syria, and were successful in establishing a strong link with Mufti al-Haj Amin al-Husayni, who had emerged as the leader of the Palestinian national movement in the early 1930s. When the Great Palestinian Revolt broke out in 1936, the Brotherhood was able to play a major role in mobilising Egyptian support for the Palestinian revolution: the Brotherhood formed committees, and collected donations from all over Egypt; they sent protest letters to the British Embassy and organised popular gatherings and protest marches. Because of these activities, the Palestinian question was discussed in the farthest corners of Egypt and in all its cities, towns and villages. This both strengthened the Brotherhood's self-confidence and alerted the traditional Egyptian political parties and the monarchy to the fact that a new popular force was emerging.

Another important factor played a role in pushing the Brotherhood into politics. Ahmad al-Sukkari, a close friend of Al-Banna's from al-Mahmudiyyah, worked in the Ministry of Education and headed the Muslim Brotherhood branch in the town. In 1938, al-Sukkari moved to the Ministry of Education's head office in Cairo. He was soon appointed as second-in-charge in the Brotherhood and his role was to supervise the organisation's daily affairs. Al-Sukkari was a gifted orator, extremely intelligent and very politically aware. It is possible that he saw al-Banna as a religious teacher who had little interest in politics. What is more certain is that al-Sukkari played a key role in establishing the Brotherhood. His influence is apparent in al-Banna's historic speech at the Brotherhood's fifth congress, in which he clearly indicated that the organisation was going to enter the fray of Egyptian politics. When the king's advisor, 'Ali Mahir, began establishing links with the Brotherhood, al-Sukkari acted as the main channel of communication. These were the Brotherhood's first steps into the political sphere, but definitely not its last. Surprisingly, the Egyptian government, which has since become the sworn enemy of the Brotherhood, was the first to encourage these steps!

'Ali Mahir's Cabinet was filled with Arab nationalist and Islamist elements who were opposed to the British presence in Egypt, including individuals such as 'Aziz 'Ali al-Misri, 'Abd al-Rahman 'Azzam and Salih Harb. When the Second World War broke out, Mahir stuck to the 1936 treaty and refused to declare war on Germany. When the British forces lost ground against German and Italian forces on the Egyptian–Libyan border and in Egypt itself, neither the Egyptian government nor its people concealed their animosity towards the British. In the summer of 1940, the British forced King Faruq to disband 'Ali Mahir's government and appoint a new one.

Early the following year, Rashid 'Ali al-Kilani and some military officers led an uprising against Britain in Iraq, resulting in a new British invasion of that country. The entire Arab Middle East seemed to be on the brink of erupting. In these conditions, the Brotherhood probably established temporary links with the Axis Powers, just as 'Ali Mahir and 'Aziz al-Misri had done. In addition, it is highly likely that Al-Banna established al-Nizam al-Khass (the Covert Structure) within the Brotherhood at around this time.

The Covert Structure was a secret armed wing that was not answerable to the Brotherhood's public leadership structures. Al-Banna initially appointed Salih 'Ashmawi, one of the Brotherhood's most prominent young members, to lead this new formation. However, it soon became clear that 'Ashmawi had too many other responsibilities, and he was replaced by another young man who was not part of the Brotherhood's leadership group, although he was well known to them. His name was 'Abd al-Rahman al-Sanadi. Thus, the Covert Structure acquired its first secret leader. This secrecy was not only illegal, it also shielded the structure from accountability. In the coming years, the Covert Structure and al-Sanadi were linked to a string of damaging transgressions, including a revolt against the leadership of the Brotherhood itself.

In the same period, al-Banna was introduced to Muhammad Anwar al-Sadat, who was then a young military officer. Sadat introduced al-Banna to a number of other military officers who were strongly nationalist and extremely angry about the British occupation. As soon as al-Banna realised how widespread this anger was within the military, he appointed a former soldier who had joined the Brotherhood, Mahmud Labib, to take responsibility for military elements linked to the Brotherhood.

At this point, even the organisational structures of the Brotherhood began to transform themselves. Shortly before the end of the Second World War, al-Banna introduced a new feature into the organisation's structure, known as the nizam al-usr (structure of families). In the first phase of the group's history, individual members had been loosely linked to various branches or groups within the organisation. With the introduction of the new structure, the Brotherhood organised itself into small primary and permanent 'family' units. In this way, the Brotherhood made a major transition from being an organisation focused on the propagation of Islam to being a multi-faceted political entity stretched across Egyptian society, both openly and secretly.

On 4 February 1942, the British used force to compel King Faruq to either abdicate or appoint Mustafa al-Nahas, leader of the Wafd Party as prime minister. British confidence in Nahas was motivated by the fact that he was a former minister and one of Britain's most faithful allies in Egypt. In addition, they had faith in the Wafd Party's liberalism, and its animosity towards the Nazis. However, this 'February 4 Incident' (as it is known in modern Egyptian history) cast doubt on the patriotism of the Wafd Party and signalled the beginning of the collapse of the king. After this, the monarch seems to have been overcome by his fear of the British. He gradually descended into corruption and hopelessness, becoming intensely withdrawn and distanced from his people.

Initially, the king retaliated against the February 4 Incident by expelling the Wafd government. While Egypt boiled over with popular activity calling for an end to British occupation, governance was passed on to parties linked to the palace that had neither parliamentary support nor popular influence, and which therefore relied on the security apparatuses to maintain control. In a climate of increasing political violence and disorder, the Brotherhood's Covert Structure (along with several other political organisations) broke out of its shell, spilling out onto the streets of Cairo. Such violence was not new to Egyptian politics. Since the assassination of then-prime minister Boutros Ghali in 1910 at the hands of a member of the Nationalist Party, regular cycles of political violence have broken out in Egypt, in which almost all of the country's various political organisations have taken part.

In 1945 a member of the Nationalist Party assassinated the prime minister, Ahmad Mahir, who was on his way to announce Egypt's entry into the Second World War on the side of the Allies. After failed attempts to assassinate al-Banna and Nahas, Husayn Tawfiq assassinated Amin 'Uthman Pasha, a former government minister and another of Britain's most faithful allies. Tawfiq was a member of a secret group to which Anwar Sadat was linked. At a time in which it was common for activists to throw grenades at British patrols in Egyptian cities, the Metro and Miami cinemas in downtown Cairo were bombed and several businesses were subjected to arson attacks.

Meanwhile, by maintaining a truce with the Wafd government for the remainder of the Second World War, the Brotherhood grew both administratively and in terms of its popular support. As the war drew to an end, the Brotherhood seemed set to emerge as a popular and very real competitor to the Wafd Party, not only among the middle classes but also in the universities and deep in the Egyptian countryside. However, as noted, Egyptian politics had begun to shifting towards chaos, violence and revolution, and, just next door, Palestine moved closer to explosion and to the first Arab-Israeli war.

In May 1948, as soon as the British Government announced its intention to withdraw from Palestine – Egypt's immediate neighbour – several Arab nations began preparing to help the Palestinian people to confront the Zionists. 'Abd al-Rahman 'Azzam, secretary general of the newly formed Arab League, called on Arab youth to volunteer for the sake of Palestine. In April 1948, the first unit of volunteers left from Cairo, crossing the Egyptian–Palestinian border. Members of the Brotherhood and its Covert Structure, as well as Egyptian military officers, participated actively in the Arab campaign, and played a prominent role on the battlefield. In addition, participation in the Palestinian War was not limited to Egypt's Muslim Brotherhood; members of the Brotherhood, which now had branches in Jordan, Syria and Sudan, also volunteered.

If the Brotherhood's participation in the Palestinian war increased their general popularity, it also boosted the confidence of elements within the Covert Structure. In January 1948, Egyptian security forces uncovered an arms cache and 165 explosives in an isolated part of the Cairo suburb of Muqattam Mountain. A battle ensued between the police and a young member of the Brotherhood, who later claimed that the weapons were intended for Palestine. Ultimately, the arms were confiscated and several people were arrested, including Al-Sayyid Fayiz, one of the leaders of the Covert Structure. We can assume that Egypt's state security apparatuses knew little about the Covert Structure or its leaders at that time, but this changed very quickly.

When Ahmad al-Khazindar, a well-known Egyptian judge, was assassinated on his way to work on 22 February 1948, the police were quickly able to arrest the two killers, who confessed to being members of the Covert Structure. A month before his assassination, the judge had passed a cruel sentence on two young Brotherhood members who were accused of lobbing grenades at the English Officers Club in Cairo on the eve of the Prophet's birthday (no fatalities occurred). Clearly, the judge was assassinated in an act of retribution. In November of the same year, the two suspects were found guilty of his murder and sentenced to life imprisonment with hard labour.

During the investigation of the assassination, al-Banna was called in for questioning, but was released without charge. However, the whole incident left him feeling extremely anxious that he was losing his grip on the Covert Structure and that it was beginning to operate as an independent body. Despite the corruption that had riddled the state and much of Egyptian politics in the 1940s, and regardless of the personal inclinations of certain judges, the Egyptian legal fraternity had managed to preserve its independence and integrity. In fact, Egypt's legal profession, from judges to lawyers, are unique in still being widely respected. Undoubtedly, the assassination of the judge was, from a certain perspective, an assault on the country's legal institutions, but al-Banna had some grounds to hope that it would still be willing to protect and show impartiality towards the Brotherhood. It is therefore surprising that, despite being tremendously concerned about the assassination, he took no immediate steps to contain the Covert Structure.

On 13 May 1948, just two days before the Egyptian Army crossed the Palestinian border to participate in the Arab campaign to protect the rights of the Palestinians, the prime minister Mahmud Fahmi al-Nuqrashi declared martial law in Egypt. In the coming weeks, the tensions in Egypt increased. The country's Political Police unit began a campaign of arrests, targeting suspected communists and Zionists. As soon as the Palestinian War began, a huge march took place in Cairo in support of the Egyptian army and in protest against the British occupation.

Then, another kind of war broke out as several districts in Cairo were turned into battlefields. Homes in the Jewish quarter were blown up and explosives were detonated on the premises of Shicoril and Orico, two large businesses owned by wealthy Jewish citizens. The premises of Benzion, Jatino and the Eastern Delta were blown up. The offices of the Marconi Telegraph Company were destroyed, as were the premises of the Eastern Publishing Company. Then, for a second time, homes in parts of the Jewish quarter were attacked.

It was widely believed that the Brotherhood was playing a central role in the bombings, and it seemed as if the Egyptian government had lost control of the capital city. In October, security officers found an arms cache on the farm of Muhammad Farghali, the leader of Brotherhood volunteers who had gone to Palestine. Then, on the afternoon of 15 November, a police vehicle spotted a suspicious-looking jeep with no a license plate, parked in front of a house in Cairo's al-Waili district. The jeep was seized and two passengers, who attempted to flee, were arrested. The house was raided and a large quantity of explosives and documents were found. Thereafter, other individuals linked to the jeep and the house were also arrested. Both the jeep and the house were found to be linked to the Covert Structure; in fact, some of the individuals arrested were known to be leaders in the organisation. The documents revealed much about the Covert Structure, and brought the Brotherhood's underground wing to the attention of Egypt's Political Police division once more.

The bombings resulted in many deaths and tremendous material losses, and continued until the end of 1948. On Wednesday 8 December, Nuqrashi issued Military Order No. 63 of 1948, banning the Muslim Brotherhood and all its branches. The first clause of the order, which contained nine sub-clauses, stated:

> The society known as the Society of the Muslim Brotherhood is immediately proscribed, along with all of its branches across the Egyptian Kingdom; premises appointed for its activities are also closed. Papers, documents, recordings, printed material and money, or more generally all of the possessions of the Society, are also seized. Members of the administrative council of the aforementioned Society, its branches, managers, members and affiliates are prohibited from continuing the activities of the Society in any form, but more specifically, are prohibited from holding meetings, branch meetings, organising such meetings and inviting people to attend them, collecting funds or subscriptions or anything of the sort. In implementing this ruling, a gathering of five or more persons who were members of the aforementioned Society is regarded as a prohibited meeting.[4]

As al-Banna and other Brotherhood leaders listened to the banning order being broadcast over the radio, police officers encircled the organisation's two buildings in al-Hilmiyyah al-Jadidah Square. The police cordoned off the buildings after confiscating their contents and arresting everyone present except al-Banna. Similar scenes played out at all the Brotherhood's branches across Egypt. Brotherhood volunteers returning from Palestine were also arrested. Although Nuqrashi's government was generally very weak, his campaign against the Brotherhood was bold and comprehensive, and it seems to have taken al-Banna and his organisation by surprise.

Since the Brotherhood's relations with the Wafd and other political parties were not at their best, no opposition was voiced against the banning order. The only protests came from a former Coptic Wafdist leader, Makram 'Abid, and these merely prompted one newspaper, the *'Akhir Sa'ah* (Final hour), to sarcastically observe that 'Abid was the Muslim Brotherhood's newest recruit. For their part, the Brotherhood, saw the banning order as a British plot, implemented by a puppet regime, and believed that Nuqrashi was attempting to harass the Brotherhood's volunteers in Palestine as a means of weakening their loyalties to the organisation. However, while the British and other Europeans in Egypt certainly welcomed the ban, no evidence has yet emerged that proves any link between the British and the issuing of the banning order.

Nuqrashi's move did not go unpunished by the Brotherhood's armed wing. On 28 December, just twenty days after the banning order was issued, 'Abd al-Majid Ahmad Husayn, a member of the Covert Structure and veterinary science student, opened fire on the prime minister in front of the interior ministry building, hitting him in the chest and back, and killing him instantly. Nuqrashi was surrounded by a police guard at the time, and ironically the young assassin was disguised as a police officer. The Covert Structure had exacted their revenge, and in so doing they took the level of political violence in Egypt to new heights, tarnishing the image of the Brotherhood so badly that the damage has yet to be undone.

If the killing of Judge al-Khazindar had made al-Banna nervous, the assassination of Nuqrashi was like a thunderbolt. Al-Banna quickly found himself isolated, not only because most of the Brotherhood's leadership had been arrested, but also because the Brotherhood's strategy had no answers to the kind of questions posed by this critical situation or the tempestuous conditions. The writing was on the wall, however. At Nuqrashi's funeral, his followers shouted 'Death to al-Banna', and when Interior Minister 'Ibrahim 'Abd al-Hadi, a close friend of Nuqrashi and former head of the Royal Court, took over as Egypt's prime minister, he unleashed an unprecedented campaign of violence against the Brotherhood and its supporters.

❦❦❦

Al-Banna's discourse was, from the outset, a general one, without clear or specific goals. In some ways, this helped broaden support for the group and increase its followers. In his lectures and writings, al-Banna sought inspiration from the Islamist reformists, whether in relation to preserving Islamic identity, internal reform or relations with Western civilisation. However, al-Banna's writing was far more obscure than that of the reformists and far more expressive of his sense that Islam was under threat and in need of protection.

In the *Risalat al-Ta'alim* (Treatise of teachings), which is regarded as one of the Brotherhood's most important early texts, al-Banna affirmed that 'Islam is a complete system that deals with all aspects of life; it is about state and homeland, government and community'. In this text, he expressed a moderate Salafi position that accepts ijtihad (renewed intellectual effort), but does not invoke it with fervour; he mentioned the principle of masalih al-mursalah (public welfare) but did not emphasise it; he rejected bida' (heretical innovations) but simultaneously rejected takfir (excommunication) if a Muslim commits sin.[5] In addition, he avoided discussing the essence of the Islamic system and did not refer to constitutions, freedoms or parliamentary systems; he did not discuss the difficult relationship between the shari'ah and the ummah, which is implicit in any acceptance of the notion of the modern nation-state. Al-Banna's general statement: 'Islam is religion and state, Qur'an and sword', was quickly accepted as the Brotherhood's motto and methodology, and was also adopted by a large number of other forces that are broadly supportive of political Islam.

In a petition presented by the Brotherhood to 'Ali Mahir on the occasion of the formation of his government in October 1938, al-Banna wrote:

> We inherited Islam and its teachings generations ago, and there is no doubt that the leadership of Islam and the Muslims has become Egypt's lot. Ideas and administrative systems emanating from Europe spread out, some of which accord with Islamic thought and some of which clash with and negate it. The Muslim Brotherhood believes that the only path to reform is for Egypt to return to the teachings of Islam and to implement them properly, in addition to drawing from all other ideas, old and new, Eastern and Western, as long as these do not negate the teachings of Islam and are to the benefit of the Muslim community.[6]

However, al-Banna very rarely specified which Islamic teachings he wanted the Egyptian state to have recourse to, nor did he clarify – even in general terms – what aspects of Western thought may be drawn upon.

In the early phase of the Brotherhood's history, it is likely that al-Banna's vision of transformation was fairly vague. In 1942, he put himself forward for nomination to participate in the elections but was forced to withdraw by the leader of the Wafd Party Mustafa al-Nahas. Al-Banna did, however, stand for election in Egypt's 1945 parliamentary elections but large-scale rigging by Ahmad Mahir's government guaranteed his failure.

His willingness to stand for election does not necessarily mean that al-Banna believed in parliamentary systems, political pluralism, or the principle of power rotation in politics. In truth, none of the Brotherhood's early writings take a position on parliamentary systems and al-Banna's views on political parties were invariably negative.

Al-Banna had expressed his opposition to the idea of revolution in his letter to the organisation's fifth congress in 1938, saying: 'Egypt has experienced its share of revolutions but has gained nothing more from them than you are already aware of.' Nevertheless, just two years later, al-Banna helped establish the Brotherhood's Covert Structure. Was he endorsing the monarchy by calling a special conference in 1937 to welcome the appointment of the new king? Or did he support the establishment of a republic, as Egypt's security forces claimed in the late 1940s? The answer to both of these questions is that we don't know.

What is clear, is that the Muslim Brotherhood injected a new Islamic fervour into the streets of Egypt, and thereafter into several Arab countries. However, their rapid growth, the danger they represented to Western interests in Egypt and the region, and the opacity of their political views were no help when violence flared up at the beginning of the 1950s, placing the future of the Brotherhood and the Egyptian state in question. These features of the organisation were also a burden when 'Abd al-Hadi's government intensified the campaign against them and the prime minister began planning to avenge the assassination of Nuqrashi, his friend and predecessor.

After the banning of the Brotherhood, and the arrest of its leadership, the YMMA welcomed al-Banna with open arms and gave him an office at their premises in central Cairo. Feeling that his safety was threatened, al-Banna was initially always accompanied by one of his brothers, who was also a police officer. However, his brother was soon arrested and his brother-in-law, 'Abd al-Karim Mansur, who was a lawyer, became his new companion.

Al-Banna soon asked the governor of Cairo for permission to leave the city and move to the home of friends in the countryside, but 'Abd al-Hadi ordered the governor to ignore the request. During those crucial days, al-Banna asked various mediators to try to find a solution with 'Abd al-Hadi, or, at the very least, to get him permission to visit the Brotherhood leaders in prison.

On 12 January 1949, everyone was taken aback when the Covert Structure attempted to blow up the appeal court building in which all the papers concerning the Brotherhood had been stored, including the files on Nuqrashi's assassination. For the next few weeks, 'Abd al-Hadi's intermediaries' primary task was to try to hoodwink al-Banna into believing that the state would let him be. They convinced him to write a strong statement condemning the murder of Nuqrashi. In this now-famous statement, al-Banna described the killers as 'neither members of the Brotherhood nor Muslim'. However, instead of circulating the statement immediately, 'Abd al-Hadi held it back, making it public a day after al-Banna met his fate, in an attempt to create the impression that his assassination was the result of an internal dispute within the Brotherhood.

At about 8:30 on Saturday evening, 12 February 1949, al-Banna left the YMMA building with his brother-in-law after meeting with one of the intermediaries involved in the crisis. One of the YMMA employees ordered a taxi for al-Banna and his companion. The two men climbed into the vehicle but before it could move off, three individuals with revolvers opened the two back doors of the vehicle and opened fire before fleeing the scene. Al-Banna and his companion were not killed immediately, and al-Banna tried to go after his attackers, even noting down the license plate number of the attackers' getaway car.

The two victims were taken by ambulance to the Qasr al-'Ayni Hospital. When they arrived al-Banna was still conscious but his brother-in-law, who eventually recovered, was not. No-one knows for certain what transpired in the operating theatre, but al-Banna's death was announced just hours later. His body was handed over to his family under stringent security conditions and they were ordered to bury him immediately. When he was carried to his final resting place by his family, the Coptic Wafdist leader Makram 'Abid was the only public figure present.

The assassination of Hasan al-Banna, founder and spiritual leader of the Muslim Brotherhood, was a result of deep-rooted crises that afflicted both Egypt and the Brotherhood in the 1940s. The Egyptian government had lost control of their country, and the leaders of the

Muslim Brotherhood lost control of their members' political actions. No Egyptian government has ever commissioned a serious investigation into al-Banna's assassination. The one investigation that did occur took place soon after the 1952 revolution, with the establishment of a criminal tribunal. The tribunal incriminated several police officers and officers from the Political Police unit for committing or conspiring to commit the assassination. However, 'Abd al-Hadi, who many believe ordered the assassination, was never implicated.

Al-Banna's assassination ended an era in the history of the Brotherhood. A new era began, in which the Brotherhood had to face challenges no less intense than those it had already confronted, but without its founder and spiritual guide, around whom it had congregated for two eventful decades.

4

The Muslim Brotherhood and the 1952 Egyptian Revolution

*O*n 27 October 1954, Gamal Abdel Nasser delivered a national address to the people of Egypt from al-Manshiyyah Square in Alexandria. As leader of the coup that deposed the Egyptian monarchy two years earlier, Nasser stood before the crowd as their new prime minister. After widespread public outcry about concessions that his government had made to the British, he was intending to use his speech to explain the gains that Egypt had made in a new agreement with Britain about their withdrawal from Egypt. Suddenly, eight shots were fired in the direction of the podium. Astonishingly, none of the bullets reached their target and no one was injured. Nasser continued speaking, raising the pitch of his voice to denounce those plotting against the revolution and the national cause.

Just hours later, Nasser's military regime accused the Muslim Brotherhood of attempting to assassinate the leader of the revolution, and embarked on a widespread campaign to arrest their leaders, cadres and members. This was the culmination of tensions that had grown between Nasser and the Brotherhood in the previous two years, and the beginning of a bloody rupture between the two that has burdened Arab politics, as well as Arab and Islamic thought, ever since. The problem is that the clash between Nasser's Free Officers and the Brotherhood was not a conflict between politically and intellectually opposed parties; in fact what they had in common far outstripped what set them apart.

Anwar Sadat was the first nationalist military officer to make contact with the Muslim Brotherhood in the early 1940s.[1] However, at that time

51

Sadat was not yet part of Nasser's group (he joined the Free Officers in the late 1940s). Nasser, on the other hand, joined the Muslim Brotherhood's Covert Structure in 1942. Other Free Officers who joined the Covert Structure include Kamal al-Din Husayn, Hasan Ibrahim and 'Abd al-Latif al-Baghdadi. Even Khalid Muhyi al-Din, later known for his leftist leanings, passed via the Covert Structure on his way to Iskra, the Egyptian communist organisation.[2] However, the majority of those who subsequently became known as the Free Officers had resigned from the Brotherhood in the late 1940s. The tedious leadership style of the leader of the Covert Structure, 'Abd al-Rahman al-Sanadi, was one reason for their disaffection. The other was their belief that they should broaden their organisation within the military and recruit non-Islamists as well. However, the most important reason is probably that Nasser, who always showed high levels of tactical acumen, had chosen to affiliate to the Brotherhood when their popularity was growing rapidly during the Second World War. When the Brotherhood was banned, and under threat from the government of 'Abd al-Hadi, he chose to cut ties with the group. However, as the idea of a military coup developed in Nasser's mind, he re-established contact with the Brotherhood in the autumn of 1951. By this time the Free Officer's Organisation had grown, and indeed included both Islamist and non-Islamist officers.

❧❦❧

Nasser was born in 1918 in Alexandria. His father hailed from the village of Bani Mur, which was under the jurisdiction of the Asyut Governorate in Egypt's Sa'id region. His father worked for the state-run postal service, which granted the family a simple but stable livelihood. As a secondary-school student, Nasser participated in protests against the 1936 Anglo-Egyptian Treaty, during which he was arrested but soon released.

In March 1937, Nasser enrolled at the military academy where officers of the Egyptian Army were trained. Prior to 1936, army officers were chosen from Egypt's upper classes and the academy, like all other military institutions, was under British administration since the British occupation began. In 1936, the Anglo-Egyptian Treaty between Egypt and Britain granted Egypt limited independence and gave the Egyptian government the freedom to manage the administrative affairs of its own army.[3] The Wafd government quickly opened the doors of the military academy to all Egyptians, and Nasser was among the first to enrol. In fact, almost all of the Free Officers were part of the school's first intake after the signing of the treaty.

After his graduation, Nasser served in the Egyptian Army in Sudan. He participated in the Palestinian War in 1948 and 1949 and played a prominent role as an officer in the Egyptian forces that were besieged in the villages of al-Fallujah and Iraq al-Manshiyyah, and which gained a legendary reputation for their steadfastness in the face of the siege. Like all nationalist officers in that tumultuous phase of Egypt's history, Nasser looked to Egypt's politicians to win full independence for Egypt and to bring about the country's renewal. He might once have been attracted to populist groups that opposed British occupation, such as those led by Ahmad Husayn of the Egyptian Youth Movement, but under the influence of 'Abd al-Mun'im 'Abd al-Ra'uf, who was an army officer and an active member of the Brotherhood, Nasser was convinced to join the Muslim Brotherhood.

The Brotherhood faced tremendous difficulties after their banning and al-Banna's assassination. Although a large number of their leaders and cadres were in prison, their under-secretary Salih 'Ashmawi tried to maintain some communication between the leaders who had not been arrested. In January 1951, the Wafd Party won the parliamentary elections with support from the Brotherhood, and the government's campaign against the Brotherhood came to an end. By December of that year, a judicial pronouncement lifted the banning order, and the Brotherhood resumed its activities. The prime minister, Mustafa al-Nahas, cancelled the 1936 treaty with Britain after negotiations between the two sides failed to make any progress, and the Egyptian nationalist forces began preparing for an armed struggle against the ongoing British military presence in the Suez Canal region. The Wafd government was well aware that the Brotherhood was willing to play a central role in this resistance.

In this way, the Brotherhood successfully restored its legitimacy, and they then began to look for a new al-murshid al-am (leader or general guide). The leadership had begun looking for a successor to al-Banna in the early months of 1951. Many aspired to the position, including: the under-secretary Salih 'Ashmawi, who was supported by the Covert Structure; Ahmad Hasan al-Baquri, an Azhari shaykh; members of the existing leadership structures; and 'Abd al-Rahman al-Banna, Hasan al-Banna's brother. In the end, technocrats within the leadership structure offered the position to Justice Hasan al-Hudaybi, one of al-Banna's closest friends and a judge in Egypt's supreme court, the country's highest legal authority. Al-Hudaybi initially rejected the position but reconsidered and accepted after sustained pressure from the Brotherhood. However, the announcement that al-Hudaybi had accepted the position as the Brotherhood's second general guide in October 1951 did not put an end to the hopes of those who still aspired to the position. Differences within the Brotherhood over who would be leader were soon outstripped by disputes about al-Hudaybi himself, including his background and his poor grasp of issues pertaining to the organisation.[4]

❦

Al-Hudaybi was born in the village of 'Arab al-Sawalihah, which fell under the jurisdiction of the city of Shibin al-Kawm in the Delta Region. His family were descended from one of the Arab tribes that had settled in the area centuries before. He graduated from law school in 1915 and worked as a lawyer for a short period. In 1924, he was made a judge, which required him to move between the various judicial regions of the country. His legal background and his constant travels helped him to develop a good understanding of the Egyptian people, including their moods and character traits. He had great respect for every aspect of the law and spent twenty-five years of his life in the judiciary. Apart from his long and close relationship with Hasan al-Banna, he is not known to have been affiliated to any of the Egyptian political parties that were active under the monarchy.

From the outset, al-Hudaybi expressed his opposition to the presence of the Brotherhood's secret armed wing and declared his desire to disband the Covert Structure. This sparked open enmity between al-Hudaybi and his supporters and the leaders of the Covert Structure.

A month after he had been chosen as leader, al-Hudaybi agreed to meet King Faruq, and his opponents within the Brotherhood quickly started a rumour campaign against him. There is no doubt that al-Hudaybi did not have the charisma of al-Banna, but he proved no less firm in defending what he saw as the Brotherhood's political and Islamic principles. It was therefore naïve to accuse him of being associated with the monarchy. Despite his elevated position in the judiciary, al-Hudaybi was from a rural, tribal background, and had no relationship with the Egyptian aristocracy. He had no relationship with the monarchy other than a passing acquaintance with some employees at the palace.

Accordingly, when Nasser and his companions began preparing to topple the monarchy, al-Hudaybi did not hesitate to support them. Al-Hudaybi's one problem, as was later made apparent by events, was his hesitation in disbanding the Covert Structure. Al-Hudaybi took over the leadership of the Brotherhood under difficult circumstances and at a time of quickly unfolding events. It is therefore not surprising that he proved unable to unite the Brotherhood, and lacked the experience to run the affairs of a group that had multiple institutions, centres of power and orientations.

On 26 January 1952, while attacks against British Forces in the Suez region were increasing, a massive fire broke out in Cairo's commercial centre, starting in Fuad I Street. Hundreds of buildings including shops, offices, hotels, theatres and restaurants were destroyed by the fire, the causes of which, like the absence of security forces in the city at the time, remain unexplained. Politically, the fire had two central consequences, one open and evident to all and one planned and plotted in secret. First, the Wafd government, which was taken by surprise by the fire, announced a state of martial law. The king exploited this to remove the Wafd from power. In the few remaining months left to the monarchy, it installed a series of short-lived minority governments to govern the country. Second, Nasser and his colleagues decided to expedite their plans to overthrow the monarchy. On the morning of 23 July, Cairo awoke to find military forces loyal to the Free Officers Movement patrolling the streets and guarding certain institutions.

The Free Officers took power in a bloodless coup that changed the face of Egypt and the entire Arab region. It is known that the leadership of the Muslim Brotherhood were the only Egyptian political group that had foreknowledge of the coup and its timing, and that, at the request of the Free Officers, members of the Covert Structure had spread out on the road between Cairo and Suez to block the British military should they attempt to intervene. Within three days, the Free Officers had entrenched their control over the institutions of state and forced the king, who was spending the summer at the Ras al-Tin Palace in Alexandria, into exile.

When the first communiqués about the revolution were issued, the Free Officers and the Brotherhood were strong allies, and many in the Brotherhood saw the revolution as their own.[5] However, within just two years, differences between the two sides had emerged and led to bloody clashes. The leaders of the Free Officers Movement, who were all middle-ranking officers, were careful to choose Major-General Muhammad Naguib as head of their revolutionary council. Naguib was generally well-known as a nationalist and he was well-liked in the army, but he was not originally one of the Free Officers, and he believed in the parliamentary system. Naguib accepted the leadership role on the understanding that the aim of the coup was to free the country from political despotism and British influence, after which the army would return to its barracks. Nasser went along with this although he probably had something different in mind.

On the Brotherhood's recommendation, former royal advisor 'Ali Mahir formed the first revolutionary government. However, 'Ali Mahir and the leadership of the Brotherhood were soon at odds with the Free Officers on the maximum amount of land ownership that would be allowable under proposed agricultural reforms. This was the first difference between the Officers and the Brotherhood, and it resulted in 'Ali Mahir's resignation. Naguib himself formed the second government and Nasser invited the Brotherhood to participate in the cabinet, offering them three ministerial positions. However, al-Hudaybi already doubted Nasser's loyalty and was suspicious about his desire to reach agreement with the Brotherhood, so he refused to allow the Brotherhood to accept the positions offered. When Shaykh Ahmad Hasan al-Baquri broke ranks and accepted an appointment as endowments minister, al-Hudaybi forced him to resign from both the Brotherhood's leadership structure and from the organisation altogether. This was the second clear indication that trust between the two groups was evaporating.

Nevertheless, the legitimacy of the popular revolution was not yet entrenched, and although clouds of doubt hung over the relationship between the Brotherhood and the Free Officers, Nasser still needed the Brotherhood's support. For this reason, when the leaders of the revolution decided to dismantle all political parties in January 1953, the Brotherhood was exempted under the pretence that it was a civic organisation and not a political party. In the same month, the Free Officers resolved to form the Hay'ah al-Tahrir (Liberation Assembly) that would act as a broad political organisation, supporting the revolution and representing its popular base.

The Brotherhood was invited to join the Assembly and to submit to its leadership. They refused, arguing that a political party formed and supported by the state would never win the confidence and support of the people. In reality, the formation of the Assembly was an attempt to weaken the Brotherhood so that the leaders of the revolution would no longer need its support. Soon, clashes took place between members of the Assembly and the Brotherhood, especially at the universities. In spite of this, Nasser still attempted to persuade the Brotherhood (or at the very least some of its members) to join the Assembly. On the first anniversary of the Hasan al-Banna's assassination, Nasser and Naguib visited his grave, and promised to launch an investigation into the assassination.

In November 1953, al-Sanadi and his closest allies were removed from their positions as leaders of the Covert Structure and new leaders were chosen. The change was an attempt by al-Hudaybi and the rest of the Brotherhood's maktab al-irshad (executive council) to regain control of the Covert Structure, which had all but become an independent organisation. However, the matter was not easily resolved. Al-Sanadi had support among some of the top leaders in the Brotherhood, including distinguished Azhari scholars such as Sayyid Sabiq and Muhammad al-Ghazali, as well as the former contender for the leadership of the Brotherhood Salih 'Ashmawi. Within a matter of days, al-Sanadi's allies – with Nasser's support – tried to force al-Hudaybi to resign but they were unsuccessful. However, while it is unclear exactly when Nasser had established ties with al-Sanadi and his supporters, it is well known that Nasser exploited the divisions within the Brotherhood to sideline al-Hudaybi, who the Free Officers Movement saw as preventing the Brotherhood from being assimilated under the umbrella of the revolution's leadership. Although the vast majority of Brotherhood members were united behind al-Hudaybi, differences among the leadership with regard to their position in the revolution continued to grow. Ultimately, these differences created chaos in the ranks and constant spats about decision-making began to weaken the organisation.

In mid January 1954, after the attempt to remove al-Hudaybi failed, and clashes at the university were ongoing between students who had joined the Brotherhood and those who were affiliated to the Liberation Assembly, the Revolutionary Leadership Council issued a resolution banning the Muslim Brotherhood. Hundreds of Brotherhood members, from its leadership to its cadres, and including al-Hudaybi, were arrested and sent to a military prison in Cairo and to al-Dakhilah prison near Alexandria.

At this point, a development within the Revolutionary Leadership Council rescued the Brotherhood. Disagreements between the leaders of the council about the future of the revolution (including the re-instatement of the constitution and the parliament) were at least as potent as the disagreements within the Brotherhood on this issue. By the end of February 1954, conflict between the Free Officers led Muhammad Naguib to resign as head of the Revolutionary Leadership Council. Naguib was the only council member who was well known and well liked by the people. Thus, while the cavalry officers supported him, his most significant support came from the streets where there was widespread mobilisation in favour of his re-instatement.

In a rare moment of co-operation, the Brotherhood and the Egyptian communist movement, played a major role in mobilising Egyptians against Nasser and the other members of his Revolutionary Council. For a while it seemed Nasser had lost control of Cairo and much of his popular support. This compelled him to reinstate Naguib and issue a number of resolutions calling for the election of an institutional assembly that would prepare a new constitution, re-establish parliamentary politics and put an end to military rule. To further ease tensions, members of the Brotherhood were released and its banning order was rescinded. These moves were later proved to be little more than a tactical reshuffle by Nasser and his supporters.

In the last few days of March 1954, with the future of the country still hanging in the balance, the Muslim Brotherhood committed a major strategic error. The Brotherhood was in a strong position after the Free Officers had been forced to reinstate Naguib. Nasser had visited al-Hudaybi's home in full view of the press, and all but apologised for the crisis caused by the Brotherhood's banning and the imprisonment of its leaders. Al-Hudaybi then delivered a speech from the Brotherhood's Public Centre, explaining the group's position on recent events and calling for a return to a civilian and constitutional dispensation. The problem was that al-Hudaybi's call lacked strength and decisiveness. Or, perhaps it is more accurate to say that the political drive shown by the Brotherhood in the days and weeks that followed did not match up to his speech.

In an unjustifiable moment of compliance, the Brotherhood withdrew from the ongoing popular protests that were calling for a return to constitutionalism and elections. Because they did so, much of the popular pressure on the Revolutionary Leadership Council fell away. Of course, the leaders of the Brotherhood, including the technocrats around al-Hudaybi, were closer to Nasser in terms of their outlook than they were to the old political dispensation. In addition, for the majority of the Brotherhood's leadership, the call for a return to a parliamentary system was not the deciding factor in their support for the revolution. The Brotherhood therefore justified their withdrawal from the popular protest movement in terms of wishing to calm the people and avert the dangers of chaos and internal division. In reality, however, their decision gave Nasser the time he needed to regroup and strengthen the position of the Revolutionary Leadership Council.

The Free Officers quickly organised massive demonstrations, attracting thousands of supporters from every corner of the country, carrying banners calling for the continuation of the revolution and condemning corruption. The protestors attacked the premises of *The Egyptian* – a liberal newspaper – and assaulted 'Abd al-Razzaq al-Sanhuri, a prominent legal expert and president of the Council of State. Nasser quickly responded to calls from his allies, (which had already been prepared in advance by his advisors), rescinding earlier resolutions that had promised the return of electoral politics and the disbanding of the Revolutionary Leadership Council. Khalid Muhyi al-Din, leader of the Cavalry Officers' Regiment (which supported a parliamentary system) was banished to Geneva, and security in Cairo was tightened. Nasser become prime minister after Naguib's resignation, which enabled him to strengthen his grip over various state apparatuses, and affirm his firm control of the army. In this manner, what later became known as the 'March Crisis' concluded, with Nasser resuming full control.

In the next few months, the Muslim Brotherhood and other forces opposed to the Revolutionary Leadership Council and military rule continued to falter. Al-Hudaybi left Egypt on a long tour visiting Brotherhood branches in other Arab countries. Upon his return, and on the advice of the organisation's leadership, the Brotherhood's new leader quickly went underground in Alexandria, leaving the organisation's massive support base to act without visible leadership. Intense debates continued within their ranks on their relationship with the revolution and with the Free Officers Movement. From July to September, the Covert Structure ran a huge pamphlet campaign to protest against the agreement reached between Nasser's government and Britain. The campaign reignited Nasser's anger and he initiated a series of arbitrary arrests of Brotherhood members, especially members of the Covert Structure.

There is little doubt that the Covert Structure's new leaders discussed the option of assassinating Nasser, and agreed not to do so. Al-Hudaybi warned all the leaders of the Brotherhood and Covert Structure who visited him while he was in hiding against any action that involved spilling blood. In light of this information, the name of the person or people who attempted to take Nasser's life in the Manshiyyah incident seems likely to remain an unsolved mystery,[6] just like the Cairo Fire.

Despite a complete lack of evidence, Nasser held the Muslim Brotherhood responsible for the assassination attempt. The Brotherhood was banned and prevented from operating legally until after the revolution of 2011.[7] Thousands were arrested and hundreds were brought before swift and farcical military tribunals. The Tribunal Assembly, headed by Jamal Salim, a member of the Revolutionary Leadership Council, and assisted by Husayn al-Shafi'i and Anwar Sadat, issued the death penalty to six of the Brotherhood's leaders, the most prominent of whom was the former judge and renowned legal theorist, 'Abd al-Qadir 'Awdah. Many others were imprisoned.

It is important to note that the Free Officers led by Nasser were not political heavyweights; they did not have the support of any particular social group or effective political party. Even the Egyptian army, to which they belonged, was not yet large enough to protect them. Were it not for their lightning-quick actions in grabbing hold of the Egyptian state, the group might not have managed to hold on to power.

Nasser realised from the beginning that no state will survive if it is caught between two centres of power. Initially, therefore, he strove to entrench the revolution through forging an alliance with the Muslim Brotherhood. In his subsequent struggle against them, he was extremely effective, if not always noble. Nasser knew what he wanted and he was assisted by the military spirit that managed to preserve a relative degree of unity within the Revolutionary Leadership Council.

As for the Brotherhood, confusion overcame their vision and they lost unity of purpose. Most of the Brotherhood's members agreed with Nasser's programme and shared his enmity for monarchies and for political pluralism. However, they did not know exactly what they wanted from the revolution or from the new dispensation. Should they be a political party or a religious movement? And was the coup their own or the army's?

The revolution occurred at the peak of the Brotherhood's rising popularity, but it took place at a time when the Brotherhood's political thinking had not yet crystallised. Its confusion led to its immobilisation and prolonged banning. However, years of banning and hostility in Egypt eventually ended, and in the meantime other branches of the Brotherhood flourished in Palestine, Jordan, Iraq, Sudan and Syria. At the same time, another Islamic political party emerged in the Arab sphere: none other than Hizb al-Tahrir.

5

Taqi al-Din al-Nabhani and Hizb al-Tahrir

t the end of March 2005, after a few days of protest that began in the south of the troubled country of Kyrgyzstan, the regime led by President Askar Akayev collapsed. The president left the capital Bishkek, and opposition leaders, comprised of individuals from the former administration, took control of the state. Kyrgyzstan was the third of the former Soviet states to witness a popular democratic revolution within the period of a year. Or so it seemed.

Washington appeared to be at sea about whether events in Kyrgyzstan represented new evidence of the Bush (Jr) administration's success or not. But soon, on either side of the Atlantic, American and British newspapers were describing the revolution as the pinnacle of Kyrgyzstan's long march to democracy. In this way, the 'Tulip Revolution' joined the series of so-called colour revolutions that took place in the former Soviet Union and Balkan states that were open to America.

A few sceptics held a different opinion. The Kyrgyzstan revolution, they argued, had been 'manufactured' by a small group of Americans. From the moment Kyrgyzstan opened its doors to American aid, an organisation called Freedom House (managed by James Woolsey, a former director of the CIA and advocate for the Iraqi invasion) established a printing press in the country's capital that soon became a hub for the printing of sixty opposition newspapers. The majority of civil society institutions in Kyrgyzstan are now financed by members of Hizb al-Tahrir (also known as the Liberation Party), whose activities had increased quite visibly in Central Asia in the preceding years. The objective of the Americans was not only to topple the Kyrgyzstan government, but also to reach the Muslims in China's Qinghai province, who have a historical relationship with the Muslims of Kyrgyzstan.

In the early 2000s, Hizb al-Tahrir returned to the political sphere, attracting widespread attention after many years of relative absence, and in Central Asia, Hizb al-Tahrir is now preoccupied with nurturing rebel movements and Islamic opposition to the political regimes. In August 1994, a branch of the organisation convened an international conference on the Islamic caliphate at London's famous Wembley Stadium, spurring widespread protests from the Jewish community in Britain. A year later, the group organised a noisy demonstration in Trafalgar Square, in which slogans opposing Western democracy and secularism were displayed and during which the British government was invited to embrace Islam. In 2003, a group of British youth was indicted in Egypt for establishing an organisational structure for the group, which was planning to overthrow the Egyptian regime. Then, after the London bombings in July 2005, the British prime minister announced his intention to prohibit the organisation from operating in Britain, even though it has never advocated the use of violence.

Despite the controversy surrounding these and other similar incidents, it would be an exaggeration to suggest that Hizb al-Tahrir poses a threat to the status quo in any of the countries in which it has a presence. The organisation, is however, a source of irritation and concern for governments and their security apparatuses. This does not apply exclusively to governments, but also to Islamic organisations and individuals, since the group addresses everyone it sees as 'un-Islamic' – from Western powers trying to control the fate of the Islamic world to Islamists who do not share their views. This comprises all the reformist scholars and intellectuals that Hizb al-Tahrir accuse of imposing Western concepts and values on Islam, including the Muslim Brotherhood, which they have often described as incapable of grasping the foundations of

Islamic thought and its greater purpose, and Islamic jihadists, who are viewed as having deviated from Islam.

After the Muslim Brotherhood, Hizb al-Tahrir was the second Islamist organisation to gain prominence in the Arab world, and probably the most politicised. It is an elitist organisation even though it claims to speak on behalf of the entire Muslim community and is hoisting the banner of the Islamic caliphate in a manner unprecedented since the 1920s.

☙❦❧

Muhammad Taqi al-Din al-Nabhani was a Palestinian teacher and Islamic judge who established Hizb al-Tahrir and constructed its intellectual edifice.[1] Al-Nabhani was born into a family of scholars in the village of Ijzam, in the municipality of Haifa in 1909. He received his higher education at al-Azhar University in Cairo between 1928 and 1932. He is also believed to have combined his studies at al-Azhar with additional classes at the Dar al-'Ulum, from which Hasan al-Banna also graduated. Although the two men were of the same generation, and both their names are linked to the contemporary Islamic Awakening, al-Nabhani outlived al-Banna by some four decades, and they differed in almost every other way. Al-Banna initiated his Islamic project while in his twenties, with no fixed vision of what the Muslim Brotherhood would become. Al-Nabhani, on the other hand, established Hizb al-Tahrir when he had reached his forties, and after having formulated a clear vision of the structure and purpose of the organisation, as well as how it would operate strategically. Whereas al-Banna was a propagator of Islam and a popular leader, al-Nabhani was an intellectual with philosophical inclinations who praised the virtues of not mixing with the masses. The Muslim Brotherhood has always been far more capable of engaging with changing realities, whereas Hizb al-Tahrir's stated objectives shrink away from indicating how its members should deal with the changing world.

After completing his studies, al-Nabhani returned to Palestine where he worked as a teacher. He later joined the Islamic Court, which fell under the jurisdiction of the Higher Islamic Council. Al-Nabhani was not a prominent activist in the Palestinian National Movement before the Nakbah, but he was known to have mixed with the followers of Mufti al-Haj al-Amin al-Husayni, and was closely associated with Arab nationalist groups. Al-Nabhani became the deputy president of the Jami'yyah al-'Itisam al-Islami (Islamic Steadfastness Society) in Haifa, which was led by Shaykh Muhammad Nimr al-Khatib, one of the most prominent Islamic figures in the city. Al-Nabhani and al-Khatib refused to affiliate the Islamic Steadfastness Society to the Muslim Brotherhood, when the Palestinian branch of the Brotherhood was established in 1945.

In 1948, after Palestine had been devastated by the Nakbah, al-Nabhani emigrated to Damascus, where he met up with two of his former comrades, Dawud Hamdan, a lawyer specialising in Islamic personal law, and Nimr al-Misri, a teacher. Both had immigrated to Syria from the city of Ramla. Together with these two, al-Nabhani began debating what needed to be done after the catastrophe that had befallen the Palestinians and the Arabs.[2] There is no doubt that the Palestinian Nakbah was the event that had the greatest impact on the group that founded Hizb al-Tahrir. Al-Nabhani's first book, *Inqadh Filistin* (Rescuing Palestine), recorded some of the early discussions between comrades who experienced the Nakbah. The book is no longer included in Hizb al-Tahrir's literature, probably because it contains Arab nationalist sentiments that the organisation is no longer committed to circulating.

Al-Nabhani returned to Jerusalem after being summoned by its governor, Anwar al-Khatib. There he was appointed as a qadi (judge in the shari'ah system) and later as a judge in the Supreme Court. During this period, al-Nabhani continued his conversations with his Damascene comrades as well as resuming his links with the supporters of Mufti al-Haj al-Amin al-Husayni and with Palestinian and Jordanian Arab nationalists, especially the early Jordanian Ba'athist groups.

At that time, the struggle over the annexation of the West Bank by Jordan was at its most intense, with supporters of the Mufti and the Arab nationalists challenging the supporters of Jordan's King 'Abdallah I. Colonel 'Abdallah al-Tal, the military commander of the Jerusalem region, was one of the nationalists' strongest supporters. When al-Tal began planning to overthrow the king of Jordan, al-Nabhani was one of two emissaries secretly sent to Syria's revolutionary president, Husni al-Za'im to request support from Syria and Egypt.

Even though Jordan was in turmoil from the effects of the Nakbah, and their king was accused of colluding with the British and the Zionists, the coup failed and King 'Abdallah succeeded in annexing the West Bank to Jordan. In July 1951, King 'Abdallah I was assassinated in the courtyard of al-Aqsa Mosque by of one of al-Husayni's supporters.

At this point, al-Nabhani resigned from his post in the judiciary and returned to teaching, as this gave him greater scope for political activity. During his tenure at the Islamic College in Amman, and later a stint at the Ibrahimiyyah Madrasa in Jerusalem, al-Nabhani succeeded in drawing 'Abd al-Qadim Zalum as well as Rajab and As'ad Bayud al-Tamimi (all of whom were from Hebron) into his discussion group to consider a way forward.

Dawud Hamdan played a central role in convincing al-Nabhani and the rest of the group to move away from Arab nationalist influences and adopt an Islamic position. They all agreed that the Palestinian Nakbah was a reflection of the level of Islamic political and civilisational decline, and that the only way to address this was to work with the entire Muslim ummah, rather than in Palestine or the Arab states alone. Their debates centred on the principle of ummah, and together they concluded that Islam was the starting point, and that the instrument for its renaissance was the formation of an Islamic political organisation. In November 1952, al-Nabhani, Dawud Hamdan, Munir Shuqayr, 'Adil al-Nabulsi and Ghanim 'Abduh applied to the Jordanian Interior Ministry for the licensing of a new political party in the name of Hizb al-Tahrir.

After the bitterness caused by the Palestinian Nakbah and the annexation of the West Bank by Jordan, the authorities had initiated a period of political pluralism and parliamentary activity in Jordan. Also at play in this shift was angry opposition to British influence in Jordan and the weakness of the young King Hussein, who had assumed the throne after his grandfather's assassination and his father's abdication. Perhaps the founders of Hizb al-Tahrir hoped these conditions might guarantee the licensing of their party. In fact, the Jordanian authorities refused their request for a licence despite the interventions of several prominent Jerusalemites in their favour. A second application made two months later was also refused.

Aware of the Ottoman law on societies, al-Nabhani and his comrades then attempted to convert the organisation into a society, similar to the Muslim Brotherhood, which had been given permission to operate and conduct activities in March 1953. The Jordanian authorities saw through the ploy. They responded by arresting and detaining the founding members for several weeks, and then placing them under house arrest. The Jordanian authorities' official reason for refusing the licence application was that the organisation's political programme rejected nationalism and Arabism, while recognising only Islam; they argued that this contradicted Jordan's constitution and threatened the unity of its people.

In fact, this was only one of the reasons for Jordan refusing to license the party.[3] Without doubt, the organisation's emphasis on Islam contained an implicit rejection of the principle of hereditary rule and therefore of Jordan's monarchy. Syria's support for al-Nabhani and his comrades was also a factor, as was their close relationship with al-Husayni, who was central to challenging Hashemite rule in the West Bank. In any case, their failure to secure a licence did not stop members of the group from continuing their activities in secret. However, al-Nabhani decided it would be futile to remain in Jordan where he would be subjected to increasing government oppression so he moved to Syria, before settling in Lebanon.

Most of Hizb al-Tahrir's foundational texts were produced in the 1950s, Apart from minor additions, subtractions or clarifications, subsequent editions of these works have not been revised. Their ideology is founded upon the belief that every community has a principle from which a system emanates, and this principle involves both a set of ideas and a way acting – a methodology. Hizb al-Tahrir's central focus is Islam, which al-Nabhani saw as obliging its adherents to establish an Islamic political system. In fact, al-Nabhani believed that politics is the foundation and backbone of Islamic thought. This motivated him and members of Hizb al-Tahrir to attack the Muslim Brotherhood and their Islamist predecessors such as Muhammad 'Abduh and Rashid Rida, for emphasising issues of education, culture and ethics.

In addition, al-Nabhani rejected Greek logic and the methodologies of the classical Islamic dialectical theologians, believing that revelation stands above reason. Nevertheless, he resorted to rational argument in his attempt to prove that Islam is the religion that complements human beings' natural disposition and that the Islamic system alone is able to provide what is in our best interests. In fact, al-Nabhani's critique of the capitalist, democratic and secular systems is based on the argument that western Europe did not derive these systems from rational principles, but through historical negotiations between intellectuals and the church. This interpretation is based on a hasty and simplistic understanding of European history, and al-Nabhani's claim that his methodology is the only one that can be derived from the way of the Prophet, is no less simplistic.

Despite the prominent place that politics occupies in the discourse of Hizb al-Tahrir, its methods for social transformation and establishing an Islamic system sprout from the world of ideas. Al-Nabhani described the sought-after Islamic renaissance as primarily an intellectual rebirth.

In any given state, Hizb al-Tahrir's project begins with a select group of elite individuals who work to build a political party. The party is necessarily factional because factionalism is implicit in the system of political parties that has been imposed on Muslims. In the following phase, the faction interacts with the community by way of publications, pamphlets and other tools of mass communication, to create a popular movement that supports it. As soon as the organisation is assured of having created such a movement, it is expected to begin working towards securing political power, which Hizb al-Tahrir refers to as the 'fulcrum'.

Perhaps influenced by the series of military coups in the Arab East in the 1950s and 1960s, al-Nabhani developed the idea that, in this advanced stage, 'seeking assistance' is an essential tactic for gaining power. What he meant by this was securing alliances within the sector that holds the most power in any modern state: the military/security apparatus. In other words, al-Nabhani envisaged recruiting a group of officers who work towards bringing the Hizb al-Tahrir to power by means of a military coup. As soon as it is in power, the organisation is expected to implement its vision of an Islamic state immediately, not in phases. What this means is announcing the realisation of the Islamic caliphate and working towards the expansion of the fulcrum – that is, the authority of the caliphate – to other parts of the Islamic world.

Al-Nabhani initially believed that his project would come to fruition within a decade or two, and therefore began writing a ready-made constitution for the forthcoming Islamic state. The constitution consists of eighty-nine articles and includes general legislation and clauses on the system of governance, economic, social and educational systems, as well as foreign policy.

Despite Hizb al-Tahrir's extreme commitment to using historical Islamic concepts in their own founding charter, their constitutional vision does not depart from the structure of a modern state, other than with regard to the position of the caliph and the institution of the caliphate. Even on this point, the constitution they propose states that the caliph must be elected and can be removed from the position by way of a resolution by the court of grievances.[4] Apart from this, al-Nabhani's vision of authority and power refers largely to an autocracy: the head of state *is* the state, and state authority is derived from the authority of the Prophet.

By 1954, the leadership of the organisation believed that they had succeeded in building a solid cadreship in Jordan, and that they could become more open in engaging with society. They began to publish a newspaper, *al-Ra'yah* (The standard), which was quickly shut down by the Jordanian authorities. In elections held in October of that year, four members stood as candidates. However, only one, Ahmad al-Da'ur was successful in gaining a parliamentary seat, and this was possibly more because of the support he received from the Muslim Brotherhood's branch in his constituency than because of any real voter support for Hizb al-Tahrir.

In the following year, the activities of the nationalist movement in Jordan increased substantially as a result of British pressure on Jordan to sign the Baghdad Pact. In the ten months between the end of 1955 and the elections in October of 1956, the king installed five different governments. First, the government of Sa'id al-Mufti collapsed. The government of Hazza' al-Majali lasted just three days. Governance was passed on to Samir al-Rifa'i, but then al-Mufti returned to power only to fall again and be succeeded by Ibrahim Hashim. When the National-ist Socialists won the October elections, Sulayman al-Nabulsi became prime minister, at the head of a government that included many na-tionalists and Arabists. At this time, the entire Arab region was fending off the Eisenhower administration and the British government, which were attempting to draw the Arab states into their camp in their war against communism. Arab leftists and nationalists, led by Nasser, op-posed forming alliances with the West, calling instead for neutrality and independence.

Al-Nabulsi's ascension to power inspired some optimism in the leadership of Hizb al-Tahrir as they saw his rise as a major setback for the monarchy despite the leftist and Arab nationalist inclinations of his government. However, the 'Jordanian Spring' was short-lived. In just a few months, al-Nabulsi resigned due to pressure from the palace. Another unsuccessful coup attempt also failed to destabilise the regime, and then a traumatic internal crisis overtook Hizb al-Tahrir.

In 1955, a facsimile of a US$150 000 cheque issued by the American Embassy in Beirut and made out to al-Nabhani was circulated openly. Rumour had it that the payment was to strengthen Hizb al-Tahrir's efforts in the fight against communism. The organisation denied receiving any funds and accused the Jordanian security apparatus of spreading propaganda. It is not easy to get to the bottom of the various claims, but the saga of the cheque, and Hizb al-Tahrir's silence about its relationships with the major powers (whose policies it criticised), certainly had a major impact on popular perceptions of the organisation. At about the same time, both Nimr al-Misri and Dawud Hamdan left the organisation, citing al-Nabhani's unilateral leadership style, a dispute about a Czech arms deal negotiated by Nasser with the Soviet Union and al-Nabhani's allegations that Nasser was an American agent. Thus, al-Nabhani lost two of his oldest comrades, and his unilateral tendencies only increased.

Hizb al-Tahrir's popular appeal continued to decline in the face of the dramatic rise in the popularity of Nasser and Arab nationalism. However, al-Nabhani believed that his organisation had entered the phase of needing to interact with society, so he developed a popular political programme aimed at undermining the legitimacy of the ruling regimes. This was based on a hypothesis concerning the world's primary states. The argument is that the primary state at the end of the Second World War was Britain, but that the USA entered the global sphere soon thereafter and began competing against the British for prominence. Hizb al-Tahrir distributed many pamphlets on this theme, arguing for example that: Syrian president Husni al-Za'im (d. 1949) was an American lackey and that Sami al-Hinnawi's (d. 1950) coup against him was supported by the British; Syrian President Adib al-Shishakli (d. 1964) was an American agent and those opposing him were supported by the British; Nasser was an American puppet, as was ʿAbd al-Karim al-Qasim, and the 1968 Baʿathist coup in Iraq that brought Ahmad Hasan al-Bakr and Saddam Hussein to power were American inspired; King Hussein of Jordan and Yasser Arafat of the Palestine Liberation Organization (PLO) were loyal to the British; and so on.

Admittedly the world did see the US actively mobilise against the antiquated colonialism practised by Britain and France in the 1950s, but to portray international politics as if it was frozen in time, and to ignore further realignments within the West in relation to the Cold War, was a gross simplification on al-Nabhani's part. Furthermore, his theory belittles the liberation struggles and sacrifices of oppressed people against colonial and neo-colonial exploitation, in favour of a conspiracy-theory-led paradigm of international politics. Ultimately, instead of strengthening popular support for the organisation, this polemic hastened its decline in Jordan and other Arab countries.

Nevertheless, the dwindling popularity did not prevent it from trying to seize power in Jordan. A coup attempt was made in 1968, a year after the painful Arab defeat, in which Jordan lost the West Bank and the city of Jerusalem. The Jordanian authorities had managed to uncover the coup plot and abort it, but another attempt was made in 1969, and yet another after the bloody Black September clashes that took place between Palestinian commandos and the Jordanian Army in September 1970 and continued into 1971. None of these coup attempts were successful and Hizb al-Tahrir generally failed to win significant support in Jordan.

This did not prevent the organisation from spreading to several other Arab and non-Arab countries. From its inception, the group regarded itself as Islamic, and, as such, unconfined by borders or nationalities. Today, it is believed that its members are active not only in Jordan, but also in Syria, Lebanon, Iraq, Kuwait, the United Arab Emirates, Morocco, Turkey, Pakistan, Malaysia, and in several Western countries, especially Britain.

Al-Nabhani died in Lebanon in 1977 and the leadership of the organisation was passed on to his friend and long-time member, 'Abd al-Qadim Zalum. Under Zalum's leadership the organisation seemed to gain a new vitality. In 1978, it sent a delegation to Libya to discuss prophetic practice with Muammar Gaddafi, inviting him to embrace their philosophy and pronounce Libya the centre of the Islamic caliphate. The delegation failed in this mission, however, and the Libyan government continued to persecute the few supporters of Hizb al-Tahrir in that country.

Also in 1978, as soon as the Islamic Revolution in Iran began to unfold, another delegation met Ayatollah Ruhollah Khomeini at his base in the Paris suburb of Neauphle-le-Château. In the middle of the following year, when preparations for the writing of a constitution for the Islamic Republic began, a delegation from Hizb al-Tahrir presented memoranda, which included copies of their Islamic constitution, to Ayatollah Khomeini and the Iranian foreign minister Ibrahim Yazdi. However, as soon as it became clear that the Iranian leaders did not take their invitation to establish an Islamic caliphate seriously, the leaders of Hizb al-Tahrir launched a vicious attack on the new Iranian regime, accusing it of sectarianism and of having links with international powers.

In the 1990s, Hizb al-Tahrir resumed its attempts to influence various heads of state. At that time, Iraq was crippled by international sanctions after its defeat in the first Gulf War. Iraqi president Saddam Hussein initiated what he referred to as the 'Faith Campaign', attempting to colour his regime in an Islamic hue, so as to win over more Arab and Islamic support. Hizb al-Tahrir thought Hussein might be sincere, and sent a delegation inviting him to subscribe to their vision and calling on him to transform Iraq into a base for the Islamic caliphate. However, as in the past, this engagement with Hussein produced no results.

Hizb al-Tahrir is still active and seizes every opportunity it can to expand in any country.[5] However, it always seems to reach a point beyond which it is not able to grow any further. Hizb al-Tahrir seems to provide a space for a small group of people who believe its teachings without asking too many questions. Despite the heated debates that the organisation has inspired, it is difficult to argue that it has influenced any of the other Islamist forces.

Probably the greatest factor undermining the group is its lack of intellectual flexibility and its failure to see the changing realities that surrounded it. An organisation that made thought its point of departure has fallen foul of the narrowness of its own intellectual horizons. Essentially, the group sees all other Islamists as flawed and has turned its back on them.

However, as is shown in the next chapter, the early growth of political Islam was never confined to the Arabs. An Islamic political force on the Indian subcontinent, the Jamaat-i-Islami, occupies an important space in the political sphere and in contemporary political Islamic thought.

6

Al-Mawdudi and the Jamaat-i-Islami

*O*n 12 October 1999, the military took power in Pakistan under the leadership of General Pervez Musharraf. This was the third military coup since the country won independence in 1947. This time the coup occurred at a time when the world had begun to believe that the era of military coups and the subjugation of the popular will to that of army officers had come to an end. Nevertheless, just as in Pakistan's previous military coups, the officers toppled the constitution and halted the democratic process.

Prior to the coup, the party-political struggle between Nawaz Sharif's Islamic League and Benazir Bhutto's People's Party had worn Pakistan out and paralysed the state. With corruption rampant, popular opposition to the coup was limited.

In fact, opposition to the coup came mainly from the Pakistani government's traditional ally, the US government. In 2001, near the end of Bill Clinton's second term in office, Washington seemed to be about to turn its back on Islamabad and begin strengthening its relationship with India, Pakistan's sworn enemy. However, Musharraf saw the events of 9/11, and America's war against the Taliban and al-Qa'ida, as a golden opportunity to rebuild Pakistan's relationship with Washington. Musharraf's government became the USA's most important partner in the 'war on terror', actively participating in dismantling al-Qa'ida cells and handing over many of its leaders to the American authorities. In Pakistan's tribal region, which runs alongside the Afghani border,

Pakistani military forces and its intelligence agency co-operated with the American forces to blockade al-Qa'ida bases and destroy its tribal allies, almost resulting in a civil war.

In Pakistan, which has deeply rooted Islamic traditions, America's global war against terrorism appeared to be a war on Islam itself. In a country whose tribes share the same roots and values as the Afghan tribes, Musharraf seemed to be declaring war on his own people to please the Americans. Musharraf faced wide opposition, not only because of his dictatorial bent and his obsession with being both the country's president and the leader of its army, but also because of his loyalty to Washington.

In 2008, after Pakistan has again installed a democratic dispensation, President Asif Ali Zardari faced opposition from his own government, which was dominated by his People's Party and the Islamic League, the two parties that Musharraf's coup had toppled less than ten years before. However, the opposition was not limited to the two main political parties, but extended to an alliance of Islamic forces, some of which (such as the Society of Pakistani Scholars) are regarded as the state's most reliable power bases. The Jamaat-i-Islami, as it is referred to in Urdu, is the centre of this alliance as well as its organisational and political mind. Most observers believe that it will be impossible to re-establish stability in Pakistan until the Islamic forces, and more specifically the Jamaat-i-Islami, are accommodated in some way.

The Jamaat-i-Islami is perhaps the only Islamic organisation that can match the Muslim Brotherhood, in terms of staying power and public support. The Jamaat was established in 1941 in the Indian city of Lahore, when the Indian subcontinent was still under British occupation, and before it had been divided into India and Pakistan. Just as the Muslim Brotherhood is linked to Hasan al-Banna, and Hizb al-Tahrir to Taqi al-Din al-Nabhani, so the Jamaat-i-Islami is linked to Abu'l A'la al-Mawdudi.

Al-Mawdudi was born in Aurangabad, in the Indian state of Maharashtra in 1903. His family was descended from a line of scholars who belonged to the Chistiyyah Sufi Order, one of the most widespread and influential Sufi orders on the subcontinent. His ancestors had served the Muslim Mughal emperors who ruled India from 1526 to 1720, establishing Islam in the region.[1]

However, the family's situation deteriorated in 1858, after the collapse of a major Muslim rebellion against British rule. They were forced to leave Delhi and move south to the Deccan region. Like his ancestors Al-Mawdudi's father was a committed Sufi, and was determined to raise his children in accordance with a traditional Islamic upbringing, distancing them from Anglican influence as much as possible. In these conditions, it was impossible for al-Mawdudi to escape India's Islamic past or his family's deep-rooted traditions, and both left a deep impression on him.

Al-Mawdudi studied the Islamic sciences and excelled at Arabic; he was still a youngster when he translated Qasim Amin's controversial book, *al-Mar'ah al-Jadidah* (The new woman), into Urdu. However, he had to abandon his studies at the age of sixteen after his father became ill and died.

The young al-Mawdudi was more interested in politics than religion, and this propelled him into the field of journalism. As a supporter of the Indian Congress Party and Mahatma Gandhi, he chose to work for the weekly *Taj* newspaper in the city of Jabalpur, which supported the Congress Party.

In this early phase of his life, he was passionate about Indian nationalism and India's need to achieve independence for all of its ethnic and religious groups. However, he soon became involved with the Khilafat (caliphate) Movement led by Moulana Muhammad 'Ali – a renowned Islamic leader who died in London in 1931 and was buried beside al-Aqsa Mosque in Jerusalem. The Movement's activities centred on inviting Muslims to join and protect the Islamic Caliphate, which was under severe threat after the defeat of the Ottoman Empire in the First World War. Even though the Khilafat Movement was not limited to the

Muslims of India, it played a huge role in reviving the spirit of solidarity and in activating the organisational capacity of Indian Muslims. The young al-Mawdudi became close to Moulana Muhammad 'Ali during his involvement in the Khilafat Movement, and the latter encouraged him to return to Delhi where he assisted in the publication of the *Hamdard Journal*, the Khilafat Movement's official publication. This was the beginning of al-Mawdudi's involvement in Islamic affairs.

From 1921 to 1924, al-Mawdudi was linked with the Jamiat 'Ulama-e-Hind (Society of Indian 'Ulama), the first organisation for religious scholars in India, and he became the editor-in-chief of their publication, *The Muslim*. The leaders of the organisation encouraged him to enter into formal training under scholars from the Hanafi Deobandi School at the Fatehpuri Mosque in Delhi but al-Mawdudi did not see himself as a scholar in the traditional sense. During this period, his writings began to reflect an interest in the conditions of Muslims in India and beyond, as well as in the Muslim renaissance and the preconditions for this. In an earnest attempt to equip himself with the necessary tools for further research and study, he decided to learn English.

In 1924, when Atatürk annulled the caliphate, the Khilafat Movement drew to a halt. These developments, including Atatürk's attempt to build a Turkish state based on nationalism and detached from its Islamic roots, left their mark on al-Mawdudi. He began to critique what he saw as nationalist chauvinism, for creating divisions within the Muslim community. He included the Indian Congress Party in this, seeing their call for an Indian nation as a mask that concealed strong Hindu nationalist inclinations. In view of the strong relations between the Jamiat 'Ulama-e-Hind and the Congress Party, al-Mawdudi decided to cut his ties with the Jamiat. There is no doubt that the rise in chauvinistic Hindu nationalism that occurred in the 1920s was unprecedented. In 1925, after two Muslim activists assassinated a bigoted Hindu leader, sectarian violence between Muslims and Hindus erupted across the country and Hindu nationalist newspapers launched a widespread campaign against Islam as a religion, describing it as a faith that advocated violence. This campaign prompted al-Mawdudi to publish his famous book, *Al Jihad fil-Islam* (Jihad in Islam) in 1927, which entrenched his reputation among Muslims in India.

The deepening of his Islamic sentiments and the widening gap between himself and the Indian nationalism prevalent in Delhi, prompted al-Mawdudi to move to Hyderabad, the last Islamic emirate in British India. There, he devoted much time to study and research. He also grew his beard and donned the traditional garb worn by Indian Muslims.

A single question seems to have occupied much of his thinking, namely: what weakened Muslim rule in India and led to its collapse? Seeking inspiration in the works of great Indian Muslim reformers, such as Ahmad Sirhindi and Shah Waliullah Dihlawi, al-Mawdudi's answer to this pressing question suggested that Muslims had been overly influenced by local traditions that had weakened the spirit and values of Islam. After reaching this conclusion, al-Mawdudi began to call for the establishment of a separate polity for Muslims and for a break with Indian and Hindu culture.

In 1932, al-Mawdudi launched the *Tarjuman Qur'an* (Exegesis of the Qur'an), a monthly journal that became the main channel for the expression of his ideas until his death in 1979, forty-seven years later. However, al-Mawdudi was fully aware that ideas alone were not enough to effect change. In 1938, therefore, he responded to an invitation extended to him by Muhammad Iqbal, a renowned Islamic leader and intellectual, and made his way to Pathankot, an ancient city in the state of Punjab, to run the Dar al-Salam Educational Institute, which Iqbal founded.

The years from 1935 to 1939 were decisive for Muslims in India. The British government finally submitted to the Indian independence movement, and agreed to hold elections for the formation of local Indian administrations with limited authority. However, the Muslim League, led by Muhammad 'Ali Jinnah, was caught unawares by this development and the Congress Party was able to attain an overwhelming victory in the elections, allowing it to form a national government under British supervision.

The Congress Party was a secular nationalist organisation, and this made Muslims anxious that their educational institutions might be closed, and that secular nationalism would then undermine their children's sense of identity. However, with the outbreak of the Second World War, the British government disbanded the national government and re-imposed direct British rule in India. Nevertheless, the short period of Congress rule served to only strengthen the secessionist inclinations of many Muslims.

By the late 1930s, political work dominated activities in Islamic circles in India. The question of secession was the dominant one for Muslims but their leaders were openly divided on the issue. The Muslim League, led by Jinnah, called for the establishment of an independent nation state for Muslims, while the Jamiat 'Ulama-e-Hind entirely rejected the idea of secession. Al-Mawdudi was convinced of the need to rebuild Islamic culture and society, but he was apprehensive about the Muslim League's secular and nationalist orientation. Amidst these tense and urgent debates, al-Mawdudi established the Jamaat-i-Islami in the city of Lahore. The most prominent members of the founding group – which included no more than seventy individuals – were Abu'l Hasan al-Nadwi, who later became one of the most prominent Muslim scholars in India, Mu'in Tufayl Muhammad, who took over leadership of the Jamaat after al-Mawdudi, and Muhammad Manzur Nu'mani.[2]

The founding members chose al-Mawdudi as their leader and agreed to set up their headquarters in the city of Pathankot. However, the spread and influence of the Jamaat-i-Islami was not strong enough to prevent the splitting of the subcontinent into India and Pakistan in 1947 when Britain finally agreed to grant independence to India. Once the split occurred, members of the Jamaat-i-Islami found themselves divided by a national border. Al-Mawdudi chose to move to Pakistan and relocate the group's headquarters to the city of Lahore, with its rich Islamic history.

When Muhammad 'Ali Jinnah became Pakistan's first president, some of al-Mawdudi's hopes materialised. However, Jinnah saw Pakistan as a Muslim state, not an Islamic one, and ruled according to a secular nationalist dispensation rather than Islamic principles. Like many other Islamic scholars, Al-Mawdudi believed that secession from India, which had incurred immense humanitarian costs, should have resulted in the establishment of a state committed to building a society saturated with Islamic views and values. It is therefore not surprising that the struggle over Pakistan's identity as a state began at the very moment of the country's birth. Al-Mawdudi joined other Islamic scholars in lobbying for an Islamic constitution for Pakistan.

However, after accusing the government of hypocrisy, al-Mawdudi was soon arrested – while calling for jihad and assisting the Kashmiri rebels, the government had simultaneously agreed to a ceasefire with India in Kashmir. After being incarcerated for two years, he was released due to increasing pressure upon the Pakistani government.

Almost immediately after his release, al-Mawdudi instigated a widespread campaign calling for the resignation of the foreign minister Zafrullah Khan (Khan belonged to the Qadiani sect, which many Muslims regard as outside the bounds of Islam). Al-Mawdudi also continued to call for the development of an Islamic constitution, announcing that Muslim soldiers and civil servants are prohibited from swearing allegiance to any state as long as that state had not declared Islam to be the basis for its authority. He was soon rearrested and prosecuted again. In court, he received a death sentence but this was overturned by the High Court in 1955. In the following year, the constitution was published with a clear statement affirming the Islamic nature of Pakistan. Al-Mawdudi saw this as a major victory for Islamisation, announcing his acceptance of the constitution and calling for a campaign to Islamise all state institutions and legislation.[3]

Al-Mawdudi's early vision of transition to an Islamic system supported the total overthrow of the existing system, but his vision was vague with regard to the methodology and means that would be involved. Al-Mawdudi held back from condemning nation states that ignored the doctrinal affiliation of the majority of their citizens. This was certainly why he refused to recognise the Pakistani state, although some accused him of opposing the split from India. His acceptance of Pakistan's constitution and Jamaat-i-Islami's participation in the elections that followed represented a major shift for al-Mawdudi, in that it essentially affirmed the Pakistani state. This shift was perhaps not only influenced by the constitution's affirmation of the Islamic nature of Pakistan, but also by the High Court decision that vindicated al-Mawdudi and rescinded the death penalty that had been hanging over him. Al-Mawdudi discovered from personal experience that the modern state was not all bad when he realised that it was the separation of powers, and the independence of the judiciary, that had saved him from the hangman's noose.

The onset of military rule in Pakistan brought about another shift in al-Mawdudi's political thinking. In 1958, the Pakistani army seized power under General Ayub Khan. The coup occurred after successive Pakistani administrations had failed to establish political stability or bring about economic development. The coup leaders quickly abandoned the constitution and imposed direct military rule.

It is widely believed that American diplomats and intelligence agents played a role in encouraging the officers to take over, just as they had in several other third-world countries at around that time. With the onset of the Cold War, and rising tensions between the West and the Communist Bloc, the Americans seemed to think that discipline and modernity would flourish under military rule in third-world countries, enabling them to develop economically and resist communist expansion. Pakistan was an important link in the allies' Cold War activities, and Washington believed that only the Pakistani army was capable of maintaining stability while driving a development programme that would shield the country from the communist ideology that had spread across many parts of East and South East Asia.

Ayub Khan wanted to establish a nation founded on Pakistani nationalism, and set about strengthening the unity of various groups that operated within the framework of the new state. He saw the ideas and activities of the Jamaat-i-Islami as an impediment to this. Drawing inspiration from Atatürk, Ayub Khan announced in a famous speech: 'We are not only Muslims; we are also Pakistanis'. It did not take long, therefore, for Ayub Khan to initiate a campaign of pursuit and repression against the Jamaat-i-Islami. Al-Mawdudi was incarcerated twice as a result, first in 1964, and then from 1967 to 1969. Interestingly, the relationship between Ayub Khan and the Jamaat-i-Islami improved briefly during the Indo-Pakistani War of 1965, when Ayub Khan declared jihad against India. In an attempt to muster additional support for this war within Pakistan, Ayub Khan did not hesitate to serenade the Jamaat-i-Islami and try to draw close to al-Mawdudi.

Under military rule, al-Mawdudi soon began to see the positive sides of democracy, and this persuaded him to join a broad alliance that aimed to bring down military rule. In the end, Ayub Khan's regime collapsed in 1969 and the crisis of East Pakistan, now Bangladesh, began to loom on the horizon.

The Jamaat-i-Islami was active in campaigning against the breakaway of Bangladesh, which India supported with all of its political and military might. In the heat of a war that raised the passions of all Pakistanis, a new star was rising on Pakistan's political horizon. Zulfikar 'Ali Bhutto was Pakistan's eloquent foreign minister at the beginning of the Bangladesh breakaway crisis, and later became its prime minister.

In 1972, al-Mawdudi resigned as leader of the Jamaat-i-Islami and Mu'in Tufayl Muhammad, another of the group's early founding members was elected to replace him. Pakistan was entering a new phase of its history and the organisation seemed to be in need of new blood.

Al-Mawdudi was now in his late sixties, and his failing health did not allow him to pursue political and intellectual work as well as keep track of the organisation. His resignation did not prevent him from writing for his journal *Tarjuman Qur'an*, or from offering advice to the organisation's new leaders. Seven years later, in September 1979 Al-Mawdudi passed away in a hospital in the USA, where he had gone for treatment. After his death, his body was returned to Lahore, where it was estimated that about a million Pakistanis took part in his funeral procession.

Despite Jamaat-i-Islami's failure to achieve tangible political power, al-Mawdudi had considerable influence both within Pakistan and beyond. This prompted the Pakistani government to award him the title of 'leading statesman'.

Between the publication of his first book in the mid 1920s and his death in 1979, al-Mawdudi wrote many other books and thousands of articles, lived an eventful political life, and engaged in many, many debates. It is therefore only natural that his ideas on the Islamic state and the role of religion in modern Islamic society were subject to revision and change.

The problem that al-Mawdudi found himself confronting before the formation of Pakistan was the contradiction between the glorious Muslim Empire, that had thrived in India in previous centuries, and the plight of contemporary Muslims who felt besieged by both the growing Hindu majority and the British occupying forces, fearing that neither safeguarded their interests with any degree of justice. It is possible to argue that al-Mawdudi's early views centred on the revival of Islam as a distinct, rejuvenating force. He did not view the Indian problem from a perspective of national liberation from imperialism, nor did he try to understand the situation of Indian Muslims as a minority group. He viewed Muslims through the lens of their history, as conquerors who had been the dominant authority for centuries.

Al-Mawdudi's objective, in establishing the Jamaat-i-Islami, was to restore a pure Islamic society. He sought to achieve this through the formation of a vanguard of elite believers, who would intermingle with the masses, spreading the vitality of Islam among them once again. Even after the founding of Pakistan, the Jamaat-i-Islami was, for a long time, more of an elite organisation than a popular movement. This probably explains its failure to attain noteworthy support during the many Pakistani elections it contested.

To build the Islamic vanguard, al-Mawdudi advocated a revival of the faith, God-consciousness and religious values, in addition to worship and good deeds. He thus attempted to limit the influence of popular Sufi practices without totally rejecting them. Al-Mawdudi affirmed the rationality of faith and argued that salvation was not an individual matter but the result of social action. In his book, *The Four Concepts*, al-Mawdudi insisted on the uniqueness of Islam, and presented definitive interpretations of the concepts of al-ilah (divinity), al-Rab (the Lord), al-'ibadah (worship), and al-din (religion), drawing links between faith in one God and al-hakimiyyah al-mutlaqah (the absolute authority) of the shari'ah in Islamic society. Without honouring this link, al-Mawdudi argued, Islamic society would revert to al-jahiliyyah (a state of ignorance).

In his early struggles to contribute to the establishment of Pakistan on Islamic foundations, al-Mawdudi articulated Islam as a comprehensive ideology, clearly influenced in this by the major Western ideologies. However, he also strove to portray Islam as a unique system, and clearly distinct from communism and capitalism. He also sensed that the struggle between Islam and its opponents would inevitably reach the point of revolution, resulting in the formation of an Islamic state that would commit to total reform, restoring honour and prosperity to humanity by introducing a utopian system that is real and sustainable. Despite adopting a discourse of differentiation, al-Mawdudi could not avoid borrowing many Western concepts pertaining to states and society, and his writings are filled with terms such as 'the Islamic coup', 'Islamic ideology' and 'Islamic state'.[4] The state alluded to here is the modern nation-state, with all the well-known institutions that prevail in Western countries and political practice, such as presidents, parliaments, independent judiciaries, constitutions, etc.

Slowly but surely, al-Mawdudi's discourse began to lose its radicalism and totalitarian bent. The concept of a total Islamic revolution vanished, and was replaced with a commitment to democracy. As a result, the Islamic state became a democratic state. Al-Mawdudi rejected violence and military coups as means to attain power. He rejected the popular revolution that brought about the Islamic Republic in Iran, regarding this as a path that would lead to chaos. He held the view that the shari'ah could not be unilaterally imposed, but should be implemented as a result of community consensus.

Nevertheless, al-Mawdudi to a large extent remained a conservative, who was committed to the Hanafi jurisprudential legacy as espoused by the Deobandi School. He believed that the social role of women should find expression in a sphere separate from that occupied by men. He rejected Western views on the role of women and on the question of minorities, just as he rejected the policies of nationalisation and agrarian reform, which he saw as short-sighted solutions to problems caused by the absence of Islamic rule, that ultimately fail to eliminate poverty and social disparity. He held that the policies of the elusive yet ideal Islamic state should be based on Islamic economics, which he believed was the only system capable of providing just solutions to social problems. In other words, politics remained the centre of gravity in al-Mawdudi's thought.

❧

When Tufayl Muhammad took over as leader of the Jamaat-i-Islami, the Pakistan People's Party led by Zulfikar 'Ali Bhutto had made a clean sweep of Pakistan's 1970 elections and Bhutto became president. Bhutto was a popular socialist who gave millions of Pakistanis hope for a better life, and vindicated their confidence in politicians once more. He was also however a truly intractable opponent of the Jamaat-i-Islami.

In the face of Bhutto's popularity, the Jamaat-i-Islami's only recourse was to initiate a campaign against the Ahmadiyyah Qadiani community and the appointment of its adherents to influential positions in the government. This drew some popular support but not enough to challenge Bhutto. This convinced the Jamaat-i-Islami to join a broad alliance of Islamic organisations under the banner of Nizam al-Mustafa (System of the Chosen One).[5]

Islamists saw Bhutto as a threat to Islam's cultural heritage – and, in fact, as a threat to the faith itself. That is, they did not see him simply as a political opponent, and bringing him down became imperative for them. In the 1977 elections, the opposition won thirty-six parliamentary seats, nine of which were won by the Jamaat. At this point, Bhutto made a fatal error in allowing his administration to carry out large-scale election fraud. Amid rising tensions and increasing opposition to Bhutto, the army intervened once again.

In June 1977, General Muhammad Zia-ul-Haq seized power and suspended the constitution and the democratic process. He then had Bhutto arrested, tried, and eventually executed. In this way, Pakistan entered a new era that tied the Jamaat-i-Islami to Zia-ul-Haq's controversial administration in many complicated ways.

Zia-ul-Haq exercised absolute authority and attempted to establish political and economic stability by suppressing all forms of opposition – leftist, centrist and right-wing. However, the ambitious general, who built the foundations of Pakistan's nuclear arms programme, was not naïve. To win the loyalty of the people, he instituted a project to encourage the Islamisation of Pakistan. It would have been difficult to advocate Islamisation without the co-operation of the Islamists, so Zia-ul-Haq positioned himself close to the Jamaat-i-Islami and appointed some of its members to ministerial positions, thus striving to transform the organisation into a political and ideological tool that would support his administration.

Another factor that justified increasingly close relations between Zia-ul-Haq and the Jamaat-i-Islami was the rise of Islamic resistance to the Soviet Union's occupation of Afghanistan. The involvement of the Soviet Union also resulted in the USA becoming a direct player in the Afghan War, and Zia-ul-Haq tried to strengthen Pakistani–American relations by tying the Afghani resistance fighters to his own administration. The majority of the Afghani resistance fighters held strong Islamic views, and had firm links with the Jamaat-i-Islami. This made the Jamaat essential to the furtherance of Zia-ul-Haq's policies in Afghanistan.

However, the warm relationship between the Jamaat and the general did not last. Being associated with a military dictator began to undermine the Jamaat's popular appeal, and it therefore became essential for the organisation to maintain a clear distance between itself and the general's administration. From his side, Zia-ul-Haq had no wish to share power and sought to use the Jamaat as a tool to strengthen his rule. The 1985 elections – called by Zia-ul-Haq to add a democratic veneer to his reign – marked the end of the fragile alliance. The Jamaat-i-Islami 'won' just ten seats in the national assembly, and this very poor result set alarm bells ringing among the Jamaat's leadership.[6]

In 1987, Qadi Husayn Ahmad took over as leader of the Jamaat. He hailed from Pakistan's north-western province, which was the Afghani jihad's main support-base. Under his leadership, the Jamaat tried to cast aside its elitist character and affirm its mass appeal. In the following year, Zia-ul-Haq died in an airplane crash. After this, Pakistan entered a new phase of democratic rule, in which the Jamaat had to compete against the People's Party led by Benazir Bhutto and the Islamic League led by Nawaz Sharif. The Jamaat regarded Benazir Bhutto as following in her father's footsteps – that is, as extremely secular and therefore a greater threat to Pakistan's Islamic character than Sharif.

The Jamaat contested the 1988 and 1990 elections in coalition with other less-influential Islamic forces, under the name of the Islamic Republic Alliance. They were unable to win more than ten parliamentary seats in both elections. Although the Jamaat undoubtedly grew stronger under Husayn's leadership, its support from voters did not reflect this. It thus became clear that Pakistani election results depend more on voter loyalty to their various ethnic affiliations and traditional leaders than on their own political and intellectual points of view. This worked to the advantage of Bhutto and Sharif.

At any rate, this phase of democracy in Pakistan lasted less than ten years. On 12 October 1999, the military once again toppled civilian rule after the head of the military, Pervez Musharraf, and the prime minister, Nawaz Sharif, disagreed on how to take forward the struggle for Kashmir. In May of the previous year, Pakistan and India had joined the set of nations that possess nuclear weapons. And because Musharraf's approach to the question of Kashmir seemed likely to increase tensions on the Indian subcontinent, Western responses to his coup were extremely negative, especially in Washington. The West imposed a trade boycott on Musharraf's government. Combined with foreign debt that rocketed to US$32 billion, the boycott posed a major threat to the Pakistani economy.

Then, the events of 9/11, and America's involvement in the war in Afghanistan, drew the USA back into an alliance with Pakistan once more. For Pakistan, the costs of rebuilding the alliance were extreme. Musharraf had to help topple the Taliban regime in Afghanistan and take direct steps against al-Qa'ida supporters in Pakistan, including the Pakistani tribes that were sympathetic to al-Qa'ida.

The Jamaat-i-Islami and other Islamic forces in Pakistan saw Musharraf's actions as extremely provocative. This was especially so for the Society of Pakistani Scholars, which had close cultural ties with the Taliban. The Jamaat responded by contesting the October 2002 parliamentary elections in an alliance with five other Islamic organisations as the United Action Assembly. The Assembly's election campaign was directed against Musharraf and his alliance with George W Bush. The Assembly succeeded in winning sixty-three of the 342 seats in the National Assembly, in addition to taking control of the local government in the country's north-western province.

These were the best election results the Jamaat (and Islamists more broadly) had achieved in Pakistan since the country was established. Their success indicated that Qadi Husayn's attempts to win over mass appeal were succeeding as well as the deep popular animosity that existed towards the government's alliance with Washington. However, the Jamaat was not able to sustain their success in the 2008 elections. These were contested by far more parties of which the two largest, the People's Party and the Islamic League, again emerged as the strongest.

The Jamaat-i-Islami has come a long way since its inception in British-occupied India at the beginning of the 1940s. It is now active in parties that honour al-Mawdudi's ideals and operate, not only in Pakistan, but also in Bangladesh, India, Sri-Lanka and the Indo-Pakistani diaspora. While Pakistan remains the Jamaat's primary sphere of influence, the road to power remains long.

The organisation is now seen as an important example of how supporters of political Islam can integrate into the structures of the modern state and adapt to state apparatuses. The Jamaat has happily adopted the democratic system and, in fact, become one of its greatest defenders, challenging many of the military coups that have plagued the Muslim world. While the Jamaat's elitist structure and the complexities of electoral politics in Pakistan have limited its electoral success in that country so far, the intellectual and cultural impact that the organisation has had on Pakistan and on modern Islamic thought should not be underestimated. They have played a key role in spreading Islam's inspiring values and confronting false practices based on superstition and faith in dervishes. Similarly, the impact of al-Mawdudi's intellectual legacy on modern Islamic thought should not be undervalued.

Surprisingly, although al-Mawdudi's thinking evolved to embrace peaceful transitions towards Islam via the practice of democracy, his early ideas have spread further in the Islamic world.

Few of those who have been influenced by al-Mawdudi's early think-ing have fully grasped the fact that his ideas developed in the context of Muslims in India *before* the establishment of Pakistan. However, his concepts of al-hakimiyyah (divine authority), al-uluhiyyah (divinity) and al-mufaasilah (disengagement) all became central to the writings of another Islamic intellectual who has had a far more pronounced impact on the destiny of political Islam: he is none other than Sayyid Qutb.

7

The revenge of the intellectual

$\mathcal{J}$ ust a few months after the events of 9/11 2001, the life and influence of Sayyid Qutb fell into the spotlight of world attention. As researchers, experts and analysts concerned with political Islam began searching for the intellectual frame of reference behind al-Qa'ida, the group that carried out the attacks on New York and Washington, it became clear that no intellectual in the modern Islamic landscape had left a legacy more stark or polarising than Sayyid Qutb.

The relationship between Qutb's thought and that of al-Qa'ida members is unsubstantiated. However, it cannot be denied that after his execution, a man who began his life as a teacher, writer and literary critic was transformed into the founding father of radical Islam. In the 1970s and 1980s, Qutb's books were circulated and sold more widely than any others in the Arab world. In fact, after his works were translated into several languages, his influence extended into the Islamic world more broadly. If the destinies of the Muslim Brotherhood and the Jamaat-i-Islami clarify the impact of social contexts on political policies and programmes, then Qutb's life and intellectual legacy emphasise the tremendous impact that the life and death of one person can have on the world. Qutb appropriated some concepts directly from al-Mawdudi's early writings, the difference being that Qutb's execution made him an intellectual martyr, and martyrdom helped to give his views an unchallengeable authority.

Sayyid Qutb was born in Egypt in 1906 – the same year as Hasan al-Banna – in the village of Musha, which lies in the governorate of

Asyut.[1] Asyut is located in the heart of Egypt's Sa'id region, where the harshness of the natural environment seems to make people both physically strong and prone to severity. Sa'idi society is generally more devout and conservative, perhaps because it is situated so far away from Cairo's cultural and political verve. The neglect of this vast region by successive governments has at times spawned feelings of marginalisation, but it has also entrenched a culture of self-reliance that strongly values both freedom and rebellion.

Qutb's father, al-Haj Qutb Ibrahim, was a village elder who owned a small piece of land. However, his generosity and family responsibilities meant that he gradually lost most of his possessions. Sayyid Qutb completed his primary education at a modern school in Musha, and had memorised the Qur'an by the age of ten. In 1919, when he was just thirteen, his village was caught up in Egypt's national revolution against British occupation, and Qutb experienced aspects of that revolution very directly.

Six years later, Egypt had been granted a semblance of independence, and a period of veiled liberalism prevailed. At this point, Qutb travelled to Cairo, which was then the capital of Western modernity in the East, to register as a student at the teacher-training college. In 1928, after having completed his studies, Qutb enrolled at the Dar al-Ulum, from which al-Banna had graduated the previous year. In 1933, at the age of twenty-seven, Qutb received his degree from the College and was immediately employed by the education ministry, within which he gradually advanced over the next eighteen years.

Qutb's early worldview was characterised by rebelliousness. He is even reported to have described his life between 1925 and 1939 as a period of atheism.[2] After he graduated, his main interests were literature and literary criticism, and he associated very closely with the renowned Egyptian writer 'Abbas Mahmud al-'Aqqad, who also hailed from the Sa'id region. Al-'Aqqad thrived on the intense intellectual battles that took place among Egypt's literary and intellectual elite in the period between the two World Wars, and Qutb became known for supporting al-'Aqqad against figures such as Mustafa Sadiq al-Rafi'i and Taha Husayn.

Qutb was acquainted with most Egyptian writers of his time and wrote articles on the works of Tawfiq al-Hakim, Taha Husayn and 'Aziz Abazah for prominent journals and newspapers. His positive review of Naquib Mahfouz's novel *Khan al-Khalili* probably introduced Mahfouz to a broader audience and helped launch his career as one of Egypt's major novelists.

Qutb never married and many believe that the reason for this was a bitter, failed relationship. His novel *al-Ashwak* (The thorns), published in 1947, is widely believed to be a portrayal of that experience. Qutb suffered from ill health and lung disease throughout his life, prompting him to choose a home in the dry Halwan district outside of Cairo. In the garden of his home, Qutb entertained visitors, friends and students. These included Gamal Abdel Nasser and other members of the Free Officers Movement, as well as the leaders of the secret Islamic organisation – an association that eventually led to Qutb being put to death in a hangman's noose in 1966.

At the end of the 1930s, Qutb returned to Islam. The events that led up to this are unclear; what is known is that his primary interaction with the Qur'an was through literature, not politics or doctrine. In 1939, Qutb began a series of articles for the journal *al-Muqtataf* entitled 'al-Taswir fi al-Finni fi al-Qur'an al-Karim' (Aesthetic portrayal in the noble Qur'an). The articles were later collected in a book of the same name. The articles present a literary reading of the aesthetics of the Qur'an, but one of the fruits of Qutb's efforts was that he became convinced of the organic structure of the Qur'anic text. After some time, and with slight development, this became one of the central themes in Qutb's understanding of Islam.

From then on, Qutb's interest in Islam developed rapidly. In 1949, he published his most famous work, *al-'Adalah al-Ijtima'iyyah fi al-Islam* (Social Justice in Islam). The book launched a severe attack on the gross class discrimination prevalent in Egypt. For the first time in the modern era, Qutb's work offered a deeply Islamic vision of social justice, calling for the establishment of a minimum wage and the redistribution of wealth. Perhaps one factor influencing the book was that Egypt, like most Arab countries, was exposed to increasing numbers of Marxist thinkers who were attempting to recruit supporters within the impoverished classes. It has been rumoured that Qutb rejected this book after the issue of doctrine took centre stage in his thinking. However, Qutb introduced several concepts in *Social Justice* that shaped his vision of Islam, and there is no doubt that he held onto those ideas until the end of his life.

The symbolic announcement that indicated the transformation of the Muslim Brotherhood from a society concerned with religious propagation to one doing political work was Hasan al-Banna's often-quoted statement: 'Islam is religion and state, Qur'an and sword'. In a similar vein, Qutb wrote in *Social Justice*: 'Islam does not separate religion from state and is not only a doctrine and a faith, but a social system as well...[a social system that calls for] the liberation of human beings.'[3] However, even at this early stage, Qutb's views were already intensely dogmatic. He condemned all Islamic history after the fitnah (the first civil war in Islam), ignoring centuries of Islam's cultural and intellectual heritage, and suggesting that Islam has an ideal core that exists independently of historical experience.

Nevertheless, *Social Justice* had a tremendous impact upon Nasser and his fellow Free Officers as they made plans to overthrow the Egyptian monarchy. The book also made a positive impression on the Muslim Brotherhood, who began to pay attention to Qutb as a potential ally. In fact, by the mid 1980s, Samir Amin, the renowned Egyptian Marxist thinker, argued that *Social Justice in Islam* was the Muslim Brotherhood's 'only ideological product'.[4]

In 1948, Egypt's education ministry gave Qutb a scholarship for a period of two years, sending him to America to study pedagogy. Qutb learned English and travelled to as many parts of the USA as his health allowed. His letters from America to his friends in Egypt, and the articles he published during this period, reflect a dark and negative view of what he saw as American lifestyle and culture. America, from Qutb's perspective, was

> the greatest lie known to the world! We are able to benefit from America only from its purely scientific inventions in mechanics, electricity, chemistry and agriculture, and so on. However, when we try to derive benefit from America in theoretical studies, including teaching methodology, I am of the opinion that we are making a mistake.

Qutb saw American culture as primitive and believed that 'all of the American genius is collected and crystallised in the field of production and work, such that nothing is left to produce anything in the field of human values'.[5]

It is not certain to what extent Qutb was aware of elements within America who were highly self-reflective and critical of their own culture, but it is known that he never read Steinbeck or Hemingway, or saw work by playwrights such as Arthur Miller being performed.

After returning to Egypt, Qutb began to express his scepticism about liberal democracy, and his critiques of the monarchy, with its acolytes and pashas also became frequent, sharp and focused. Nasser and his comrades made a considerable effort to win him over before they launched their revolution. After the coup, Qutb was appointed as an advisor to the Revolutionary Leadership Council and was given an office at their headquarters in al-Jazirah.

However, Qutb – like al-Hudaybi – quickly lost confidence in the Free Officers, and began to question their commitment to establishing a just order based on Islamic principles. In fact, Qutb began to suspect that Nasser and his fellow officers had links with the US government, and speculated that the Americans might have backed the coup.

In 1953, Qutb officially joined the Muslim Brotherhood. As a sign of their respect for him, they asked him to take responsibility for their official newspaper, *al-Ikhwan al-Muslimun*. As tensions and differences between the Brotherhood and the Free Officers escalated, Qutb strove to transform the Brotherhood into a mass movement that would be able to express the demands of the people and defend them should any confrontation with the Officers arise.

The differences between the two groups quickly transformed into open conflict, forcing Qutb to close down the newspaper. He then began to produce another publication, *al-Ikhwan fi al-Ma'rakah* (The Brotherhood in battle), which was published in secret and contained thunderous attacks on Nasser. When Nasser was exposed to an assassination attempt in Alexandria, Qutb suggested that it was nothing more than a plot concocted by foreign elements intent on destroying the Muslim Brotherhood. Nonetheless, like thousands of other Brotherhood members who were rounded up in widespread arrests, Qutb ended up in prison, and the Brotherhood was banned towards the end of 1954.

Qutb was placed in the Liman Tarrah Prison close to Cairo. Probably because of his intellectual stature and his earlier relationship with the Free Officers, Qutb was not subjected to abuse or torture like many of his fellow Brotherhood members. He did, however, spend lengthy periods during his incarceration in the prison's hospital, and when his health deteriorated further, the prison authorities were forced to transfer him to Al-Manial University Hospital in Cairo. This allowed Qutb to remain in touch with the political, cultural and social developments in Egypt under Nasser's rule.

To attribute his radical transformation in the 1960s to the isolation imposed on him in prison doesn't ring true; in all probability, his radicalisation developed as a result of his awareness and rejection of what was transpiring around him.

In terms of his vision for Egypt's future and its role in the Arab region, Nasser was an ambitious leader. However, he was not a gambler and at the outset of his rule, he probably assumed it would be possible to avoid clashing with the Western powers that held sway in the Arab region. His assumption was far from correct. As soon as Nasser came to power he found himself embroiled in a major political battle against policies that the Western allies were trying to implement in the Middle East to protect their spheres of influence and restrict the encroachment of the Soviet Union.

With the outbreak of the Algerian Revolution in 1954, Egypt extended its support to the Algerian revolutionaries, thereby incurring the animosity of France. In 1955 after an upsurge of Israeli attacks against Egyptian forces in the Gaza Strip, Nasser took the Western bloc by surprise when he began to procure weaponry from the Eastern Bloc. Then, when Washington and the World Bank refused to finance the building of the Aswan Dam, Nasser announced the nationalisation of the Suez Canal Company, which was then owned by France and Britain. At this, Egypt's relationship with the West hit an all-time low. In 1956, the world was shocked when Britain, France and Israel attacked Egypt and occupied Gaza, the Sinai Peninsula and the Suez Canal region.

The entire world, including Washington and Moscow – albeit for their own reasons – opposed this war because of its potential to destabilise the entire Middle East region. Within a few months, the tripartite alliance withdrew from areas they had occupied. Although Nasser was defeated militarily, he emerged from the conflict having won a major political victory. This strengthened his legitimacy in Egypt and made him the undisputed leader of the Pan-Arab movement.

A year thereafter, Syria's political leaders asked Nasser to establish a single Arab state that would unite Egypt and Syria. This was indeed achieved and the United Arab Republic was born in February 1958. By supporting Arab unity, and its participation in the Non-Aligned Movement, Egypt became an active Arab and third-world power and Nasser's confidence grew, along with his belief in the astuteness of his polit-ical decisions. For a while, Nasser became a uniquely powerful leader, whose strength was compounded by his infectious charm and huge popular appeal. Egyptian artists, such as Umm Kulthum, Muhammad 'Abd al-Wahhab and 'Abd al-Halim Hafiz, played a role in entrenching the strong links between Nasser and the people. The film *al-Nasir Sa-lah al-Din*, by the Egyptian film producer Yusuf Shahin, even tried to portray Nasser as a modern-day Salah al-Din by imbuing him with the characteristics of the historical hero.

Not even the collapse of the United Arab Republic (after the coup that took place in Syria in September 1961) was able to weaken Nasser's powers. Egypt's strained relationship with the West, and the fact that the Soviets were willing to help fund the building of the Aswan Dam, led to the establishment of closer ties between Egypt and the USSR. In the latter half of 1961, Nasser announced a string of legislation that gave the state control over the economy and industry and placed Egypt on a path to socialism. This socialist orientation became the framework for Nasser's internal policies and provided the ideological foundations of his vision for Arab nationalism and the Arab region.

This dual emphasis on nationalism and socialism did not necessarily mean that Nasser was opposed to Islam. When he banned the Muslim Brotherhood, for example, other non-political Islamic organisations such as the Jam'iyyah al-Shari'ah (Islamic Law Society) and the Ansar al-Sunnah (Upholders of the Prophetic Tradition) were unaffected. In fact, during Nasser's rule, more mosques were built in Egypt than in previous eras. Al-Azhar, the traditional stronghold of Islamic educa-tion, was transformed into a major university and several new institu-tions were added to it. In addition, delegations from al-Azhar were sent all over the world.

However, this expansion of Islamic influence was, like almost everything Nasser undertook, heavily orchestrated by the state. In re-turn for every achievement, Egyptians were expected to submit ever more readily to the will of the government. For example, in return for free education, the state took control of all education institutions; in return for industrial development and job creation, the state assumed control of the economy; in return for the development and growth of al-Azhar University, the institution was made a tool of the state. And the full might of Egypt's security forces was brought to bear on any independent thinking and citizens who dared to question state policies.

From his cell in Liman Tarrah and later from his hospital bed in Cairo, Qutb felt the effects of Nasser's system and saw few of its achievements. He saw a deified leader, socialist ethos overpowering Islamic culture, and a state trying to almost place itself in the position of the all-powerful Creator. These rapid changes probably reinforced the psychological break between Qutb and Nasser's regime as much as Qutb's experiences in prison.

At the beginning of June 1957, after a dispute with the prison authority, prisoners in Egypt who were also Brotherhood members held a sit-in in their cells. Qutb saw the prison guards respond by charging the cells and firing randomly at the prisoners. By the time the massacre ended, twenty-three prisoners had been killed and forty-six injured. On that day, the break between Qutb and the Nasserist state became irreparable. In fact, it heralded Qutb's rejection of all incumbent regimes, and ultimately led to the publication of his most well-known work, *Ma'alim fi al-Tariq* (Milestones).

In 1964, after Qutb's health had deteriorated even more, he was released from prison, and the Iraqi president, 'Abd al-Salam 'Arif – who was one of his admirers – intervened on his behalf. In the same year, *Milestones* was published in Cairo. It was rumoured that when Egyptian censors tried to ban the book, Nasser overturned their decision and insisted that its publication go ahead.

In this small volume that has had a tremendous impact, Qutb argues that Islam cannot be actualised by simply declaring one's faith in Allah as Lord and Creator. He states that faith also has to encompass a belief in Allah as the ruler and driver of human affairs, and as the source of all laws and moral values. Borrowing from some of al-Mawdudi's early writings, Qutb referred to this conception of faith as al-hakimiyyah (divine governorship), and affirmed that:

> All of this world is living in a state of jahiliyyah [ignorance], from the perspective of the authentic state wherefrom all the elements of life and its systems emanate…this ignorance is founded on transgressing the authority of Allah on earth and transgressing the most basic characteristic of divinity, which is divine governorship; such ignorance ascribes divine governorship to humankind.…Everything around us is ignorance, the perspectives and beliefs of people, their habits and traditions, the sources of their culture, their art and literature, their laws and legislation, even much of what we regard as Islamic culture, Islamic frames of reference, Islamic philosophy, Islamic thought, are all products of ignorance.[6]

Qutb also denounced nationalism, stating that as far as Muslims are concerned, their only form of citizenship is their faith, and called for this to be the point of departure for all Islamic praxis. He argued that the call to Islam in Mecca was made on this basis, and that it should therefore always be made on this basis, and especially in an era in which ignorance was again so dominant.

An overwhelming sense of isolation shrouds the pages of *Milestones* and many of Qutb's later writings reflecting his sense of isolation from the world in general, and not only from Nasserist Egypt. Qutb was a son of the modern world par excellence, a product of modern education, modern culture, a student of modern literature, and yet he chose to rebel against modernity. Nevertheless, Qutb's oppressive sense of isolation from the world was, in essence, an entirely modern phenomenon.

Qutb had come a long way from calling for liberation from oppression, exploitation and dictatorship in his book *Social Justice*, to calling for the total liberation of humanity in *Milestones*. Qutb's relationship with a world that he saw as lacking a higher, more transcendent frame of reference progressed in a similar manner. He saw the world as dominated by a dictatorship of the human intellect, and increasingly in crisis. It is therefore not strange that the opening lines of *Milestones* state that: 'Humankind stands today on the brink of the precipice.' Note that Qutb refers here to all of humankind, and not to any specific country or society. The problem is that Qutb did not speak like a modern philosopher; he did not use the language of Heidegger or Sartre, he drew from a very specific semantic field belonging to Islamic luminaries from the classical era such as al-Ash'ari, al-Isfira'ini and Ibn Taymiyyah. Qutb spoke as a modern Islamic dialectic theologian, using the parlance of Islamic doctrine. The problem was that this was not something he was necessarily qualified to do.

Milestones makes decisive and uncompromising statements, expressed in a language of utmost certainty, and lacking in the caution and relativism that characterises Sunni doctrinal texts and positions. Its tone and language are closer to those used by the Kharijite sect[7] than to general Sunni discourse. Qutb did not advocate takfir (excommunication) for individuals, regimes or rulers deemed to be sinful. In fact, he specifically denied making such a pronouncement against anyone.

Certainly, when Nasser approved the publishing of *Milestones*, there were no indications that he saw it as promoting takfir. In fact, Kamal al-Din Husayn, a member of the Revolutionary Leadership Council and a former minister who left government due to his differences with Nasser, was so impressed with the book that he bought several copies and distributed it among his friends. Husayn later affirmed that he did not see the book as promoting a takfiri position. Nevertheless, the internal logic of Qutb's text undoubtedly legitimises takfir.

Milestones is written in captivating prose by the pen of a professional writer using angry language that does not adhere to the conventional
idiom of Islamic doctrinal debate. All that *Milestones* needed to be interpreted as advocating takfir was a new context – a context in which
the level of popular anger was increasing and in which believers were
increasingly distanced from the conventions of Sunni doctrinal debates.
These very conditions arose just months after the book was published,
and were heralded by the execution of its author.

In the late 1950s, when most of the Brotherhood was in prison, supporters of the organisation who had not been arrested continued to meet
in secret. Most of their energies focused on supporting and helping the
families of the prisoners and detainees, but certain individuals were
intent on seeking revenge against Nasser and his regime.

In 1963, two small Brotherhood groups came together; the first was
led by a young university student, 'Ali Abduh 'Ashmawi, and the second
by a grain merchant from a village in the governorate of Dumyat, 'Abd
al-Fatah Isma'il. Both men had been associated with the Brotherhood before its banning in 1954. The leaders of this small secret band made contact with Zaynab al-Ghazali, who founded and led a cultural and charitable organisation called Jam'iyyah al-Nisaa' al-Muslimaat (Muslim Wom-
en's Association). Al-Ghazali had close family ties with several leading
figures in the Brotherhood, including the household of its leader Hasan
al-Hudaybi and with Sayyid Qutb's sisters; she also had strong links with
members of the Egyptian elite. Al-Ghazali reportedly assured 'Ashmawi
and Isma'il that they could count on al-Hudaybi's support if they were to
try to build a secret Brotherhood structure. Subsequently, many Brotherhood members, including Farid 'Abd al-Khaliq, who was then very close
to al-Hudaybi, have flatly rejected the claim that al-Hudaybi supported
the building of a secret Brotherhood structure at that time.

Nonetheless, 'Ashmawi and Isma'il's group began searching for a
prominent Brotherhood personality or leader who could help to legitimise its activities. Al-Ghazali attempted but failed to recruit 'Abd al-

'Aziz 'Ali, a former member of the Nationalist Party and a minister in the first revolutionary government for this role. The group then agreed to approach Sayyid Qutb. Al-Ghazali had given Qutb's books to members of the group, after having helped his sisters to obtain the books from him in prison. Thus, as soon as Qutb was released from prison, 'Ali 'Ashmawi and 'Abd al-Fatah Isma'il offered him the leadership of the group, and Qutb immediately accepted. However, he also began working to change the group's orientation away from seeking revenge and attempting to overthrow Nasser's regime. Instead, he attempted to convince them to adopt what he saw as correct beliefs. Qutb believed that the transition to an Islamic system would be prolonged, and that activists who wished to try to bring this about required firm foundations in faith before they thought about taking political control.

The only violence Qutb agreed to was the possibility of using weapons in self-defence if the state's security structures tried to launch another offensive against the Brotherhood. For this reason, Qutb approved of group members being trained in the use of weapons, and agreed to the hiding of guns, ammunition and explosives. In addition, in the event that the regime attempted another clampdown on the group, plans were drawn up to assassinate leaders of the regime and to destroy key infrastructure such as power plants.[8]

In the summer of 1965, various centres of power within the regime began to compete with one another. The security apparatuses, including the military police, under direction of army commander Field Marshal 'Abd al-Hakim 'Amer, launched a wide-ranging campaign to clampdown on the secret activities of the Muslim Brotherhood. However, internal security was not the responsibility of the armed forces, and Shams Badran – the director of 'Amer's office and the person appointed to lead the campaign – did not have a very clear idea of what to search for. What Badran did know was that 'Amer's position in the state hierarchy had been undermined by the collapse of Egyptian–Syrian unity four years before, and he was keen to help strengthen 'Amer's position.

A series of random arrests quickly uncovered the secret structure led by Qutb. Just days before, Qutb had called a halt to the assassination and sabotage plans he had previously endorsed, convinced that the group was incapable of making any impact on the stability of the regime. Although he was fully aware that his arrest, and execution, was inevitable, Qutb refused to flee the country. The intellectual and writer almost seemed to be seeking release from this world, a world that he had condemned with his every breath, calling for a state of conscious rupture with all it contained.

Thousands of members of the Brotherhood, as well as their family members and people closely or distantly connected with them, were subsequently arrested. Whether they were members of Qutb's grouping or the earlier Brotherhood structures made no difference. Even members of the Islamic Law Society and the Tablighi movement, which were not political organisations and had not previously been targeted by the regime, were arrested. In addition, Rashad Mahna, the former custodian of the monarchy, and Fu'ad Siraj al-Din, a prominent Wafdist leader, were also jailed. Interrogations were conducted at the military prison, and the matter was placed under the jurisdiction of military intelligence and the military police, rather than the civil judicial institutions. In the absence of any legal restrictions, and despite the fact that 'Ali 'Ashmawi made a full confession, the interrogators used horrific methods to torture detainees and many died.

The whole situation was a terrible disgrace for a major Arab nationalist regime that was fighting imperialism and saw itself as defending Arab unity and independence. The outcome of the subsequent trials only brought the regime further into disrepute. The accused were tried before a military court, presided over by Lieutenant General al-Dajawi, which sentenced Sayyid Qutb and 'Abd al-Fatah Isma'il, as well as Muhammad Yusuf Hawwash, Qutb's former prison mate and one of his close associates, to death. Three other accused were also given death sentences, but these were later commuted to life imprisonment. Despite attempts at mediation by several Arab and Islamic leaders, as well as protest marches that took place outside Egypt, Nasser's regime insisted on carrying out the sentence against Qutb and his two comrades. All three were executed in the summer of 1966, just a year before the devastating 1967 war in Palestine.

There is no doubt that a secret organisation existed and that plans for assassination and sabotage had been drawn up. However, no one had yet taken any actions that justified a death sentence. In fact, Hawwash had played no role whatsoever. He was not even part of the secret group. His only crime was his close and longstanding relationship with Sayyid Qutb. If these sentences are placed alongside the systematic torture and incarceration without trial of thousands of individuals for years on end, it is not difficult to imagine the impact that the trial and subsequent executions had on the relationship between Islamists throughout the Muslim world and the rule of Gamal Abdel Nasser.

In the next few years, the concept of takfir spread rapidly among Islamists – whether or not they were affiliated to the Muslim Brotherhood. The adoption of the idea among detainees in al-Qanatir and Liman Tarrah prisons, some of whom had previously met Qutb, is indicative of the impact that Qutb's ideas had on them. In the depressing atmosphere of incarceration, the ideas in *Milestones* were driven to their logical conclusion. The state tried to confront this by asking scholars from al-Azhar to give lectures in the prisons and engage detainees in debate concerning their beliefs and their leanings towards takfir. However, Azhari scholars who co-operated with the regime in this way simply lost much of their credibility. In the end, the strongest and most effective response to the issue of takfir came from the Muslim Brotherhood and its leader, Hasan al-Hudaybi.

Al-Hudaybi was detained again in the summer of 1965, and in spite of the fact that no charges were laid against him, he was sent to Tarrah Prison. Given his age and ill health, he spent most of his time in the prison hospital, and this meant that members of the Brotherhood had an opportunity to meet with him from time to time. Al-Hudaybi was soon informed of the strong spread of leanings towards takfir and its link with Qutb's ideas. He ordered the formation of a committee, made up of scholars among the Brotherhood prisoners, and asked them to write a detailed refutation on the subject and on the position of its propagators. In fact, the refutation was partly written by al-Hudaybi himself, and was later published in his name as a book entitled *Du'at La Qudat* (Propagators not judges).

In this vital text, al-Hudaybi argued that the notion of al-hakimiyyah (divine authority) is not a Qur'anic concept, noting that it is not mentioned in either the Qur'an or the Sunnah.[9] He also affirmed that the position of the Brotherhood is identical to the general position held by the ahl al-Sunnah doctrinal school. That is, whoever pronounces the affirmation of faith is to be regarded as a Muslim; no Muslim has the right to question the sincerity of another's intentions; and no Muslim can be expelled from the fold of Islam by virtue of an action. He also pointed out that the open pronouncement and prevalence of sin in society does not vindicate passing judgment that the general populace has fallen out of the fold of Islam and into a state of disbelief. The circulation of this text amongst detainees assisted tremendously in quelling the flame of takfir, even if it did not extinguish it entirely. There is no doubt that al-Hudaybi's initiative prevented the Muslim Brotherhood from descending into the pit of extremism, and also played a major role in re-establishing support for the organisation in the 1970s.

The 1960s saw the rise of the postcolonial state in most countries in the Islamic world. In Egypt, Pakistan, Algeria and Indonesia, governments promised their people development and prosperity, independent national decision-making and protection from external threats. In return, these states asked for loyalty from their people and for their acceptance of security forces being used to maintain stability. However, by the end of the decade, crises of governance were already apparent in most of these countries and the status quo could not hold. The crises raised questions about the legitimacy of the newly independent states and the futility of keeping silent about their methods of control and subjugation. Several regimes faced increasing internal opposition, and one of its main sources was political Islam. Interestingly, Egypt, where the suppression and elimination of Islamic forces was strongest, was precisely where political Islam re-emerged once more.

8

The closing of the circle

etween 5 and 10 June 1967, Egypt, Syria and Jordan engaged in one of the shortest wars in Arab history, and in the history of the Arab–Israeli conflict. The war, which began with a comprehensive Israeli strike on Egyptian air-force bases, ended in a painful defeat for the three Arab nations. When the ceasefire was announced, the Israeli forces were lined up on the eastern side of the Suez Canal, having occupied the Gaza Strip and the whole of the Sinai Peninsula. The Egyptian army, which had been the largest of the Arab forces, was forced to leave convoys of destroyed military hardware dispersed across the desert, and thousands of their soldiers were killed or captured. From Syria, the Israeli forces took control of the Golan Heights, and from Jordan, they took Jerusalem and the West Bank, thereby completing their occupation of Palestine.

What was astounding about the June 1967 war was not only the extent of the Arab defeat, but its unexpectedness. During the build-up to the battle, popular opinion in the Arab world held not the slightest doubt that an Arab victory was certain. In fact, before the war began, all three Arab regimes informed their citizens that they were on the road to victory. In the final weeks of May, Arab armies lined up around the edges of the Zionist state and held noisy military processions in the streets. Prior to Israel's attack on Egypt, Syria had been under constant Israeli attack for several weeks, and was pushing Egypt to help them counter Israeli aggression. After the Israeli air strikes, Iraq, Saudi Arabia and

Algeria quickly dispatched units from their armies to the front to show their support for the Arab military effort. Even during the first hours of the battle, when the extent of the catastrophe that had befallen the Arab regimes was already crystal clear, radio stations in Cairo, Amman and Damascus, continued broadcasting totally false reports about enemy losses.

The defeat was felt on many levels, militarily and morally the Arab sense of honour was displaced, and their hopes of resuming the place they deserve on the international stage were dashed. Millions more Palestinians now found themselves under Israeli occupation; Jordan had lost the city of Jerusalem with all that this means to Arabs and Muslims; and Israeli forces were just a short distance from Damascus. Yet, the sense of loss felt by the Egyptians exceeded all this. Egypt was the largest Arab state, and even Arabs opposed to Nasser still saw Egypt as a kind of father figure, holding it responsible for their protection from misfortune.

Nasser was fully aware of this. He announced his resignation and stepped down on 9 June, before the war had even officially ended. No matter what Egypt went through after his resignation speech, the massive popular demonstrations asking Nasser to stay on were a clear expression of Egypt's rejection of defeat. Egyptians wanted to tell the world that if their defeat was intended to punish Nasser for his policies, his people were ready to stand by him. They also wanted Nasser to know that, just as he had taken his country to war, he now had to stay on and restore their country to its rightful place in the world.

In March the following year, while Egypt was rebuilding its army and its lines of defence, judgment was passed in a case of dereliction of duty against the leaders of Egypt's air force. On hearing the outcome, Egyptians were of the opinion that the judgment did not match the level of neglect or the ensuing defeat, and noisy demonstrations broke out in all corners of the country calling for a retrial. For the first time since the clampdown on the Muslim Brotherhood and Qutb's execution in 1966,[1]

Islamic slogans were again prominently displayed on the streets. However, the people holding banners and chanting slogans were not members of the Muslim Brotherhood; they were ordinary people affirming their faith in Egypt at a moment of calamitous crisis that had overcome the country and the Arab world.

Nasser saw signs of this Islamic Awakening and might have thought he could use it to help his people to confront the burden of defeat and prepare for war once more. His speeches to soldiers at the front took on an Islamic character as he called on them to show confidence in, and depend on, Allah. He began organising voluntary citizens' brigades that included Azhari scholars and du'aat (Islamic propagators) from the Suez Canal region and other areas who would visit army camps. One such individual was Hafiz Salamah, an imam from one of the mosques in the city of Suez who later played an important role in the popular defence of that city in the October 1973 War. In early 1969, the state also tried to demonstrate its interest in religious matters by encouraging both Muslims and Christians to visit al-Zaytun Church (in Salim I Street in Cairo) after it was rumoured that the Virgin Mary had appeared there for a few brief moments.

❦

The emergence of the Palestinian resistance movement, and the popular Arab and Islamic support that gathered around it, was a development that clearly indicated the changing balance of forces between Arab states and their people. Shortly after the emergence of resistance in Palestine, it was clear that the Fatah Movement enjoyed the strongest and the most widespread popular support.

Fatah was born at the end of the 1950s, from within the ranks of the Palestinian branch of the Muslim Brotherhood. At different points in their lives, many of Fatah's founding members, such as Khalil al-Wazir (Abu Jihad), Muhammad Yusuf al-Najjar (Abu Yusuf) and Salah Khalaf

(Abu Iyad), were affiliated to the Muslim Brotherhood. Yasser Arafat (Abu 'Ammar) also had had a strong relationship with the Brotherhood, while Khalid al-Hasan (Abu al-Sa'id) was a leader in Hizb al-Tahrir.[2] All of these individuals agreed on the need to establish a Palestinian national liberation movement, similar to the Algerian National Liberation Front, which comprised a group of organisations that were united by the goals of liberation and national independence rather than any ideological agreement.

At the beginning of 1965, Fatah began to carry out guerrilla attacks on the Zionist state, using Syria as its base. Unlike the authorities in Damascus, those in Cairo and Amman tended to see Fatah in a negative light. This was probably linked either to the Brotherhood background of its founders or to the desire of the Arab frontline states to maintain security and stability on their borders with the Zionist state. Either way, Fatah's operations contributed to rising tensions along the border between Syria and the Zionist state. Egypt then intervened to protect Syria from Israeli counterattack, and the June 1967 war broke out.

Soon after the Arab defeat, Fatah leaders realised that the Arab people urgently needed a military force to resist the Zionist state. They also noted the weakness of the incumbent Arab regimes and their unwillingness to muster any resistance to Israel and its allies. Fatah began establishing bases for its commandos in the Jordan Valley, from where they launched limited attacks against Israeli forces on the Palestinian side of the river. In March 1968, Fatah commandos resolved to stand fast in the face of the much larger and better-equipped Israeli forces who were crossing the Jordan River with the intention of destroying Fatah bases. A battle ensued near the town of Karamah, which lasted just one day. The commandos received strong back up from the Jordanian Army and the battle assumed mythical proportions that ignited the passions of the Arab masses. Thousands of Palestinians and other Arabs volunteered from across the region, hoping to join the ranks of Fatah and other resistance organisations.

The Islamic backgrounds of Fatah's leaders had not gone unnoticed by Arab Islamists. A strong and amicable relationship developed between Khalil al-Wazir (Abu Jihad) and the Syrian Brotherhood leader, 'Isam al-'Attar, when the two were in Beirut in the early 1960s. After the Egyptian branch of the Muslim Brotherhood was banned, and its leaders were either in jail or in hiding, al-'Attar acted as the co-ordinator for the Brotherhood's various branches in the Arab world, and therefore played an important role in determining their joint policies.

After the Battle of Karamah, members of the international co-ordination team met under al-'Attar's leadership and made a decision to participate in the resistance under the banner of Fatah. Fatah welcomed the Brotherhood, and established several bases for the Islamists in the areas of Marwu, al-Rafid, Hartha and al-'Aluk in Jordan, which became known among Fatah's ranks as the 'Bases of the Shaykhs'. These bases welcomed hundreds of Islamist volunteers from Jordan, Syria, Sudan and elsewhere who performed well in resistance operations. Some, like the Syrian Marwan Hadid, went on to play a prominent role in the escalation of Islamist violence in Syria, and a member of the Palestinian Brotherhood, 'Abdallah 'Azzam, later emerged as one of the central Islamist figures in the Afghani jihad.

The Palestinian resistance movements were capable of absorbing immense amounts of popular anger, as well as people with Islamic revivalist inclinations. When Nasser opened Cairo to the resistance movements and offered them his protection, this was exactly what he had in mind.

In September 1970, battles broke out in Jordan between the Palestinian resistance forces, represented by the organisations that made up the Palestine Liberation Organization (PLO) and the Jordanian government troops in what is known as 'Black September'. Nasser called an emergency Arab Summit in Cairo to try to find a solution to the conflict and to put an end to the fighting. Hours after the conclusion of the summit, Nasser suddenly died of a heart attack. With his death, a phase of Egyptian and Arab history ended and another began. Anwar Sadat, Nasser's replacement in Egypt, did not have the same elevated stature as his predecessor in Arab circles. Although promising to follow in Nasser's path, Sadat's political compass simply did not point in the same direction.

In mid 1971, the Jordanian army launched a huge campaign against Fatah bases in the Jordan Valley and the Northern Mountain area. This ended with Fatah being expelled from Jordan entirely. With Fatah being the largest of the organisations within the PLO, the Palestinian leaders then chose Lebanon as an alternative base. However, this upset the balance of power among Lebanese sectarian forces. A destructive civil war quickly flared up, sucking the Palestinian resistance movement into its vortex. The PLO adopted one policy change after another, with the goal of achieving international recognition and initiating a political process that would find a peaceful resolution to the Palestinian question.

The absence of an Arab or Islamic discourse calling for the liberation of Palestine, combined with the PLO's involvement in the mire of the Lebanese civil war, helped to quieten the flame of resistance. Support for Palestine among the Arab masses began to shrink, thereby creating space for the Islamists to re-emerge. The Egyptian arena, where political Islam began its resurgence, reflects the immense complexity that contributed to the return of the Islamic perspective.

From the inception of his rule in October 1970, Sadat found a leftist bloc within the Egyptian regime that strove to secure his support. By nature, however, Sadat stood to the right of the Republican regime, and he had little time for the left. In May 1971, tensions erupted between the two blocs. Sadat decisively rid himself of the left by hurling them into prison and was then free to steer the state in the direction he saw fit.

Israeli occupation of Egyptian and Arab land was still a major issue, and Sadat felt responsible for redeeming Egypt's honour after its 1967 defeat. Over the next two years, two huge waves of student demonstrations demanded that Sadat make a move to finish off the Israeli occupier.[3] At first, most of the activists behind the student demonstrations were members of the Communist Party, but Islamist students quickly gained prominence, and stood at the forefront of the student movement.

Shabab al-Islam (the Muslim Youth Society) was born in January 1973 within the Engineering College of Cairo University. This student group, which was led by 'Isam al-Ghazali, Wa'il 'Uthman, 'Adli Mustafa and Sayyid Mutawwali 'Azazi, became a focal point for political activity as Islamist students shrugged off their fears and took the initiative. In just a few months, Islamist students took control of most of the religious groups affiliated to the Student Union in the majority of Egypt's universities.

The activities in the universities were also supported from outside. An extremely influential Islamic figure at that time was Shaykh Muhammad al-Ghazali, who had been born in al-Buhayrah in 1917 and graduated from al-Azhar in 1941. Al-Ghazali was an active member of the Muslim Brotherhood and saw himself as a student of Muhammad 'Abduh, Rashid Rida and Hasan al-Banna. However, in 1954, during a period of internal strife within the Brotherhood, Al-Ghazali was expelled from the organisation for opposing its leader, Hasan al-Hudaybi, on the issue of the new revolutionary government.[4]

Al-Ghazali was a powerful preacher and a prolific writer whose thinking was characterised by renewal and an attempt to comprehend the changing times; he was a political scholar in all respects. Al-Ghazali reached the rank of director of propagation at al-Azhar University and was a commissioner in Egypt's Ministry of Endowments. He managed to maintain a cordial relationship with the state, even during the most violent years of Nasser's rule.

In the 1970s, with the strong support of many volunteers, Al-Ghazali decided to revitalise the 'Amr ibn al-As Mosque, the oldest and undoubtedly the largest mosque in Egypt. Neglect had left it in a poor state. After the renovations were completed, al-Ghazali began to lead the Friday prayers. Soon hundreds of thousands of Cairenes began at-

tending each week, spilling out into the surrounding streets and following the prayers via loudspeakers, in a demonstration of the depth of
Islamic revivalism at the time.

Apolitical Islamic organisations also made an important contribution to this Islamic revival. In Cairo's Anas ibn Malik Mosque, where
the headquarters of the Tablighi Jamaat was located, thousands of individuals gathered around Shaykh Ibrahim 'Izzat. Similarly, the mosques
of the Jami'yyah al-Shari'ah (Islamic Law Society), which were spread
across the country and numbered more than a thousand, were exceptionally well attended.

In addition, the student unions began organising Islamic camps on
various university campuses, inviting the likes of al-Ghazali, 'Izzat and
other prominent Islamic figures to address them. In this period 'Abd
al-Halim Mahmud, one of the most influential Azhari shaykhs in the
Republican era, was made the head of al-Azhar University. Mahmud
was a Sufi of the Shadhili Order. Having studied in Paris, he was well
acquainted with the ways of the world and fully aware of the difficulties
confronting religious institutions in the contemporary period. Mahmud
won back much of the respect that the ancient institution of al-Azhar
had lost. He defended Islam and al-Azhar in his writing and his lectures
and initiated a major project to expand Azhari education to all levels,
from primary school to university.

Even *al-Ahram*, a newspaper that was a bastion of officialdom,
could not ignore what was happening. The editors therefore asked one
of their young correspondents, Fahmi Huwaydi, a former member of
the Muslim Brotherhood, to edit the *Religious Thought* column that was
published in its widely circulated Friday edition. The column quickly
became a platform for the discussion and debate of issues and trends in
contemporary Islam.

Sadat's regime was not necessarily out of touch with what was happening. After his clash with the leftists in government in May 1971,
Sadat worked hard to eliminate the influence of the Egyptian left in uni-

versities and in state media and cultural institutions. He quickly realised that the left was more widespread, and its influence far greater, than he had anticipated. It is believed that Sadat complained to his friend Muhammad 'Uthman Isma'il, then governor of Asyut, about left-wing dominance of the media and cultural institutions, etc. Isma'il reportedly advised Sadat to allow the Islamists more latitude, as only they would be capable of undermining the influence of the left. To enable Isma'il to implement this policy Sadat then appointed him as the head of the Arab Socialist Union, the only political party permitted to operate in Egypt at that time.

For a time in the mid 1970s, the regime maintained silence with regard to the increasing activities of Islamist organisations, and Sadat even began portraying himself as a 'believing president', devoted to praying at the appointed times, as well as protecting and defending family values. In addition, Muhammad Mutawalli al-Sha'rawi, an influential Azhari shaykh, returned to Egypt from exile, and allied himself with Sadat. For several years, Sha'rawi's speeches and reflections were broadcast to millions of Egyptians via the country's public television channel.

However, Sadat was fully aware that Nasser had left an occupied Palestine and thousands of Muslim Brotherhood members detained or serving prison sentences. Sadat also realised that the state's persecution of the Brotherhood had left many Egyptians feeling marginalised and oppressed. After Sadat had dispensed with the left-wing opposition party, his regime began releasing Brotherhood members, especially those that had been detained without trial and those who had already served part of their prison sentences. The leader of the Brotherhood, Hasan al-Hudaybi, and the lawyer 'Umar al-Tilmisani were among those released.

In October 1973, Egypt and Syria declared war on Israel. Most of the fighting took place in the Sinai and Golan, which Israeli forces had occupied since the 1967 war. Egyptian soldiers crossed the Bar

Lev Line shouting Allahu Akbar (God is great). The war took place during the holy month of Ramadan, thereby giving it a strong Islamic overtone. When Israeli forces succeeded in reaching the city of Suez, Shaykh Hafiz Salamah, the imam at one of the city's mosques, played an important role in mobilising the resistance and defeating the Israelis. His role was widely broadcast by the Egyptian media, and Sadat was pressed into awarding him the Order of the Sinai Star – a medal traditionally awarded for bravery and heroism in the military.

The war was not a convincing victory for the Arabs. However, the Egyptian forces succeeded in storming the Suez Canal and gathered together on its east side, while Egypt and Syria engaged the Israelis in a series of devastating tank battles. With these victories the armies and regimes of the two countries won back some respect and strengthened Sadat's legitimacy. With this, he became more confident about dealing with Egypt's internal situation, and initiated a project to leave his personal mark on Egypt.

At the beginning of 1974, all Brotherhood members who were still in prison were gathered at the Turrah Farm Prison, where conditions were slightly better than those at other facilities. Represented by officers from state security, and specifically by Fuad 'Alam, the state began to negotiate with the Brotherhood's leaders with the aim of resolving issues once and for all. The two sides reached an unwritten agreement that entailed certain obligations. The state agreed to free all Brotherhood members, dropping all charges against them, and allowing them to return to their vocations and their places of work. In addition, none of these individuals would be prevented from propagating Islam or from preaching in mosques and on public platforms. For their part, members of the Brotherhood undertook to denounce violence, stop opposing the government and never again bear arms against the state.

Soon, all Brotherhood members were freed and matters seemed to have been resolved. However, the agreement held for only a short period. The negotiations, for some reason, did not fully address the question of the Brotherhood's political status, and this issue remained unresolved for years to come.

Nonetheless, the release of the Brotherhood prisoners had a tremendous impact on Islamic revivalism in the country. Even though the Brotherhood was not accorded the status of a political party, the regime chose to turn a blind eye to some of its activities. The Brotherhood reorganised itself, and after the death of al-Hudaybi at the end of 1974, 'Umar al-Tilmisani – a lawyer – was elected to lead the organisation. Al-Tilmisani was a gentle, refined person, non-confrontational and very knowledgeable about the exhausting struggles that had taken place between the state and the Brotherhood. He therefore made every possible effort to avoid repeating those experiences and, for a while at least, Sadat tolerated the Brotherhood's activities without feeling personally threatened.

The Brotherhood resumed publication of its journal, *al-Da'wah*, and this became its unofficial voice. Meanwhile a group of former Brotherhood intellectuals, including Mahmud 'Abd al-Halim Abu Shaqqah and Jamal al-Din 'Atiyah, established a journal in Kuwait called *al-Muslim al-Mu'asir* (The contemporary Muslim). This, too, was distributed in Egypt, and was important in providing a forum for critical Islamic intellectual debate and moderate Islamic thought. Moderation was essential at this time. The Brotherhood's return to public life in Egypt was not without its challenges, especially since it was accompanied by the return of a range of orientations, including small groups of takfiri extremists.

The first of these extremist groups to gain prominence in Egypt became known as the Majmu'ah al-Kulliyah al-Finniyah al-'Askariyyah (Military Technical College Group), and was led by Saleh Sirriyah. Sirriyah was of Palestinian origin and had been an officer in the Iraqi army. He was also interested and active in politics, having helped establish the Palestinian Liberation Front, one of the early Palestinian guerrilla organisations, and participated in several military coups in Iraq in the

1960s. After this, Sirriyah left the army and continued his university studies until he obtained a PhD in educational psychology. At the same time, he joined an informal Islamic study circle and studied the science of hadith (Prophetic tradition). In the early 1970s, when Sirriyah joined the Arab League's Educational, Cultural and Science Organization as an education expert, he had reached the conclusion that the priority for Muslims should be to establish an Islamic state, rather than focus on the struggle for Palestine. Around this time, Sirriyah became acquainted with several young Egyptians who had strong jihadist inclinations. The most prominent of these was Karim al-Anaduli, a student in the Military Technical College for military officers.

Sirriyah was also influenced by Qutb's writings and wrote a short essay called *Risalatul Iman* (Epistle of faith), which illustrates clearly how Qutb came to be understood in a radical, doctrinal way.[5] Sirriyah denounced the ruling Arab regimes, arguing that they had put themselves outside the fold of Islam. Describing society as jahili (steeped in ignorance), he came very close to rejecting most ordinary people, perceiving them as outside the fold of Islam. While Qutb used the term al-jahiliyyah (state of ignorance) in a general cultural sense, Sirriyah strove to develop it conceptually and doctrinally. Thus, while Qutb believed that the path begins by spreading Islamic doctrine, Sirriyah justified the use of revolutionary force in establishing an Islamic order.

In 1974, Sirriyah approved of a plan formulated by a group of his followers from the Military Technical College to take control of the institution, and then use the College as a base from which to overthrow the regime and establish an Islamic republic in Egypt. The plan was not only naïve, but also extremely risky. Not surprisingly, it failed. Most of the group's members were arrested and tried. Sirriyah and Karim al-Anaduli were executed; several others were imprisoned.

Perhaps the most well known of the extremist groups of the 1970s was led by Shukri Mustafa. The group called itself the Jama'ah al-Muslimin (Society of Muslims) but was widely known as the Jama'ah al-Takfir wa al-Hijrah (Society of Excommunication and Exodus). Mustafa, a graduate of the College of Agriculture, had been imprisoned with the Muslim Brotherhood in the 1960s and had also been influenced by Qutb.

However, when Mustafa left prison, he labelled everyone disbelievers, except for those that believed in his version of Islam and affiliated to his group. Mustafa viewed the present in terms of his vision of Islam's first era, and believed that the duty of his band of supporters was to withdraw from the disbelieving and ignorant world, and establish the community of Medina anew. Mustafa and his group were eventually accused of kidnapping and killing Husayn al-Dhahabi, then minister of endowments and a senior Azhari scholar. Mustafa and several of his followers were arrested and executed after a sensational trial, but al-Dhahabi's murder remains shrouded in mystery. It is unclear why Mustafa would have targeted this particular minister given his declaration that he and his followers were disinterested in the world and, by implication, in the fate of any political state.[6] In any event, the execution of Shukri Mustafa led to the steady disintegration of his group.

These radical and extremist Islamic groups had little impact on the development of the wider Islamist movement. Accordingly, Eid prayers organised by al-Jama'ah al-Islamiyyah fi al-Jamiyyah (University Islamic Group) in the early 1980's, and held in the squares of the 'Abidin and Mustafa Mahmud mosques, reflected great public support for the Islamic Awakening. After this, Islamist students quickly took control of the student unions at most universities.

The publication of al-Hudaybi's book *Proselytisers not Judges*, combined with the Brotherhood's uncompromising dedication to peaceful action and strict adherence to orthodox Sunni doctrine, helped undermine and marginalise the radicalism of those who believed in takfir. The Brotherhood then began to welcome into its ranks many of the new generation of Islamist university students. By the end of the 1970s, student leaders such as 'Abd al-Mun'im Abu al-Futuh, Essam el-Arian, Hilmi al-Jazzar and Abu'l 'Ala Madi had joined their ranks. These individuals later became prominent both as student leaders and Brotherhood members. However, a group of active Islamists in al-Minya and Asyut universities in the south of the country refused to affiliate to the Muslim Brotherhood. Two prominent individuals in this group were Najih Ibrahim and Karam Zuhdi. Both helped to establish al-Jama'ah al-Islamiyyah (Islamic Group), an independent Islamic organisation that was destined to play a decisive role in Egypt's history and in contemporary Islamist violence.

Islamic revivalism was not limited to Egypt, even if this was its starting point. The number of Muslims who were interested in political Islam grew throughout the Islamic World during the 1970s, even reaching Turkey and Tunisia, where it was believed that secularisation and modernisation had irrevocably destroyed Islam's role and influence.

As noted, the birth of the Islamist movements between the First and Second World Wars was, in some ways, indicative of the weakening of the institution of 'ulama (religious scholars), as well as of its representation of Islam and its right to speak on behalf of the faith. To a certain extent, the widespread nature of the Islamic Awakening in the 1970s and 1980s reflected the fragmentation of the Islamic frame of reference. The organisational and individual voices speaking in the name of Islam multiplied in an unprecedented way, as did their modus operandi and their political programmes. In the next three decades, the Islamic Awakening manifested itself in the following main trends: popular revolution, military coups, resistance to foreign domination, internal violence, transcontinental violence, and democratic political participation. Perhaps the greatest surprise during these years was that the first and largest Islamist state was not established in Egypt, where the first Islamist movements were born, but in Iran, with its Shi'a majority.

9

The revolution of the jurist and the people

The first day of February in 1979 was no ordinary day in the Iranian capital of Tehran. The streets of the city were crowded. Millions of people had been gathering since the night before, many pouring in from other Iranian cities and villages, near and far. It seemed as if the entire nation had united into a single mass, bound by inherited legacies, hope and spiritual desire, as they awaited the return of Imam Ruhollah Khomeini from exile, whom they had chosen as their leader. The world had not seen a popular revolution of this scale and staying-power for a long time, nor had it witnessed a revolution that revolved around a religious leader, much less one who was already over seventy years of age.

When Khomeini emerged from his airplane, he radiated humility and determination. As he proceeded in convoy among millions of people, it was clear that he was comfortable in their midst. And when he began addressing the Iranian people – and the world – from the Behesht-e Zahra Cemetery, he spoke in the astonishing way that always characterised his speeches: at once simple, direct, clear and decisive. For the next ten days, Khomeini led the revolution against what was left of the King-of-Kings' regime with courage and consummate skill. As soon as the revolution was victorious, he began constructing a new government. Unfortunately, the results did not always correspond with the dream.

Iran's Islamic revolution was a major achievement for the forces of political Islam, and one that had been unforeseen by anyone in the

Islamic world or beyond, in terms of both scale and location. Before the revolution broke out in early 1978, Iran hardly featured on any map of the Islamic political revival. In addition, the regime brought down by the revolution was one of the strongest in the Islamic world, not only in terms of its own resources but also in relation to the support it enjoyed among the world's most powerful states.

The revolution succeeded because of its ability to unite people of different ethnicities, classes and political views within an Islamic framework that had clear Islamic objectives. Its forces attained power without resorting to violence, and despite the gross state violence that was used against it. Several narratives intertwine behind Iran's Islamic revolution including: Khomeini's deep sense of responsibility and his inclination towards free thinking; the king who was not rescued by the strength of the modern state despite its capacity for control and domination; the people's overwhelming desire for a renaissance and to recapture their historical status; and finally the injustice of international powers and their foreign policies.

Like those of Hasan al-Banna, Sayyid Qutb and Abu'l A'la al-Mawdudi, Ayatollah Ruhollah Khomeini's story began in the first decade of the twentieth century. He was born in 1902, in the village of Khumayn in the centre of Iran, into a family of Shi'a scholars who claim to be descended from the Al al-Bayt (the household of the Prophet).[1] His father Mustafa, who was also a religious scholar, was killed in a local dispute seven months after the birth of his son, and when Khomeini was sixteen, his mother passed away too. As a young child, he received his early education at the local kuttab (traditional primary school) and at the local government primary school. He then travelled to the city of Arak to begin his religious training under the tutelage of 'Abd al-Karim al-Ha'iri al-Yazdi (1859 – 1936), an accomplished Shi'a scholar who had attained the rank of mujtahid; which meant he was an independent religious authority not bound by any specific doctrinal or jurisprudential school. When al-Yazdi relocated from Arak to Qum, one of the central learning centres for Twelver Shi'a, Khomeini followed him. There, Khomeini completed three levels of study, reaching the status of al-ijtihad al-mustaqil (an independent religious authority) before the age of thirty.

In the early 1920s, Khomeini witnessed the final years of the Qajari dynasty and the chaos that swept through Iran as a result of its collapse and the machinations of the global powers during the First World War. He was also aware of the coup carried out by Reza Khan, once an obscure military officer, who seized power in Iran in 1921. Khan eliminated his opponents soon after taking power and established a new autocratic order, appointing himself as shah. Influenced by Mustafa Kemal in Turkey, Reza Shah began his own modernisation project in Iran in the 1930s. This involved asserting state control over many aspects of society, including forcing women to abandon the niqab (full veil) *and* even the simpler hijab (head covering).

In the 1940s, Khomeini began expressing his opposition to the shah. His interest in politics developed during the Second World War, after the allied forces toppled Reza Shah in 1941 (because of his sympathy towards Nazi Germany), and replaced him with his son, Muhammad Reza Shah. During the war years, Khomeini saw Iran being laid to ruin once again, as it was coveted by the Soviet Union on one side and Britain and America on the other.

Soon after the war, from April 1951 to August 1953, Iran went through an exceptional time of independent nationalist awakening. After parliamentary elections that were deemed to be relatively fair, Mohammad Mosaddegh became prime minister of a government led by the opposition National Front. The National Front was home to a number of populist, nationalist politicians who believed in constitutional rule and were opposed to Western influence in Iran.

At that time, Western influence in Iran's oil industry was clear. The sector was dominated by the British Petroleum Company, which was involved in extraction, refinement and sales. British workers lived like lords in southern Iran, and Iranians had no share in the wealth being generated from the oil resources in their country – they acted only as servants to their foreign masters. Nevertheless, in the face of tremendous Western opposition, as well as opposition from the shah and his entourage, Mosaddegh nationalised the oil industry.

Mosaddegh and his government had the support of the general population and several religious scholars, led by the influential marja' (Shi'a religious authority), Ayatollah Kashani. Under pressure, the shah fled the country. However, American CIA agents, together with loyalists in the Iranian army were able to successfully launch a coup to oust Mosaddegh. The shah returned, heralding a dark epoch in the history of modern Iran, with the country falling under the control of the security apparatus and their American advisors. Khomeini played no significant role in support of Mosaddegh or his government, as he was not yet counted among the more influential religious authorities. However, none of those religious scholars who were seen as influential did much either.

The reasons behind the limited involvement of the religious establishment in politics lie within Shi'a thought itself. Most Twelver Shi'a scholars are affiliated to the Usuli (Rationalist-Juristic) School, which had gained a decisive victory over the Akhbari (Traditionalist) School at the end of the eighteenth and beginning of the nineteenth centuries. The Usulis uphold the notion of ijtihad (rational interpretation) and believe that the masses need qualified religious scholars to interpret the texts and teach them about their faith. The Akhbaris reject this and affirm instead that the textual teachings handed down by the Prophet and the Shi'a imams sufficiently explicate religious matters in the absence of al-Mahdi al-Muntazar (the Awaited Saviour).

Furthermore, the Akhbaris accept no formal pledging of allegiance to religious scholars, and believe that no authority or legitimate rule can be established in the name of Islam until the Mahdi appears. The Usulis agree that any state not led by the Mahdi is illegitimate, but they also believe in limited allegiance to religious scholars, especially in matters pertaining to legal judgements, authority over orphans, and issues pertaining to the general public interest – including commanding good and forbidding wrong.

For this reason, the rise of the Usuli School is often linked with the religious establishment playing an increasingly active role in society. For example, at the end of the nineteenth century, religious scholars played a role in nullifying the Tobacco concessions and in 1906, they were active in Iran's constitutional revolution.[2] However, this does not mean that the Usulis advocate an absolute allegiance that allows religious scholars to establish Islamic governance in the absence of the Mahdi. Therefore, with the exception of Mulla Ahmad al-Naraqi (d. 1829), they do not endorse the concept of velayat-e-faqih (the custodianship of the jurist), whereby a jurist is able to represent and act fully on behalf of the absent Mahdi. However, twenty years after the coup that ousted Mosaddegh, Khomeini declared and explained the basis for his belief in velayat-e-faqih al-mutlaqah (the absolute custodianship of the jurist).

With the return of the shah to full authority, the regime strengthened its grip on state power and the economy by means of an oppressive security apparatus that was backed up by strong support from several Western states, and led by the USA. The National Front was banned, and hundreds of Mosaddegh's supporters were arrested as the regime regrouped. In 1957, Iran's intelligence and state security organisation (popularly known as SAVAK) was established, which integrated military intelligence personnel into the Criminal Investigation Bureau. Initially, SAVAK's activities were limited to keeping an eye on national security in general. However, SAVAK gradually became octopus-like, with tentacles reaching into all aspects of Iranian life, until they controlled Iran's media, the parliament, all the political parties established by the regime, the universities, the economy, and even many of the prominent religious scholars. To give just one example of their reach,

in the year in which SAVAK was established, an Iranian writer published an article in *The Diplomat* entitled 'What do the people want?'
He was soon summoned to appear before SAVAK's head of publications, Brigadier-General Kiyani, where he was told that the head of
SAVAK, General Teymur Bakhtiar, had ordered him to be summoned
and informed that 'the people' are dead.'[3] SAVAK officers were indoc-
trinated with the idea of the 'death of the people' until the organisation's
collapse. SAVAK also had secret assassination squads who were above
the law and carried out every conceivable form of torture in various Iranian prisons. By the end of the 1970s, when it was headed by General
Nematollah Nassiri, SAVAK's budget had grown to US$500 million,
and American sources estimated that the number of informers providing it with information numbered four million – about a tenth of Iran's
total population.

The shah linked his country's economy and political orientation
to that of the USA, while simultaneously trying to appease the Soviet
Union by offering it a share in certain commercial and industrial programmes. It has been estimated that by the 1970s, as many as forty
thousand American military and civilian advisors were in Iran, where
they were involved in all aspects of the state. It was an open secret that
the shah had established relations with the Zionist state. These encompassed arms deals and military and security co-operation, as well as
trade relations; he also gave the Israelis thousands of hectares of land in
the fertile Qazvin province for an experimental farm. Openly inciting
the Iranian people, the shah also supplied both the Zionist state and
South Africa's apartheid regime with oil. It was even alleged that Israeli
tanks ran on Iranian fuel during the June 1967 War.

Despite these actions, the shah wanted the Iranian people to see their
'King of Kings', and the monarchy as a whole, as personifying Iranian
nationalism and not simply as a system of governance. In a book published in his name, entitled *Toward the Great Civilisation: A Dream
Revisited,* the shah noted that 'if there was no monarchy, there would

be chaos, minority rule and dictatorship', and added that monarchy was 'the only possible means of governing Iran'.

The shah, like his father, realised that religious scholars were his main competitors for authority. He therefore made every effort to win their favour and contain, or if needs be, to subjugate them. In addition, he developed a string of initiatives aimed at weakening Islamic culture and reviving the spirit of ancient Persian nationalism.

On 6 September 1961, during a parliamentary recess, the prime minister, Asadollah 'Alam, annulled the obligation for candidates who had won seats in parliamentary elections to be sworn in on the Qur'an, and making it permissible for them to take their oath on any similarly recognised revelatory text. This sparked extreme anger within the religious establishment. Ayatollah Borujerdi was the official religious authority of the time, but his advanced age meant that he had largely withdrawn from public affairs. This opened the way for Khomeini, who quickly took lead in a growing movement against the shah and his prime minister. By then, Khomeini was undoubtedly already politicised, arguing that 'Islam is politics; without it, it would be nothing'.[4]

First, Khomeini sent a telegram to the prime minister, protesting against the change in the swearing-in process. He then sent two more telegrams, one to the shah and another to the prime minister, in which he criticised the state's control of the media and foreign control of state resources. In a public statement made at the same time, he said:

> I announce by way of my legal responsibility that there is an imminent danger confronting the Iranian people and the Muslims of the world. The Noble Qur'an and Islam are facing the peril of falling into the hands of the Zionist grasp that has appeared in Iran in the form of the Baha'i sect...soon they will dominate the entire economy of this nation with the help of their collaborators and they will destroy the Islamic nation...If anyone should succumb then he is responsible before the All-Powerful and will be

regarded as one who has passed the death sentence on himself in this world.[5]

After fifty days of tension, during which citizens began preparing for a general strike, the cabinet rescinded their annulment.

Khomeini continued his opposition to the regime, however, shifting his focus to other issues related to the state's political orientation. In December 1961, he announced in a lecture at al-Faydiyyah Madrasa in Qom, where he taught, that the struggle continued and that the shah's regime had not renounced its sins.

Nonetheless, the shah was still confident that he would be able to meet the challenges facing him. Between 1960 and 1962, the regime toppled the second National Front and arrested its leaders: Mehdi Bazargan, Yadullah Sahabi and Ayatollah Mahmoud Taleghani. The shah began to dream of becoming a popular leader, like Nehru, Castro and Nasser, with his people rallying behind him, and not simply obeying him for fear of the consequences. In January 1963, with encouragement from the Kennedy administration, the shah announced the beginning of the so-called White Revolution – 'the Shah's and the people's revolution'. His aim was to achieve limited agrarian reform, implement several measures to protect workers and encourage Iranian women to liberate themselves from prevailing traditions. The White Revolution was opposed from the outset by religious scholars and the conservative establishment, who saw it as strengthening the state and propagating Western culture.

On 21 March 1963, which marked the Iranian New Year, Khomeini announced in a statement that religious scholars would not celebrate in protest against the shah's policies. The next day, which coincided with the commemoration of the death of Ja'far al-Sadiq, the sixth Shi'ite imam, soldiers attacked thousands of mourners at a memorial ceremony being held at al-Faydiyyah Madrasa. Many men, women and children were killed. The attack was a crude attempt to topple Khomeini but served to strengthen his position instead.

On 3 June, during the commemoration of the martyrdom of Imam al-Husayn, Khomeini delivered a public speech heard by about a quarter of a million Iranians, in which he condemned the government's policies and its relationship with Israel. The following day, protests broke out in Qom and several other cities, including the capital, Tehran. People began referring to Khomeini as Bit Shakan (Idol smasher). That evening, Khomeini was arrested and taken to Eshrat Abad in Tehran. On the morning of 5 June, as news of his incarceration spread, massive protests broke out calling for the death of the shah. The state's security apparatus responded with unrestrained force. By the end of the day, which is known in Iran as the Uprising of 15 Khordad, more than fifteen thousand people had been killed.

After a month of tension the regime was forced to release Khomeini and he returned to Qom. From his podium at al-Faydiyyah Madrasa he once again attacked the state. A crucial opportunity arose when parliament ratified a draft resolution presented by the government of Hassan-Ali Mansour. The legislation granted American military personnel in Iran full immunity from prosecution in any Iranian court, thus reviving memories of similar concessions granted to foreigners in the past. This prompted Khomeini to deliver a harsh speech criticising the legislation and the state's subservience to foreign influence.

On the night of 4 November, regime forces descended on Khomeini's home and led him to the Turkish border, casting him into exile. He stayed in Turkey for about a year, before being granted permission by the government of 'Abd al-Salam 'Arif to settle in the Iraqi city of Najaf.

Strangely, the major Shi'a leader of the time, Ayatollah Muhsin al-Hakim, was strongly opposed to the Iraqi government. Other religious scholars in Najaf, some of whom had strong relations with the shah's regime, were fully aware that Khomeini might cause trouble, and would never give up his opposition to the regime in Tehran. In the thirteen years that Khomeini spent in Najaf, his relationship with religious authorities there largely remained cool. The Najaf scholars' differences with Khomeini were related not only to his views on the shah, but also to his position on other political and intellectual issues.

Despite an unofficial ban placed on him by Iraq's religious establishment, Khomeini began holding classes in Najaf as he had done in Iran. In addition to Iranians already in Najaf, many more travelled to Najaf to study under him, some of them secretly. In his lectures, Khomeini began to discuss questions of state and governance and, in 1970, he published a book on these issues entitled *Hokumat-i Eslami* (Islamic government).

Khomeini's notion of the custodianship of the jurist is regarded as a real revolution in Shi'a political thought. Previously, this was always linked to the appearance of the Mahdi and the establishment of the 'just Islamic state'. In contrast, Khomeini argued that religious scholars are heirs of the prophets and therefore have legitimacy in the time of occultation (that is, until the Mahdi appears). Khomeini affirmed that, until the Mahdi appears, religious scholars are obliged to work towards the establishment of an Islamic state that upholds divine law and justice until the Mahdi appears. He also affirmed that any state that takes the most highly qualified religious scholars as its frame of reference should enjoy full legitimacy. In other words, Khomeini held that the custodianship of the jurists was all encompassing, and not deficient or limited in any way. He thereby nullified the effects that the doctrine of waiting for the Mahdi had had on everyday life and jurisprudence for the Shi'a community.

Khomeini's views elicited strong responses from Shi'a religious scholars, many of whom rejected his views. However, his ideas found increasing support among those Iranian religious scholars who were opposed to the shah. There is also no doubt that the Islamic Republic in Iran would not have come into existence without the concept of velayat-e-faqih. Throughout his stay in Najaf, Khomeini issued statements to the Iranian people on important political and religious occasions. He also maintained his interest in the Palestinian issue, expressing his support for the Palestinian resistance, especially in the late 1960s and early 1970s.

In Iran, while the regime directed all its efforts at confronting leftist forces, Islamist activity began to permeate all aspects of society. Several organisations emerged, most of which were very small and had limited effect, but religious scholars at all levels, who saw themselves as Khomeini's followers, worked hard to spread his ideas. These included Mahmoud Taleghani, Hussein-Ali Montazeri, Mohammad Hossein Beheshti, Morteza Motahhari, Ali Khamenei, Ali Akbar Hashemi Rafsanjani, Muhammad Muftih and many others. Through their efforts and encouragement, Islamic groups and societies spread across Iran's universities and among Iranian students studying in Europe and America. Similar groups formed within Iran's working class – importantly among bazaar traders and especially in Tehran.

From a husayniyyah irshad (private tuition centre), Ayatollah Motahhari and 'Ali Shariati, a professor of sociology, presented new Islamic texts, ideas and language that strengthened the confidence of the youth in a revival based on Islamic foundations. These texts also offered new perspectives on Iranian history that helped undermine the Iranian left's hegemony over the country's cultural and intellectual spheres.

The regime, on the other hand, while becoming more isolated from its citizens simultaneously became increasingly confident. In 1971, the shah commemorated the legendary founding of the Persian Empire in an atmosphere that was itself little short of legendary. Many of the world's presidents and kings were invited to the celebrations, with catering provided by the finest Parisian restaurants – this at a time when the majority of Iranian villages had no access to running water or electricity.

In the mid 1970s, in an attempt to entrench Western ideals within a spirit of Persian nationalism, the state also launched a campaign against Islamic culture and values. As part of this, the Gregorian calendar was annulled, and replaced with the Calendar of the King of Kings. In the following year, as part of the annual arts festival in Shiraz, a group of actors presented a street-theatre performance in the nude.

Meanwhile, the White Revolution was having a disastrous effect on Iran's economy, which suffered gross agricultural setbacks, increased foreign influence, and the concentration of wealth in the hands of the few. At the end of the 1970s, despite tremendous increases in Iran's oil revenues, the average lifespan was just fifty years and the infant mortality rate was 139 in every thousand children (the same as India's at that time). Forty-five families owned 85 per cent of the country's industrial sector and Iran, which had been an agrarian country for thousands of years, was producing just 7 per cent of its citizens' nutritional needs. High inflation meant that more than 80 per cent of the Iranian working class was in debt to the banks.

The regime seemed oblivious of the extent of these crises. In 1977, two years after the Rastakhiz Party was established as the ruling party (and also the only party) in the country, the shah claimed that five million Iranians had joined the party. The shah also kept Amir-Abbas Hoveyda on as prime minister for fourteen continuous years. The fact that Hoveyda was a member of the Baha'i faith was an added source of tension. When Hoveyda was finally relieved of this post in 1977, the shah immediately made him a minister of court.

Meanwhile SAVAK continued to tirelessly pursue the regime's opponents. In 1976, it launched an extensive campaign to liquidate leftist forces. As a result, countless crimes were committed, including the assassination of opposition figures inside the country and abroad. On 19 June 1977, 'Ali Shariati was found dead in his London flat. It is widely believed that this influential thinker had died at the hands of SAVAK assassins; the regime refused to allow his body to be returned to Iran, and he was buried in Damascus.

On 23 October Mustafa Khomeini, the Ayatollah's eldest son, and closest assistant, died in Najaf in mysterious circumstances similar to those suffered by 'Ali Shariati. Khomeini responded to messages of condolence, including one from Yasser Arafat, saying, 'We are living through difficult days with frightening calamities and we should [therefore] not make mention of our personal calamities and pains.'

On 15 November, the Shah visited Washington DC, where he was assailed by protesting Iranian students before television cameras and in full view of the world. Back home in Qom, a huge memorial ceremony was held at the end of December for Mustafa Khomeini, at which Ayatollah Mohammed Sadegh Khalkhali, one of Khomeini's followers, delivered a fiery speech, relentlessly attacking the shah and his regime. From then on, it was clear that Islamist voices were becoming far more brazen and the spirit of Khomeini seemed to have returned to haunt the shah.

After a visit to Iran by US president, Jimmy Carter, in which he heaped praise on the shah and showed his full support for the regime, the *Ittila'at* newspaper surprised its readers on 7 January 1978 with an article written by Daryoush Homayoun, one of the Shah's most loyal supporters. Published under a pseudonym, the article was entitled, 'Iran, Red Colonialism and Black Colonialism', with reference to the left and the religious establishment. The article praised the shah's reforms and attacked Khomeini, mocking the memorial event that had been held for his son. Homayoun concluded his article by calling for the implementation of more progressive legislation, such as allowing abortion, obliging women to abandon their headscarves and punishing any that donned a hijab. In a matter of hours, the article was pasted on the walls of Qom so that it could be read by anyone who had not seen the newspaper. The next day, a storm of anger broke, heralding the beginning of a popular revolution that continued for more than a year.

In Qom, a large number of students from religious schools gathered, moving from the home of one major religious authority to the next, shouting 'Durud par Khomeini (Peace be upon Khomeini). The next morning, on Monday 9 January, another protest march took place in Qom. This time the security forces sealed off Fatemi Square and opened fire on the protestors, killing 155 people and wounding at least six hundred. This was to be the first blood spilled in the revolution. One of the victims wrote in blood on the wall of the square: 'May Allah cause blood to flow from the neck of whoever wipes away this blood'. The protests spread from city to city. On 22 January, Khomeini issued a statement from Najaf, announcing that the revolution would continue until victory was achieved. However, it is difficult to know whether or not, at this early stage, Khomeini was aware of the extent and possible outcome of the sudden uprising.

Protests took place in one city after another, in honour of martyrs who had been killed, or during traditional ritual commemorations of the fortieth day after martyrdom, or in response to any of the many political or religious events that occurred. In some instances, protests were also organised in response to propaganda spread by the state. For example, when the regime began blaming the communists, religious scholars lined up in large numbers to lead the protests. When the shah claimed that the protestors were backward and opposed to women's rights, women took part in massive protest marches that took place on 7 March in Tehran, Tabriz and Mashhad.

On 10 April, during another massive rally in Tehran, the Religious Society of Iran announced a fourteen-point declaration, calling for social and political justice, the release of incarcerated leaders and the return of exiles, with Khomeini at the top of the list. It was a modest list of requests that was typical of Khomeini's leadership style of incrementally escalating demands as support for the revolution grew, and making absolutely no concessions on any of the demands already made.

On 19 August, state repression took a novel turn when the Rakas Cinema in the city of Abdan was burned in an arson attack that killed hundreds of people. The attack was probably staged by the state in an attempt to take the revolution into the heart of the oil region, thus raising Western concerns about the situation, and justifying further repressive security measures. In fact, the outcome was exactly the opposite; the massacre served to further inflame the revolution and widened its support base. By the end of the month, Khomeini was explicitly calling for the departure of the shah.

On the morning of Eid al-Fitr on 4 September 1978, Tehran witnessed its first million-person protest rally. Protestors shouted slogans including 'Allahu Akbar, Khomeini rahbar' (God is the greatest, Khomeini is our leader) and 'Istiqlal, hurriyah, hukumah Islamiyyah' (Independence, freedom and Islamic government).

Four days later, hundreds of people were killed in a just few hours in Tehran's Jaleh Square on what has since become known as Black Friday. This marked the turning point at which resistance to the shah shifted from being a popular movement that was making specific demands into an open revolution seeking to overthrow of the regime.

On 24 September the shah was able to convince Saddam Hussein to expel the Ayatollah from Iraq. When Kuwait refused to receive him, Khomeini went to France, where he settled in the Paris suburb of Neauphle-le-Château. Delegations descended upon his home from all over the world, including mediators from Iran who returned home having been convinced of the need to rid Iran of the shah and his regime.

Inside Iran, Khomeini's speeches and statements continued to reach millions via pamphlets and cassette recordings. As the Iranian people united behind him, his traditional dress, unshakable resolve and language – saturated in the heritage of Islam – elicited the amazement of the world, while the shah's regime and its US allies were increasingly confused and incapacitated.

The shah tried appointing Sharif Imami as prime minister, and when this failed to calm the situation he appointed General Gholam Reza Azhari to head a new government. Azhari began a campaign to root out corruption that soon affected some the of the shah's closest associates, including Hoveyda. However, a large number of individuals, whom Azhari had banned from travelling, managed to smuggle their wealth abroad and fled the country via Tehran International Airport. In the eyes of the people, Azhari's campaign was a futile act, but it did undermine the morale of the state and deepen fractures within the regime. The shah's wife visited Najaf to try to convince Ayatollah Abu al-Qasim al-Khu'i to intervene; Khu'i was at the time the highest Shi'a religious authority and one of Khomeini's few opponents. He refused to co-operate. The shah himself also failed to win over leaders within the National Front such as Karim Sanjabi and Mehdi Bazargan. After another million-person protest took place in Tehran in December, the military establishment itself, which until then had been an impenetrable fortress, began to crumble. The air force was the first military institution to announce its support for the revolution.

On 6 January 1979, Shahpur Bakhtiar, a long-time member of the National Front, was made head of state. It was clear to all that this was a last ditch attempt to prevent Khomeini and the Islamists from coming to power. However, Bakhtiar insisted that the shah should abdicate in favour of his son and leave the country. On 14 January Khomeini formed a council to lead the revolution.[6] On 16 January the shah left Tehran for the last time, defeated and broken. Khomeini returned to Iran on 1 February. On the same day, the Islamic Revolutionary Guard Corps (IRGC), which was to play a very active role in the future of Iran, was born. For the next ten days, Khomeini led the final battle against the Bakhtiar government from a madrasa in Tehran where he was staying. The decisive confrontation took place on 10 and 11 February when Khomeini refused to listen to his advisors who wanted him to ask people to evacuate the streets for fear of rising casualties. Khomeini did exactly the opposite, issuing a fatwa stating that taking to the streets at this time was a religious obligation. About twenty thousand people were killed before the government collapsed and Bakhtiar fled to France.[7]

The first few years of the Republic were restless, tense and extremely difficult. Khomeini strove to establish the new government in accordance with the will of the people and by consultation, so he ordered a referendum to test the idea of establishing an Islamic Republic. Elections were then held to choose a Council of Experts to write the country's constitution. When the Council had completed its task, the constitution was put before a people's referendum. The constitution was then enacted, establishing a system that divided power between several institutional authorities and founded the Republic on the principle of velayat-e-faqih, which later became cause for much contestation.

The first few years of the Republic were restless, tense and extremely difficult. A few months after the liberal Mehdi Bazargan became prime minister, Islamist students occupied the American Embassy in Tehran where they held its employees captive for 444 days. Having heard that Bazargan had held consultations in Algeria with Zbigniew Brzezinski, a US security advisor, the students' objective was to prevent external intervention in Iranian affairs and ultimately liberate the Iranian consciousness from American hegemony. The occupation of the embassy led to the collapse of Bazargan's government and was the prelude to a long period of enmity between the USA and the Islamic Republic.

In September 1980, Saddam Hussein's army attacked Iran, seizing a large portion of the southern part of the country in a few weeks. Those behind the Iran–Iraq War believed the conflict would be short lived and result in the collapse of the Islamic Republic. Instead, the war continued for eight long, bloody and costly years. Then, on the second year of the war, and during a dispute over governance and the authority of the jurist-leader, the president of the Republic, Abolhassan Bani-Sadr, sided with the Mojahedin-e Khalq Islamist-Marxist opposition group. Bani-Sadr was removed from his position and fled to France. In response, the Mojahedin-e Khalq began a campaign of assassinations, targeting the leaders and key supporters of the Islamic Republic. This civil war led to the deaths of the Republic's second president, Mohammad Ali Rajai, his prime minister Mohammad-Javad Bahonar, as well as more than seventy members of the Republican Party and key figures in the state, the most prominent of whom was Ayatollah Beheshti. The

Mojahedin-e Khalq was eventually banished from Iran but only after it had exacted a frightful toll.

In the context of these battles with the Mojahedin-e Khalq and against Iraq, the Islamic Republic slowly began to change. From being an open and popular government, it turned into a closed, security state. With so many Islamist leaders assassinated, many overtly traditionalist religious leaders obtained positions in state institutions.

In terms of aiming to achieve dominance and social control, the regime was no different from many other modern states around the world. The difference was that the new state ruled and exercised control in the name of Islam. This was perhaps what inspired some of its key figures with a misplaced sense of righteousness. Religious scholars, who hailed from the ranks of the masses and had lived among them for centuries, quickly formed a new ruling class that was firmly attached to its own wealth and power.

The new regime's impact had two sides to it. On the one hand, the Islamic Republic dealt justly with the weak and impoverished and promoted their social and political mobility. It liberated Iran from foreign influence, and was able to preserve the nation's independence. On the other hand, agents of the state committed widespread transgressions including imprisoning, torturing and killing opposition figures and most state institutions were riddled with corruption. In addition, because the Islamic Republic had chosen to impose its image of Islam on Iran by invoking state powers, a kind of flaunting of Islamic standards became characteristic of Iranian society. This was certainly the direct opposite of the ideal of an Islamic Republic.

In July 1988, the US fleet in the Gulf shot down an Iranian passenger aircraft, thus making clear their support for Iraq. By the beginning of August, the leaders of the Islamic Republic had to admit that Iran would not be able to win a war against Iraq and their US allies. It therefore fell to Hashemi Rafsanjani, the influential statesman and speaker of parliament, to convince Khomeini to accept a ceasefire. In response,

Khomeini delivered his famous speech in which he said that accepting the ceasefire was 'like drinking poison'. The war ended, having caused tremendous destruction in both countries, with over a million casualties and costly delays in all development projects.

However, Khomeini, who had become a symbol of Islamic defiance in the face of Western hegemony, was unable to sustain this defiance for much longer. In February 1989, he issued his infamous fatwa against British novelist Salman Rushdie for insulting the Prophet of Islam in his novel *The Satanic Verses*. The West again found themselves at a loss in terms of how to respond, but this was Khomeini's final battle. At the beginning of June 1989, after a series of heart attacks, his soul departed this world. The Iranian capital reverberated with grief as millions of mourners flooded into Tehran on the day he was buried, creating a spectacle not seen before in modern times. In death, just as in life, and in spite of the critical situation the country was in, the people embraced their leader. Like those of other great spiritual figures in Islam, Khomeini's gravesite in the south of Tehran has become a site of pilgrimage that is visited by many.

The Council of Experts chose Ayatollah Ali Khamenei, who had been the third president of the Islamic Republic, to fill Khomeini's position, and Iranians elected Hashemi Rafsanjani, the powerful speaker of parliament, as the country's fourth president.

The relationship between Rafsanjani and Khamenei was characterised by understanding and agreement, and this helped the president to take the country into a new phase of development. Rafsanjani led Iran under the slogan 'Rebuild' for two successive terms, filling his cabinet and the president's office with a group of young ministers and assistants who came to be known as the 'Building Cadres'.

With their help, Rafsanjani gradually loosened the state's grip on the country's economic and commercial sectors, establishing a limited alliance with market forces. His government also opened Iran to foreign investment, especially in the oil and industrial sectors. Meanwhile, the margins of civil liberties were expanded and a campaign to rebuild Iran's main cities was launched. Externally, Rafsanjani's government strove to restore relations with most of the Arab and Islamic countries, and developed a special relationship with Saudi Arabia. At the same time, Rafsanjani strengthened Iran's economic and political relations with Europe, Japan, Russia and the Central Asian states and established close relations with China. Throughout this time, Iran continued to fulfil its obligations towards Palestine and Lebanon, which meant that its relations with Washington remained as tense as ever, and charged with mutual mistrust.

Iran's rebuilding policy was implemented at the cost of a marked increase in foreign debt, but this was sustainable given the size of Iran's economy. After years of revolution and war, Rafsanjani contributed to the normalisation of Iranian life, and the increased freedoms he allowed contributed to the resumption of debates about the policies and the foundations upon which the Islamic Republic was built.

Three major trends emerged: conservatism, reformism and centrism, with Rafsanjani and his allies representing the latter. The reformist bloc was comprised of a range of forces calling for change. Starting in 1997 and ending in 2005, this bloc was able to win two successive terms as president for their candidate Muhammad Khatami, a religious scholar and son of the revolution. Throughout this time, the reformists used a new popular discourse to campaign for increased freedoms and for an end to the influence of the Council for the Protection of the Constitution, through which conservative religious scholars had dominated the drafting of legislation. While some reformists remained committed to the ideal of an Islamic Republic with its constitutional edifice, others were sceptical of the possibility of establishing democratic governance in the shadow of the institution of the velayat-e-faqih, and called for the practice whereby the highest leadership positions are held exclusively by religious jurists to be nullified.

The political divisions in Iran are, from a certain perspective, related to the discourse on civil liberties that arose in the post-Cold War world, and the embracing of democracy as an expression of utopia. However, the political divides also reflect an essential problematic in Shi'a political thought. In the absence of an imamate (political leadership under the authority of an imam), which is the greatest source of legitimacy in Shi'a doctrine, there is no way to establish Islamic legitimacy.

Khomeini located this legitimacy in velayat-e-faqih; however, this limits the authority of the people; that is, their authority is ultimately exceeded by the authority of the jurist. The opponents of velayat-e-faqih call for the people to hold absolute custodianship, that is, for fully democratic rule. However, the Islamists cannot conceive of the possibility of preserving the Islamic character of a republic without a legitimate Islamic authority who is able to fulfil the role of imamate.

During Khatami's first term in office, debates between the conservatives and reformists escalated sharply, reaching a level where many observers believed that the Islamic Republic was about to implode from within. However, the Iranian political establishment revealed a high level of cunning and experience as Khatami refused to be a proxy for attempts to collapse the Republic and instead exposed the extremists in his ranks.

The conservatives then quickly regrouped and, in 2005, Mahmoud Ahmadinejad, a former officer of the IRGC, won the presidential elections and the conservatives took control of the parliament. Ahmadinejad promised a new revolution that would bring justice to the poor and protect both Islam and the Republic. The debates continued, however, not only because they are about who rules and controls the state, but also because they centre on the foundations of Shi'a political thought. As long the questions of legitimacy and sovereignty remain unresolved in the Shi'a conception of the state, Iran will remain trapped in struggles between those affirming the authority of the jurist-leader and those affirming the authority of the people.

The Islamic Republic lost much of its early resplendence. However, this does not negate the reality that the country has retained the authority to act independently and that its people enjoy significant levels of civil liberty. This is very different from what prevailed at the end of the 1970s, before the people's revolution overthrew the shah. It is highly likely that no event since has left a greater impression on the millions of Muslims in the world than Iran's Islamic revolution. However, while the revolution had succeeded in Iran, no one expected its echo to be heard in Saudi Arabia, the country of oil, prosperity, stability and the repository of the Sunni Islamic legacy.

10

Crisis in the kingdom of plenty

*A*t dawn on the first day of the holy month of Muharram 1400 (20 November 1979), a convoy of cars made its way to the holy sanctuary in Makkah. Close to two thousand men and women, even some children, alighted from the vehicles and made their way to the entrance of the mosque, loudly chanting Allahu Akbar. As soon as they were all inside the precinct of the ancient sanctuary, they quickly closed all the gates and attempted to take control of the mosque.

The holy sanctuary was already overflowing with other worshippers and pilgrims, and the newcomers waited until the end of the congregational prayer, which was led that day by Shaykh Muhammad al-Subayyal. They then pushed forward and took control of the public-address system. One of the group, believed to be its leader, began addressing the crowds, both within and around the holy sanctuary. The man announced his rejection of the rule of the Saudi family, denouncing its corruption and deviation from the guidance of Islam, which he said was apparent in the way the country was being run and in the behaviour of its rulers. He called for an end to Saudi rule and claimed that allegiance to the Saud family was invalid because it was based on coercion and duress. The man then also called for the cutting of all ties with Christian governments, specifically the USA, and for the expulsion of all foreigners from Saudi Arabia, along with the stamping out of corruption and the implementation of religious rulings. At the end of his speech, the man introduced a figure he called the Mahdi, spelling out the characteristics that verified his claim, and asking all present to recognise and pledge their allegiance to him. Members of the man's entourage did indeed pledge their allegiance, and quickly thereafter, arms and ammunition that had previously been smuggled into the basement of the mosque inside funeral biers were distributed to the men of the group. These men then took up positions in the minarets and along the walls of the sanctuary, and prepared for battle.[1]

No other city in the world embodies Islam's history and symbolism in the way that Makkah does. Blessed by Allah, this was both the abode of Abraham, father of all the prophets, and the birthplace of the Prophet Muhammad. The city unites Muslims in ways that no other site can. This is where revelation descended, and the Qur'an came down for the first time. It is where all Muslims must go at least once in their lifetime to perform the hajj. The site of the Holy Sanctuary, whose foundations were established for all of humanity by Abraham, is the direction Muslims face daily in prayer; the centre of their pilgrimage and circumambulation.

The timing of the siege was also highly symbolic. According to the Islamic Hijrah calendar, the siege began on the first day of the fifteenth century. There is no doubt that the group that stormed the Mosque chose to announce itself at this place and time, because both were so charged with meaning. The siege occurred just nine months after the Islamic Revolution in Iran and it provided further evidence of the Islamists' capacity to take the world by surprise.

The leader of the group that besieged the Holy Mosque was Juhayman ibn Sayf al-'Utaybi, a son of the 'Utaybah tribe and a former corporal in a battalion of the Saudi National Guard. The battalions are a kind of militia associated with the National Guard, whose purpose is to tie the Bedouin tribes to the apparatuses and institutions of the state. Juhayman was in his forties and had left the National Guard several years before.

After leaving his battalion, he became a regular participant in study circles run by religious scholars and had gained an informal Islamic education. It is unclear whether the ideas he expressed in his writings were distilled before he left the National Guard or during the period he devoted to his study of Islam. What is clear is that, in the few years before the Holy Sanctuary incident, he strove to form a group that shared his ideas. The group referred to itself as the Ikhwan (The Brotherhood), which has a very specific meaning in Saudi history, and it is important not to confuse this Saudi phenomenon with the Muslim Brotherhood (al-Ikhwan al-Muslimun), which is far more widespread and well known.

The collection of epistles that Juhayman wrote before the Holy Sanctuary incident presents an almost complete portrait of his intellectual orientation and motives. He made several references to the writings of Muhammad Ibn 'Abd al-Wahhab (1703–1792), the founder of the Wahhabi movement, borrowing some of his terminology, but also departing from Ibn 'Abd al-Wahhab's teachings in several ways. Juhayman relied primarily on a direct understanding of the Qur'an and the Sunnah, and his writings reflect no consideration of usul al-fiqh (Islamic jurisprudential source methodology) as followed by Muslim jurists in interpreting and understanding the foundational texts.

Juhayman also attacked Sufism, strict adherence to specific schools of jurisprudence and the practice of blindly following such schools. He did not suggest replacing blind following with absolutely free thought, but rather with taking recourse to the Qur'an and the Sunnah. Juhayman's writings reveal his interest in tawhid (monotheism), and specifically in tawhid al-Uluhiyyah (the uniqueness of divinity) and tawhid al-Rububiyyah (accepting only God as worthy of deification). He discussed the concept of shirk (ascribing 'partners' or helpers to God) and the problems associated with this in great detail. However, Juhayman's discussion of all these concepts had a political slant that was specifically related to his views on the ruling Saudi family.

Juhayman argued that imamah (absolute rule) has ultimate status in Islam as the ummah rallies and unites behind it. For him two types of imamah existed: one that leads with the guidance of the Qur'an and the Sunnah and one that

> does not lead people by Allah's Book and does not demand allegiance to serve the religion of Allah, but only makes claims without taking action; that does not seek to be guided by the guidance of the Prophet or by his traditions.[2]

He went on to argue that 'monarchy, by contrast, is in most instances coercive', noting that in the contemporary era, Muslims do not choose their caliphs but caliphs impose themselves on Muslims who are then forced to pledge allegiance to these rulers. People's displeasure with the caliphs' rule does not compel them to step down. Contemporary leaders, Juhayman asserted, cannot be considered imams because their leadership is invalid and an abomination that should be rejected. They do not entrench the faith or enjoy the support of Muslims; they simply subjugate people in pursuit of their own interests. They have abandoned jihad, and entered into alliances with Christians (namely, Western powers) and have brought every form of evil and corruption into Muslim society.

Juhayman's understanding of political action is based on the principle of inkar (repudiation). Thus, he did not declare the rulers to be infidels and he warned against being hasty about declaring anyone an apostate and engaging in takfir (excommunication). He also affirmed that scholars within the ahl al-Sunnah (followers of the Sunni doctrinal school) should generally avoid civil strife and obey rulers who are proven to be within the fold of Islam because they establish prayer. However, he also stated that it is obligatory to repudiate rulers who contravene the laws of Allah. He affirmed this by quoting the famous hadith from the Sahih Muslim collection in which the Prophet said:

> Whosoever among you should see a wrongdoing should change it with their hands; if you are unable to do so, then with your tongue;

and if you are unable to do this, then with your heart [that is, at least feel remorse] and this is the weakest form of faith.

Juhayman's strategy was to use all means possible to confront and repudiate what he saw as Saudi Arabia's wrongdoing and deviation from Islamic rule. There is no doubt that his understanding of this hadith contradicts the general Sunni understanding that he had previously affirmed. Interestingly, Juhayman did not explicitly enjoin the use of violence. He in fact asked his followers to declare their views, and be patient and restrained, but neither did he dismiss the possibility of resorting to arms.[3]

Juhayman actively propagated his views in Riyadh and Makkah, but Madinah was his focus. He was active both among Saudis and other Muslims visitors and pilgrims to the Holy City. Several of those who took part in the siege at the Holy Sanctuary were non-Saudi Arabs.

The Saudi state knew of Juhayman's views and activities before the Holy Sanctuary incident. In fact, afterwards, the Saudi minister of the interior, Prince Nayef bin 'Abd al-'Aziz, remembered that the authorities had previously incarcerated him but were forced to release him after pressure from religious scholars.

No one knows for certain how Juhayman's ideas evolved to embrace the use of force or what convinced him that the Mahdi had appeared. Unlike most of the Salafi school, who tend to pay little attention to prophecies about the future, Juhayman composed a long epistle entitled *The coming turmoil: Accounts of the Saviour and the great imposter (dajjal), the return of Jesus (upon whom be peace) and signs of the final hour*.[4] In this text, he outlined many prophetic traditions on these metaphysical issues, which the Muslim community had long overlooked. Nevertheless, the text made no claims that the Mahdi had been born or that Juhayman had met him; nor did it call for allegiance to the Mahdi. It is believed that, shortly before the Holy Sanctuary incident, Juhayman experienced a vision in his sleep, a vague dream that he later interpreted in an equally vague way.

In 1979, Muhammad ibn 'Abdallah al-Qahtani was a young man in his early twenties from a noble family allied to the powerful Qahtan tribe, which lived in the area between Saudi Arabia's eastern province of al-Ahsa' and Yemen. Juhayman probably met al-Qahtani at a religious study circle meeting in Makkah or Madinah. It is believed that al-Qahtani had a birthmark on his shoulder blade, which Juhayman saw as highly significant.[5] In addition, al-Qahtani's name was the same as that of the honoured Prophet, and he was of noble birth from the Hashemite clan. It seems the possibility had never crossed al-Qahtani's mind before, but Juhayman saw the birthmark as a seal of sorts and was convinced that that al-Qahtani was the Mahdi. Juhayman then persuaded al-Qahtani that his view was the truth, and began inviting people to pledge their allegiance to the new saviour.

Once he believed that the Mahdi had appeared, Juhayman became bolder and began to act in haste, believing that the time had come to put an end to Saudi rule and to establish a state based on Islamic justice. His messianic vision motivated him to lay siege to the holy sanctuary, and to concoct naïve plans to overthrow a well-entrenched state. He may have believed that the crowds of pilgrims on the one hand, and the claimed appearance of the Mahdi on the other, would provide all the support he would need. He was wrong on both counts. Although Makkah's holy sanctuary has been subjected to calamities throughout history, Muslims have never been sympathetic to anyone who fails to respect the inviolability of their spiritual centre and attempts to turn it into a contested space for the sake of some personal project.

It is unlikely that any of those gathered for the congregational prayer at dawn on the day of the siege joined the besiegers. As soon as they were allowed to do so, all the congregants left the holy sanctuary, leaving Juhayman and his group to face their fate alone. As news of the siege spread, tension and confusion spread throughout the Islamic World.

The Saudi authorities learned of the siege hours after it began. At the time, Saudi Arabia's strong crown prince, Fahd ibn 'Abd al-'Aziz, was in Tunis attending an Arab League Summit. His absence from the country added to the confusion in the official Saudi response. The confusion was intensified and complicated by the fact that the siege coincided with acts of civil disobedience in several cities and villages across the Eastern province of the Saudi Kingdom, where the Shi'a minority is concentrated. The success of the Islamic revolution in Iran had inspired Islamic forces generally, but it instilled a particular sense of confidence in Shi'a Muslims around the world. This newfound confidence prompted some Saudi Shiites to revive the traditional Shi'a mourning rituals to commemorate Imam Husayn in the first ten days of the month of Muharram. The Saudi state, like several other Islamic governments, condemns and prohibits these rituals as transgressing the teachings of Islam. Thus, while the Saudi authorities strove to find a solution to the siege at the holy sanctuary, Shi'a mourning processions began in the cities of Sayhat, al-Qatif and Safwa, and were due to last for at least two days. Clashes ensued between Saudi security forces and the marchers, who carried banners condemning the state. Several people were killed and others injured, creating the impression that the entire kingdom was about to explode.

Although the official Saudi statement indicated that only a handful of protestors were involved in the siege, security forces with armoured vehicles surrounded the Holy Sanctuary on the first day of the siege. The Saudi interior minister, Prince Nayef, seems to have believed that the matter would be resolved swiftly and with minimal effort on behalf of the troops. He had miscalculated; the protestors were well armed and strongly motivated. They managed to hold their ground through the night and inflected heavy casualties on the Saudi forces.

The next day, the Saudi authorities issued a statement indicating that they had 'taken every possibility into consideration to gain full control over the situation, and would proceed on the basis of a fatwa approved unanimously by all of the religious scholars'. Obtaining a fatwa was essential because violence within the grounds of the Holy Sanctuary is prohibited by the shari'ah, and the Saudi state bases its legitimacy on its observance of Islam and the shari'ah. For some reason, however, the fatwa was not issued until 24 November – four days after the siege began. The fatwa was signed by thirty senior religious scholars who, as per tradition, confirmed that they had issued it in response to a question directed at them by King Khalid ibn 'Abd al-'Aziz, and that it was based on information he had given them after inviting them to his office. With regard to the protestors, the scholars affirmed that

> It was obligatory to call upon them to surrender and lay down their weapons and if they did so this should be accepted and they should be imprisoned until their matter could be decided in terms of the law; but if they refused it was then obligatory to exercise all means to capture them in accordance with God Most High's pronouncement: 'And do not fight them in the Holy Mosque until they fight you therein, and if they fight you then fight them and that is the just recompense for those who disbelieve' (Q2: v 91).[6]

The operation to regain control of the Holy Sanctuary became increasingly costly and complicated; whenever the security forces attempted to storm the place, heavy gunfire was directed at them causing many casualties. Hundreds of armed militants remained inside the mosque and, even though they had failed to win popular support, most fought to the end, preferring death to surrender.

The repeated failure of the Saudi security forces to resolve the situation meant that Jordanian and Pakistani backup was required and in the end even French support was requested. Fighting continued at the holy mosque for twenty-two days. It was eventually brought to an end with the use of gas grenades and by flooding the lower levels of the sanctuary with water. Hundreds of protestors and security force personnel died during the siege.

It is believed that al-Qahtani was killed in the clashes but Juhayman and several of his followers were captured alive. Juhayman showed no remorse for his actions and remained convinced of both the correctness of his actions and the illegitimacy of Saudi rule until his death. It is not known how many people were executed with him, but some were definitely from his tribe, the 'Utaybah. This raises the question of the extent to which a tribal dimension and its heritage of collective memory motivated Juhayman to change from being a soldier in the National Guard, which is one of the state's most important institutions, into a hard-core activist against the ruling Saudi family.

In a passage overflowing with bitterness, from one of his epistles entitled, *The emirate, allegiance and obedience: Exposing the deception of the rulers towards seekers of knowledge and the masses*, Juhayman attacked King 'Abd al-'Aziz Al Sa'ud, the founder of the Saudi kingdom, recounting how the king had

> called upon the Ikhwan (may God have mercy on them) that had migrated from the villages for the sake of God (the Honoured and Sublime), to pledge allegiance to him on the basis of the Qur'an and the traditions of His Prophet, and they used to strive and conquer the lands, sending to him the due of an imam [leader] in terms of spoils, taxes, plunder and so forth on the understanding that he was the leader of the Muslims. Thereafter, when his authority was established and he had achieved his goal...he prohibited the jihad in God's path beyond the borders of the Arabian Peninsula and when they set forth to fight the idolaters...he labelled them – he and the ignorant scholars of religion with him – with a title that is detested by the people of Islam, as khawarij [dissenters].'[7]

Juhayman then described the king's destruction of the Ikhwan as follows:

And when he fought them and dispersed them, and his dictatorial authority was entrenched, he forged an alliance with the
Christians and disbanded jihad in God's path; and he opened the
sealed doors of evil and his sons followed in his ways until the
land of the Muslims reached the point of evil and corruption it
is at today.[8]

What inspired Juhayman, and perhaps every political crisis that has
befallen Saudi Arabia since the late 1970s, goes back to the birth of
the modern state. Before 'Abd al-'Aziz was crowned, a bloody clash
occurred between 'Abd al-'Aziz and his former allies, the Ikhwan
(Brotherhood). The Ikhwan were among the most religious and coura-
geous of 'Abd al-'Aziz's brigades and the vanguard of his armed forces. Most belonged to Bedouin tribes. Since 1913, and on the advice of
'Abdallah Al al-Shaykh, who was the qadi (chief justice) of Riyadh
at that time, 'Abd al-'Aziz had begun settling the tribes in religious
hajr (rural co-operatives). Abandoning warfare, raiding and fighting,
the Bedouin tribes settled in the hajr to work the land and be educated.
Religious teachers and legal scholars mingled with them, calling them
to Islam and judging disputes that arose between them on the basis of
the shari'ah. The stability of these new rural communities was based
more on a sense of fellowship than on tribal ties, and their members
were therefore referred to as the Ikhwan. The hajr were characterised
as religious centres, and modelled on the settlements established by
the first Muslims who emigrated from Makkah to Madinah. They were
gradually transformed into ideological and military training centres.

Al-Artawiyyah, which was founded around a constellation of wells
in a fertile valley on the caravan route between Qasim and Kuwait,
in the pasturage of the powerful Matayr tribe, was the first such community. The first members of the community were descendants of the
Matayr but groups from other Bedouin tribes soon joined them, including members of the 'Utaybah tribe, many of whom also settled there.

By 1920, twenty hajr had been established. By 1929, when clashes began between 'Abd al-'Aziz and the Ikhwan, 120 hajr had been established by members of the Shammar, Harb, 'Utaybah, Matayr, Qahtan, al-Dawasir, Bani Khalid, al-'Ajman, al-'Awazim, Bani Hajir, and al-Zafir tribes, among others. In the years between the establishment of the first hajr and 'Abd al-'Aziz Al Saud taking control of the Hijaz region, the Ikhwan played a leading role in Saudi expansion, and in the project to unify the Arabian Peninsula. However, conflict between 'Abd al-'Aziz and the Ikhwan became inevitable.[9]

The clash began immediately after 'Abd al-'Aziz, assisted by his Ikhwan brigades, took control of the Hijaz region in 1926. The Hijaz region was very different from the Najd area. As a former Ottoman province, in which the Sufi orders were widespread, its economy depended on pilgrimage and trade. This meant that life there tended to be far more relaxed and cosmopolitan, with Muslims from many countries and cultures mixing freely in its cities.

Given their religious zeal, it should not have been surprising that, on encountering this, the Ikhwan began confronting people in the streets, and attempting to stop them from what they saw as deviating from appropriate Islamic behaviour. To strengthen the rule of law and prevent the Ikhwan from being overzealous (thus besmirching the reputation of Saudi rule in the territory that holds Islam's holiest site), 'Abd al-'Aziz established the Jama'ah al-Amr bi al-Ma'ruf wa al-Nahiy 'an al-Munkar (Group for Encouraging Good and the Prevention of Wrongdoing), in 1926. However, the problem of the Ikhwan was far greater than he seemed to realise.

In 1927 'Abd al-'Aziz signed the Jeddah Treaty with Britain. Britain was represented in the negotiations by a well-known Arabist officer named Gilbert Clayton. Even though the Jeddah Treaty was better than the Darayn-al-'Aqir treaty that 'Abd al-'Aziz had previously signed with Percy Cox, in that it included British recognition of the independence and sovereignty of the Saudi state, the new treaty also defined the borders of the Saudi state, and expected the Saudis to refrain from further efforts at expansion.

In November of the same year, several of the Ikhwan gathered in Al-Artawiyyah under the leadership of Faysal al-Duwaysh, the Matayr leader, Sultan ibn Bijad, the 'Utaybah leader and Ibn Hathlayn, the shaykh of al-'Ajman. Those gathered wrote down their criticisms, and addressed them to 'Abd al-'Aziz. These included the Ikhwan's objection to the halting of their march to Kuwait, Iraq and Jordan (where they wished to further their religious mission) and the imposition of customs taxes in the Najd region. They also objected to the levels of tolerance prevalent in the Hijaz and the country's Eastern Provinces, to the use of the 'tools of the disbelievers' such cars, telephones and telegraphs, and to 'Abd al-'Aziz's son Faysal's trip to London. In the months that followed, 'Abd al-'Aziz tried to find a compromise with the Ikhwan and succeeded in winning many of them over. However, some members of the group continued to launch attacks on communities inside the Kuwaiti and Iraqi borders. Britain lodged a strong objection to this, via 'Abd al-'Aziz's advisor Hafiz Wahbah, and this brought matters to a head.

'Abd al-'Aziz sought and obtained the support of fifteen religious scholars, which allowed him to use force to put an end to the Ikhwan rebellion at the heart of his realm. The two sides met in March 1928 in the Battle of al-Siblah; the Ikhwan were defeated and their leader Faysal al-Duwaysh fled. However, the crisis did not subside completely. Al-Duwaysh tried to invade the neighbouring territories once more: members of the Matayr tribe laid siege to the road between Riyadh and al-Hufuf while members of the 'Utaybah tribe blockaded the road between Najd and Hijaz.

Around this time, 'Abd al-'Aziz heard that the leaders of the Ikhwan planned to divide the country between them if they succeeded in defeating him. From July 1929 to the end of that year, 'Abd al-'Aziz launched a series of campaigns against the Ikhwan that resulted in their dispersal and defeat. He then confiscated all their wealth, livestock and weapons, and forbade the rebels from returning to their land.

Several Ikhwan leaders were killed in battle or captured and died in prison. Juhayman al-'Utaybi's grandfather is believed to have been killed in the battle of al-Siblah. Whether this is true or not, the Maṭayr and 'Utaybah tribes played a leading role in the Ikhwan's rebellion, and they suffered major losses. In the decades that followed, those Ikhwan who survived continued to tell the story of the rebellion and its motives in the cities and villages of Najd, developing a narrative that runs parallel to that of the founding of the Saudi Kingdom.

Be that as it may, the Saudi crisis of the 1970s was motivated not only by the country's painful past but also by the Saudi state's gradual departure from the foundations on which it was established. 'Abd al-'Aziz's problem with the Ikhwan, like most of the crises that the Saudi state has experienced since, comes back to the contradiction between the Saudi attempt to establish a central state and the Islamic vision on which its legitimacy was originally based.

Saudi expansionism reached its fullest extent in 1928 under the leadership of 'Abd al-'Aziz, in an era when all the neighbouring countries were still under imperial rule. 'Abd al-'Aziz then realised that further attempts to expand his territory would bring him into conflict with Britain (in Palestine, Iraq, South Yemen and the Gulf emirates) or France (in Syria and Lebanon), or both. 'Abd al-'Aziz knew that he did not have the strength to win such a confrontation so he put an end to his expansionism. Along with this, his da'wah (religious mission), which his armies (and especially the Ikhwan brigades) had been led to believe was jihad in the path of God, also had to stop. Instead, 'Abd al-'Aziz then decided to consolidate his authority in the areas under his control.

Inevitably, this strategic re-alignment of the Saudi ruler's vision generated opposition and anger among the many devout members of his forces, especially those who were not ready to submit to the authority of a modern state or abandon their essential aim, which they saw as encouraging their fellow Muslims to practise what they believed was 'correct Islam.' The Ikhwan did not acknowledge 'Abd al-'Aziz's huge achievement in unifying the Arabian Peninsula, nor were they inclined to reflect on their place in the balance of forces in a region that was otherwise under the control of the imperial powers.

In the coming decades, the modern Saudi state relentlessly strengthened its powers and its influence.[10] Having planted the seeds of a standing army in the mid 1920s, the regime established a Directorate of Military Affairs in 1935, which became the Ministry of Defence in 1946. 'Abd al-'Aziz took upon himself the installation of radio transmitters capable of linking to outlying areas of the kingdom to speed up the transmission of information. Abd al-'Aziz was also impressed by the modern schooling system, which he had been exposed to for the first time in the Hijaz, and he established the General Education Administration in 1926, while also consenting to the establishment of several modern schools for boys in Riyadh and in other parts of Najd. In 1953, the General Education Administration became the Ministry of Education. Seven years later, a General Presidency for Girls' Schools was also established.

After 1933, when the finance minister 'Abdallah al-Sulayman signed an agreement with the Standard Oil Company of California granting them oil-prospecting rights, American and European experts flooded into the country. While the influx of foreigners served to reignite religious sensitivities, the oil revenues that came with them were highly effective in consolidating the power of the state.

It can be argued that the crowning of Faysal ibn 'Abd al-'Aziz in 1964 initiated an era of modernisation par excellence. Faysal became king in 1964 (and ruled until 1975), but in reality he had been making the key decisions since the beginning of the 1960s, while his brother Sa'ud was still king. Faysal strove to bring formal education to all corners of the Kingdom, and especially to the most isolated regions. Faysal's modernising agenda consolidated state authority, enabling this to reach even into the heart of the religious establishment. In 1970, for example, Faysal established the Ministry of Justice, consisting of seventeen members. This was at a time when colleges of Islamic Law and Islamic Studies in the new universities began to absorb the role of Islamic higher learning, pulling this away from the traditional study circles of religious scholars. Between the early 1950s and the mid 1970s, seven universities were established across the Kingdom, all under state control. In addition, it was during Faysal's reign, that the traders' organisations of the Hijaz were thoroughly undermined by the fact that all state institutions and related agencies were consolidated in the capital Riyadh, rather than being spread out over several cities. Faysal was also responsible for launching the Saudi television service and for ordering the opening of schools for girls.

In the mid 1960s, however, a dangerous new internal enemy arose within the Saudi state. In 1963, protests broke out in the Burayda region against girls being educated in the new formal schools. In the following year, Khalid ibn Musa'id ibn 'Abd al-'Aziz, a nephew of King Faysal, led a violent protest movement against his uncle, attempting to seize control of the country's television and radio stations, branding these as institutions for transmitting 'unIslamic values'. Khalid ibn Musa'id was captured and executed. (A little over a decade later, one of Khalid ibn Musa'id's younger brothers took revenge by assassinating the king.)[11]

However, the protests were just the beginning of a serious crisis. From within the heart of the educational and other modern institutions, such as the universities in Madinah, Riyadh and Dhahran, engineers, doctors and young scientists began challenging Saudi modernity, splitting it from within. Reformists also began to criticise the monarchy's monopoly of political authority, its extraordinarily strong relationship with the USA, and its shifts away from the values of Islam. This time, however, the critics joined almost secret Islamic organisations.

The idea of Islamic organisations was introduced into Saudi society by Arabs from other Islamic countries living in the kingdom who

had different political backgrounds. Such individuals include Manna'
al-Qattan and Najib al-Muti'i from Egypt, and Muhammad Lutfi al-Sa-
bagh and Muhammad Surur Zayn al-'Abidin from Syria. Some were
members of the Muslim Brotherhood, others were Salafis, and some
were both. In the end, the kingdom's strong Salafi heritage meant that
almost all of the Islamic organisations that came to the fore had Salafi
leanings.

Most of the organisations were formed in the 1960s, but were tak-
en aback by the 1979 siege of the holy sanctuary and suspended their
activities for some years. However, by the 1980s they had begun to
spread into the mosques and universities. The sheer size of the kingdom
meant that some organisations had influence in the Hijaz while others
gained support in Najd, the Eastern Province or al-Ihsa. Several of the
country's most prominent personalities, from 'Abdallah Nasif, 'Abdallah al-Turki, 'Ayid al-Qarni, Salman al-'Audah, Safar al-Hawali, Nasr
al-'Umar and Sa'd al-Faqih all the way to Osama bin Laden were associated with these organisations in some way.

From the beginning of the 1980s, Islamic sentiment in the country
was directed against the Soviet occupation of Afghanistan. The leaders of the mujahidin, including Gulbuddin Hekmatyar, Burhanuddin
Rabbani and Abdul Rasul Sayyaf were known for their strong Islamic beliefs, and the Afghani cause was supported throughout the Saudi
kingdom. In fact the Saudi state took up the Afghani cause, but calls to
support the jihad in Afghanistan consolidated the Islamic atmosphere
inside the Saudi kingdom too, and popular support for Islamic organisations spread. The fact that the Afghani issue came to the fore while
Saudi Arabia was opposing the Egyptian–Israeli Peace Treaty, and during the Iran–Iraq War (in which Saudi Arabia sided with Iraq), helped
contain the tensions that arose after the holy sanctuary incident, but not
for long.

With the unprecedented oil boom of the 1970s and 1980s the wheels
of modernisation spun faster, and corruption spread rapidly too. In-

creasing modernisation compounded the sense that the kingdom was steadily moving away from its Islamic roots. Thus, although the tribes were substantially weaker, tribal values had not disappeared, and tribal values re-emerged strongly after being adopted by some of the ruling family's most important princes. In fact, the ruling family itself behaves as if it is a kind of tribe. These factors contributed to an increasing lack of transparency in state circles and the royal family's rejection of any kind of popular representation in government.

The oil price collapsed in 1986 and led to a crippling economic and political crisis that was exacerbated by demographic factors. That is, from the mid-1990s, 60 per cent of the kingdom's citizens were below the age of twenty. This, together with rising levels of education, placed tremendous pressure upon the job market. The unemployment rate increased to 14 per cent, and the fact that the country was the world's largest oil exporter could do nothing to change this.

These issues were all intertwined when the Gulf Crisis exploded in 1990. Saudi Arabia found itself transformed into a huge military base for American forces and their allies, providing the perfect opportunity for the Islamic reformists to express their opposition to the state. Despite the return of sporadic terror attacks perpetrated within, the real challenge the state faced was from reformist forces. In truth, the reformists rose to prominence in many of the Islamic countries because their organisations were able to articulate popular sentiment more effectively than anyone else. However, reformist discourse seldom emerged before the onset of a wave of bloody violence, and during the 1980s and 1990s, violence spread from Syria to Egypt, to Algeria and Saudi Arabia.

11

The spread of violence

From the late 1970s to the late 1980s, violence gained prominence as a basic tool of expression in the Islamic world. In fact, for states and opposition groups alike, violence seemed to be their only tool. Reckless carnage caused havoc in cities stretching from Damascus to Hama, to Cairo and Asyut, from Algiers to Madinah, Riyadh and al-Khobar, with thousands of young Islamists confronting state security structures. Many young activists justified the use of violence using a discourse that mixed a simplistic appropriation of the Islamic heritage with a modern reading of politics, economics and international relations. State authorities, in turn, justified their recourse to repression on the basis of their duty to ensure national safety and stability. However, the contexts within which violence were escalating were probably more influential than the justifications used by either side.

This violence left a huge mark on political and economic life, on the relationship between state and society, and on the relationships between various sectors of society. In many cases, the violence began when state domination and tyranny had already reached unprecedented levels; yet when it subsided, many states had become even more repressive and tyrannical. Instead of bringing change and reform, the violence deepened the divisions within Arab and Muslim societies. In this whirlpool of destruction, an entire generation of youth was lost – to exile, to the dark cells of a prison or to death.

On 2 February 1982, loudspeakers rang out from mosques in the Syrian city of Hama calling the city's inhabitants to engage in jihad at the behest of its religious scholars. Within hours, small groups of armed Islamists and droves of sympathisers took to the streets, making their way to the city's military bases and police stations, aiming to seize all the weapons they could find. By evening, the city was no longer under state control, and armed Islamists held sway for the next ten days.

On the tenth day, Syrian armoured forces and defence brigade units under the leadership of the president's brother, Major General Rifaat al-Asad, arrived to reclaim the city. Their attack was brutal and bloody; heavy artillery and intensive firepower were deployed. Soldiers and officers who refused to comply with commands to fire on the city's inhabitants were executed. Clashes extended out from the mosques into homes, and from alleyway to alleyway, and large parts of the city were destroyed. Unofficial estimates suggest that the number of civilians and armed Islamists killed in the process reached twenty thousand. On 24 February, then-president, Hafiz al-Asad, announced that his troops had regained control of the city. Sources within the Islamist opposition indicated that the clashes continued until the end of the first week of March.[1]

The battle of Hama took place at the height of clashes between the Syrian authorities and their Islamist opponents, and was an indicator of what lay in store for other Arab countries. However, the armed conflict in Syria was not inevitable. It can be argued that no other Islamist group is more civilian in inclination, or peaceful and democratic in character, than Syria's Muslim Brotherhood; and the Brotherhood was the main Islamist group opposing Hafiz al-Asad. Furthermore, no revolutionary republican regime in the Arab world could claim to have a president more pragmatic than Hafiz al-Asad. Nevertheless, Syria's recent history had been so troubled that both the Brotherhood and the state were dragged into a vortex of violence and confrontation.

The Muslim Brotherhood of Syria was founded in the mid 1940s. Born from a collection of Islamic organisations in Damascus, Aleppo, Homs and Hama, the group's members encompassed several contrasting Islamic tendencies, from Sufi to Salafi to liberal. Its leader, until the late 1950s, was the prominent thinker and intellectual, Mustafa al-Siba'i. Al-Siba'i (1915–1964) was born in the city of Homs into a family of religious scholars. His father was the khatib (preacher) at the city's Great Mosque, where the young Mustafa become known for his opposition to popular Sufism and to the strong influence of the Sufi fraternities over people's lives. Inspired by the memory of the great Islamic reformer Ibn Taymiyyah, the people of Homs gave al-Siba'i the title of 'Ibn Taymiyyah Jnr'.

In 1937, al-Siba'i travelled to Cairo to study at al-Azhar University, where he got to know Egypt's great Islamic scholars of the time, including Hasan al-Banna. However, when the Second World War was declared, the British authorities arrested al-Siba'i as a precautionary measure, due to his political activities. After three years of incarceration, he was expelled from Egypt and forbidden to return for seven years. Back in Syria, al-Siba'i led the Syrian Brotherhood's volunteers in the 1948 Palestinian War. Two years after this, having been allowed back into Egypt, he obtained his doctorate from al-Azhar University. Al-Siba'i returned to Syria once more, and in the years that followed, he became one of Syria's most prominent and independent thinkers. In addition to leading the Brotherhood, he became a university professor and later dean of the College of Islamic Law at Damascus University.

Al-Siba'i was a freethinking Islamic intellectual, very learned and intellectually engaged. He is perhaps the most important thinker to emerge from the Muslim Brotherhood after Hasan al-Banna. Al-Siba'i wrote and published many books, articles and academic studies, and is remembered for two of his works, namely: *Ishtirakiyyatul Islam* (The socialism of Islam) and *al-Sunnah wa Makanituha fi al-Tashri'* (The Sunnah and its position in Islamic legislation), which were published in 1959 and 1960 respectively.

Al-Siba'i was a firm believer in the legitimacy of the parliamentary system – a belief that flowed from his vision of the shari'ah and the authority of the ummah. He affirmed in his writings that the shari'ah does not strip people of their right to manage their worldly affairs, arguing that

> Islam is a legal code that has been made permissible by God Most High and it is left to the community, to be affirmed by people of knowledge and opinion and leadership through mutual consultation. Authority, in truth, belongs to the ummah; if it is possible to consult the ummah on a matter and they agree thereupon then there can be no other alternative. Not even the caliph – let alone any other ruler – is able to negate consensus or go against what has been decided upon by those who have binding authority.[2]

Al-Siba'i was also of the opinion that Islamic legislation is civil in the sense that it establishes laws on the basis of human interests and in recognition of human dignity. He saw no sense in differentiating between people's religions, languages or ethnicity, and worked to find a balance between the interests of individuals and groups. This was what probably motivated him to get involved in an intense debate over an article in Syria's 1950 constitution. The article was about the relationship between the state and religion. Al-Siba'i proposed modifying the words that stated that Islam was the religion of the state to read instead that Islam was the religion of the *head* of state, and that the shari'ah was the fundamental source of legislation. For several years to come, Al-Siba'i continued to defend the 1950 constitution as Islamic, even though many others regarded it as secular.

Al-Siba'i expressed deep concern for society in his writings and in the views he held. He believed that the objective of Islam's legal legacy was to ensure public welfare; which encompasses the welfare of people, the attainment of justice and principled social development. He also affirmed that the goal of Islam was not the distribution of charity but rather the eradication of poverty.

These positions prompted him to defend the role of the state in redistributing wealth, and to enter into an alliance with the socialist Ba'thist Akram al-Hawrani in defence of agrarian reform. The Brotherhood contested Syria's 1949 elections led by al-Siba'i, under the party name, the Islamic Socialist Front. Al-Siba'i was consequently referred to in certain circles as the 'Red Shaykh'. In reality, al-Siba'i was a staunch opponent of communism and believed that Islam would protect Syria from Soviet expansion by achieving social justice. After the Egypt–Syria Union, Nasser's government, which was by then the Egyptian Brotherhood's arch enemy, printed and distributed thousands of copies of al-Siba'i's book, *The Socialism of Islam*, to students at al-Azhar in an effort to convince them that their socialist policies and legislation were consistent with Islam.

The Syrian Muslim Brotherhood grew markedly in the 1950s. Unfortunately, al-Siba'i became terminally ill in 1957. His deputy, the Damascene 'Isam al-'Attar, become the de facto leader of the Brotherhood even before al-Siba'i passed away. Al-'Attar led the Brotherhood on the basis of the same civil parliamentary principles established by al-Siba'i. Despite the clash between the Egyptian Brotherhood and Nasser's regime, the Syrian Brotherhood supported the Egyptian–Syrian Union in 1958 and acceded to Nasser's request for the disbanding of all political parties.

When the two countries separated again in September 1961, al-'Attar refused to sign the separation covenant that was agreed to by a large number of Syrian politicians, including the leadership of the main nationalist party, the Ba'th Party. In 1964, this led to difficulties for the Syrian Brotherhood when the Ba'thist regime prevented al-'Attar from re-entering the country on his return from the haj. Al-'Attar settled in Beirut and tried to maintain his connections with elements of the Brotherhood in Syria, but leading the Brotherhood from the outside and in the shadow of a belligerent regime was not an easy task; from the mid 1960s the Syrian Brotherhood began to fracture and fall apart.

Marwan Hadid was a member of the Brotherhood who rebelled against the organisation at an early stage.[3] Born into a relatively affluent family of cotton growers in the city of Hama, Hadid met and was influenced by Sayyid Qutb while he was studying agricultural engineering in Egypt. At the end of the 1960s Hadid acted against the advice of the leadership of the Syrian Brotherhood, and joined a guerrilla group at a training camp that had been set up in Jordan by Muslim Brotherhood branches from various Arab countries under the umbrella of the Palestinian Fatah Movement. At the camp, Hadid, along with several other Syrians, received basic military training and then participated in guerrilla activities in Palestine. In 1970, the camp was shut down after a clash between the Jordanian government and the guerrilla forces, so Hadid and his comrades returned to Syria to begin a new phase in their lives. Syria was then entering its third epoch under Ba'thist rule.

The Arab Socialist Ba'thist Party had seized control of Syria in March 1963 by way of a military coup. However, the party was soon overcome by an internal struggle between two wings, which the Ba'thists described as their right wing, led by President Amin al-Hafiz, and their left wing, led by military strongman Major General Salah Jadid. When the struggle between the two wings intensified, the right wing contacted the Muslim Brotherhood, and attempted to pull the organisation into their camp.

Some of the Syrian Brotherhood's leaders might have been attracted by the idea of co-operating with al-Hafiz as a first step towards securing control of the state but, in February 1966, the left took action, overthrowing al-Hafiz in a military coup that turned Damascus into a battleground of artillery fire. Jadid's vision of Syria was more akin to that of a leftist gang member than that of a traditional Ba'thist nationalist. Under his rule, the state launched a widespread campaign against religion, undermining and denigrating Islam.

When the religious scholars of Damascus held a gathering in the Umayyad Mosque to protest against this, Jadid clamped down on them mercilessly. However, after Syria's defeat in the June 1967 War and the complete loss of the Golan Heights to Israel, the rule of the Ba'thist left wing lost whatever legitimacy it might ever have had in the eyes of the people. Therefore, when relations between different groups within the regime deteriorated to the point of crisis in the closing months of 1970, Brotherhood leaders, such as 'al-'Attar did not conceal their support for Hafiz al-Asad when he toppled Jadid and his regime.

Al-Asad was a practical ruler who did not pay much attention to ideological delusions of the type that drove Jadid. His objective from the outset was to attain stability and security and to rebuild internal unity within the Syrian state. However, al-Asad was not able to rule alone, and he had inherited a party inflamed with leftist Arab culture that was strongly opposed to Islam. Instead of normalising Syrian political life by granting more freedoms, al-Asad strengthened the authority of his security apparatuses, including the special military forces. In 1973, vociferous debate broke out again over wording of the new Syrian constitution concerning the relationship between Islam and the state.

Hadid and his comrades organised a general strike in Hama, in which various Syrian opposition forces participated, including the Muslim Brotherhood. The strike turned violent with rioters attacking the offices of the Ba'th party and organisations associated with it. In response, al-Asad agreed to ensure the inclusion of an article in the constitution stating that the religion of the Syrian president should be Islam but this had no effect on Hadid who refused to engage with the authorities. As far as he was concerned, the regime was beyond the pale of Islamic legitimacy and the only means of dealing with it that he saw as valid was war.

In 1975, Hadid established his own organisation called al-Tali'ah al-Muqatilah li Hizbillah (The Fighting Vanguard of God's Party) with the aim of conducting this war. As soon as the Brotherhood understood the nature of Hadid's activities, he was quickly expelled along with everyone that had been associated with him. This did not stop Hadid. In June of the same year, he was arrested following a clash with security forces. A few months later, he was pronounced dead in the prison hospital. Many believed that he died as a result of torture.

Shortly before his death, Hadid smuggled a letter out of prison, in which he called on religious scholars and Islamic groups to announce a Jihad against the 'disbelieving regime'. On 8 February 1976, the Fighting Vanguard, which was now being led by 'Abd al-Satar al-Za'im, assassinated the head of military intelligence in Hama. At that time, the group was not yet well known, but with the infamous massacre of students at an artillery school in Aleppo on 16 June 1979, this changed completely.

The attack on the school was undoubtedly planned for political as well as military effect. The attackers divided the students into groups according to their sectarian affiliations and went on to kill only the Alawites. In what was probably an attempt to drag the rank and file of the Muslim Brotherhood into battle against the regime, responsibility for the attack was claimed in the name of the Fighting Vanguard.

If the Fighting Vanguard can be construed to have achieved any sort of success, it was limited to undermining both the Muslim Brotherhood and the regime in a single act. Prior to this, the links between the Brotherhood and Hafiz al-Asad's regime had not been completely severed. The regime was fighting an extremely complex struggle to control Lebanon while its supposed ally, Egypt, unilaterally made peace with Israel. Al-Asad was well aware of the strength of the Brotherhood and strove to win it over to his side; the Brotherhood had come to his aid in the 1978 referendum[4] in return for the release of their prisoners. However, the artillery school incident put an end to any possibility of further co-operation. In the coming years, unprecedented sectarian divisions shattered Syria.

Of course, the Brotherhood denied any responsibility for the artillery school incident, but six days after the incident, the country's interior minister, General 'Adnan al-Dabbagh, announced that the Muslim Brotherhood would be held responsible anyway. The regime's police and intelligence services as well as their military forces pursued anyone who had had any relations with the Muslim Brotherhood, no matter how marginal. Military and security blockades sprang up on streets and avenues and the Syrian cities turned into battlegrounds.

Thousands of people were incarcerated. Some died from torture, others were cut off from their lives and kept in prison for years on end. Summary executions were carried out at Tadmur Prison in Palmyra for which the defence brigade units were later blamed. The security forces demonstrated the lengths to which they were willing to go when they attacked the home of the former Brotherhood leader 'Isam al-'Attar, on 17 March 1980, in the German city of Achen, killing his wife, Bannan al-Tantawi, in the process. This was in spite of the fact that al-'Attar had distanced himself from Brotherhood structures and from events in Syria.

Essentially, the Ba'th Party put all its forces on high alert and set out to utterly destroy what it called the 'Muslim Brotherhood Gang'. Even young women from the Ba'th Party joined the battle by attacking veiled women in the streets. In July 1980, the Syrian People's Assembly ratified Law 49, which advocated the death penalty for anyone affiliated to the Muslim Brotherhood. In this way, the killing of Brotherhood members, or anyone suspected of belonging to the organisation, became a legitimate practice.

The Brotherhood found itself targeted from all sides and its members began to look to the Fighting Vanguard without waiting for direction from its leaders in exile. In the end, the Muslim Brotherhood officially threw their weight into battle against the regime, using all the means at their disposal. They organised strikes and protest marches. Then, using explosives and booby-trapped cars, they attacked the Cabinet building, the airforce headquarters and a site used by security forces in the Azba-kiyyah district. They assassinated as many government employees and security force officers that they could, and, in June 1980, they attempted to assassinate the president in a hand-grenade attack.

While Asad's regime was engaged in open battle against Jordan and Iraq, the leader of the Fighting Vanguard 'Adnan 'Aqlah, and the leader of the Muslim Brotherhood, 'Adnan Sa'd al-Din, saw no harm in entering into alliances with the regimes in Amman and Baghdad. Jordan and Iraq not only offered the Islamists a safe base for organisational work, but also supplied many of the car bombs that struck Syrian targets.

However, while Ba'th Party voices shouted their support for the use of revolutionary violence to confront the reactionaries, al-Asad could see the depth of the crisis that the country had descended into. Ba'th Party structures in most of Syria's northern cities were collapsing and the security forces were the only state structures that still functioned. When general boycotts occurred in most Syrian cities in the first two months of 1980, al-Asad realised that he had to seize the political initiative. He therefore called for national reconciliation, and affirmed that perpetrators of violence should be distinguished from Muslim Brotherhood members who did not participate in such acts. Mediators between the two sides began mobilising. The most important of these was Amin Yakan, a former deputy superintendent-general of the Syrian Muslim Brotherhood.

Meanwhile, 'Ali Sadr al-Din al-Bayyanuni, one of the Brotherhood's key leaders, returned to his hometown of Aleppo, which had become an Islamist base. His goal was to supervise the Brotherhood and negotiate with the regime. However, behind the scenes, the superintendent general of the Muslim Brotherhood, 'Adnan Sa'd al-Din, was working with members of a cell that had penetrated the president's security detail and was trying to assassinate him. This meant that the efforts put into negotiations and reaching a mediated settlement were very limited.

In February 1982, during the siege of Hama, the conflict reached fever pitch. The city was all but destroyed and everyone suspected of having Islamist leanings was arrested. This, combined with huge losses inflicted on Islamists in Aleppo and Damascus, settled the conflict in favour of the regime. The Fighting Vanguard leader 'Adnan 'Aqlah was captured with a large number of his supporters and their fate remains unknown.

The years of conflict settled heavily on Syrian society, casting a cloud of fear and division over the country. The Islamists' failure in Hama was not only a military or security one, it also indicated their inability to spark a comprehensive national rebellion. In the next few years, levels of violence slowly abated. From the mid 1980s, most Islamists came to realise the futility of violence and the grave consequences it holds for them and for society as a whole. The leaders of the Muslim Brotherhood undertook a painful revision of their policies, which created longstanding disputes, but eventually culminated in the election of al-Bayyanuni as the new superintendent-general. However, the regime's attitude towards the Brotherhood did not change substantially.

࿇

The surge of violence that occurred in the 1970s was not limited to Syria. Egypt, the world's largest and most important Arab country, also entered a whirlpool of destructive conflict between the Islamists and the state as several radical Islamist groups emerged and began to follow a path of violence. However, the violence that occurred from 1981 was of a totally different order.

On the afternoon of Tuesday, 6 October, while millions of Egyptians watched a huge military parade commemorating their country's victory in the 1973 Arab–Israeli War, things took a very strange turn. The master of ceremonies was praising the artillery force units as they passed before the podium where President Anwar Sadat was seated with a large group of his ministers and guests. Suddenly, one of the artillery vehicles drew to a halt and a well-built officer rushed forward firing a machine gun at the podium. Moments later, two more soldiers followed the first, and grenades began to fly through the air. Another soldier joined in, firing from the vehicle. The gunfire and explosions continued for forty seconds, killing Sadat and injuring many of those seated near him.

The officer who led the assassination team was Khalid al-Islambuli, a lieutenant in the 333 Artillery Brigade. The other three were 'Ata Tayil, 'Abd al-Hamid 'Abd al-'Al and Husayn 'Abba 'Ali – all former soldiers that al-Islambuli had managed to smuggle into the parade using bribery. The group undertook what they believed would be the first step in an armed Islamic revolution that would do away with Sadat's regime and establish an Islamic state in Egypt. The plan was not firmly rooted in any way, but the violence spurred by this incident went on for about twenty years, leaving tremendous destruction in its wake.

A conglomeration of small Islamic jihadist movements, that came to be known as al-Jama'ah al-Islamiyyah (Islamic Group), was behind the assassination.[5] It was made up of a large group of Islamist students from the southern universities of Asyut and al-Minya in Egypt's Sa'id region. While the Muslim Brotherhood had been successful in recruiting most Islamist activists in Cairo's universities and in the cities of the north in the 1970s, few southern students were willing to join its ranks. Among the more prominent students affiliated to the Islamic Group were Najih Ibrahim, Karam Zuhdi, 'Isam Darbalah, and Usamah Hafiz. Most of its members were affiliated to the science colleges, and were studying for degrees in medicine or engineering, for example. Like Marwan Hadid in Syria, these students had also read and been influenced by Sayyid Qutb, and especially by his ideas about al-jahiliyyah al-mu'asirah (the contemporary state of ignorance). However, for them Qutb's work was simply a starting point. Influenced by an incorrect understanding of a fourteenth-century fatwa issued by Ibn Taymiyyah that concerned fighting the Tartars, members of the Islamic Group believed it was legitimate to take up arms against governments in the Islamic world. They believed that they were the true bearers of Salafi doctrine, arguing that the Muslim Brotherhood was tainted by liberalism and its leaders were past their prime.

At the beginning of 1981, the leaders of the Islamic Group met with Muhammad 'Abd al-Salam Faraj of the engineering department at Cairo University, who was the leader of a small and secretive cell called the Tanzim al-Jihad (Jihad Group). Faraj had also read Ibn Taymiyyah and applied his fatwa on the Tartars to contemporary regimes. He was of the opinion that what he called the 'Islam of the rulers' was similar to the Islam of the Tartars, and therefore not true Islam. Whereas Ibn Taymiyyah had allowed fighting against the Tartars because they were attacking the Mamluk state, which protected the caliphate, Faraj believed that jihad against contemporary Arab rulers was a religious obligation incumbent on every Muslim. He wrote a book titled *al-Faridah al-Ga'ibah* (The neglected duty) in which he argued that confronting the colonial powers was futile, and that it was more of a priority to fight the enemy at hand than any distant enemy. In the same work, he also stated that the control of the colonial powers over the Islamic lands would be impossible without the collusion of its rulers.[6] This logic was reversed several years later by another jihadist who had studied under Faraj, a medical doctor named Ayman al-Zawahiri.

Muhammad Shawqi al-Islambuli, a member of the Islamic Group who often visited Cairo, enjoyed a cordial relationship with Faraj and admired him very much. Muhammad Shawqi al-Islambuli reportedly took part in the 1979 siege of the holy sanctuary in Makkah and was the first person to circulate Juhayman al-'Utaybi's writings in Egypt.[7] Muhammad Shawqi was the one who noticed signs of a newly found religiosity in his younger brother Khalid al-Islambuli, who was an artillery officer based in Cairo, and introduced him to Faraj.

After reaching an agreement, the Islamic Group and the Jihad Group began working together to stockpile weapons and secretly train their members in how to use them. A former military intelligence officer, Major 'Abbud al-Zamar, helped them with planning and training. However, Faraj was caught off guard at the end of September when Khalid al-Islambuli informed him that he had been chosen to participate in the

6 October military parade, and that he believed that he would be able to assassinate the president. In the next few days, after some hesitation, all agreed to the assassination plan, on condition that it be followed by an armed insurrection that would spark a popular revolution and bring down the regime.

During his years in power Sadat had angered many Arabs and Egyptians and used up all the goodwill he had accumulated during the 1973 War. Sadat believed that the war had won him absolute rights to determine state policy. He therefore proceeded to revise Egypt's image and attempted to position the country globally as the USA's central ally in the region. In so doing, he adopted liberal economic policies that resulted in massive social upheaval. In the few years after the 1973 war, the poor became poorer and a new class of millionaires rose to prominence, with corruption reaching levels unseen in Egypt since the establishment of the Republic. Sadat, meanwhile, lived like an emperor, not like a president who knew that his country was overburdened with problems. Even his wife, who was extremely active in elite social circles, was nicknamed Egypt's 'first lady'. On top of all of this, Sadat signed a unilateral peace agreement with Israel that not only opened the door to the normalisation of relations between the two countries, but also created massive tension between Egypt and all the Arab states.

Although Sadat opened up certain civil liberties and made space for a degree of political pluralism in Egypt, he often seemed to be completely out of touch with the Egyptian people. For example, when widespread popular protests broke out in January 1977 in response to inflation, Sadat insisted on referring to the protesters as 'criminals'. After the success of the Islamic Revolution in Iran, Sadat hosted the hated Shah of Iran, to whom even the USA had refused asylum.

Just weeks before his assassination, Sadat issued orders for the incarceration of more than fifteen hundred members of various Egyptian opposition groups, from the Nasserite Muhammad Hasanayn Haykal to the Muslim Brotherhood's 'Umar al-Tilmisani, and from the Coptic writer Milad Hanna to feminist novelist Latifah al-Zayyat. In a speech after these widespread arrests had taken place, Sadat described religious scholar, Shaykh Ahmad al-Mahlawi, as languishing in prison like a dog. At this point, many analysts observing developments in Egypt believed that Sadat had lost his balance entirely. As for the jihadists, they required no further evidence to condemn Sadat as an apostate, even though he liked to be referred to as the 'believing president'.

Nevertheless, the jihadists hopes of sparking a popular armed insurrection after the assassination of the president failed dismally. A few days later, armed Islamists were involved in bloody clashes with security forces in Asyut, but failed to take control of the city or any of its key state institutions. While the jihadists anticipated a popular revolution, most Egyptians were stunned into silence by the president's assassination and the violence that followed. The security forces were quickly able to regain control, and had soon captured Faraj and all the members of his assassination team, as well as all the leaders of the Islamic Group and the Jihad Group, along with many others affiliated to the two organisations. A trial was held and al-Islambuli, 'Faraj and their comrades were executed; many others received prison sentences of various lengths.

On 14 October 1981, Hosni Mubarak was made president of Egypt. From his first days in power, Mubarak tried to ease the tensions in the country and bring an end to the extreme political polarisation that prevailed. He released everyone who had been arrested under Sadat's orders the previous month, as well all the young Islamists who had not been officially prosecuted.

After Sadat's assassination, the Islamic Group did not carry out any further attacks. Those who wanted to continue the armed struggle left for Afghanistan. Instead, in this new and relatively open political atmosphere, the second-tier leaders of the Islamic Group began concentrating on civil and charitable activities. Groups of volunteers assisted service organisations and medical clinics, and they made some impact in the cities of the Sa'id region and in Cairo's poorer neighbourhoods. However, their thinking does not seem to have changed much.

Whereas the Muslim Brotherhood chose to participate unofficially in the 1984 and 1987 parliamentary elections, making tangible gains in the process, the Islamic Group boycotted the elections and neither fielded candidates nor participated in voting. During the late 1980s, the security forces again began to harass members of the Group and attempted to disrupt their activities, especially in Cairo's poorer neighbourhoods. Many thought that the security forces were trying to push them into a confrontation. In August 1990, 'Ala Muhyi al-Din, the Group's official spokesperson, was killed in a shooting that many believe the security forces to have been responsible for. Whether or not this was the case, the shooting made it clear that the seeds of violence had not yet been eradicated in Egypt.

Two months later, the jihadists responded by assassinating Rif'at al-Mahjub, the speaker of the Egyptian People's Assembly, in broad daylight in front of the Semiramis Hotel in the heart of Cairo. With this, the door to violence was thrown wide open once more. The Islamists attacked security officers and security officers used tremendous force in pursuit of the Islamists. Many were jailed where they were subjected to interrogation and torture.

The targets of violence widened to cover state weapons' depots, video-rental stores, jewellery stores owned by Christians, bars and liquor stores, the mausoleums of saints (the establishment of which contravenes Prophetic practice) and even wedding celebrations. The jihadists assassinated the writer Faraj Fudah – an arch enemy of the Islamists – and grievously injured the famous novelist Naguib Mahfouz. The sugar plantations in southern Egypt became the site of exceptionally violent clashes between jihadists and security forces.

During the first few months of 1993, Egypt's interior minister 'Abd al-Halim Musa tried to address the situation. He announced that the time had come for reconciliation between the Islamists and the state, and he facilitated a meeting in prison between a delegation of senior religious scholars, led by Muhammad al-Ghazali, and the leaders of the Jihad and Islamic Groups. The minister attempted to listen to the demands of the armed groups and hoped to find an agreement that would stop the violence. Unfortunately, a wave of retrenchments passing through the state unseated Musa and he was replaced by Zaki Badr al-Din.

The violence then began to re-escalate, reaching a climax in June 1995 when a group of Islamists, supported by certain circles within the Islamist Sudanese regime, tried to assassinate President Mubarak in Addis Ababa. In the same year, the Egyptian embassy in Islamabad was bombed.

However, these incidents proved to be little more than desperate attempts down a road that led nowhere. Several of the Islamic Group's leaders in prison began to acknowledge that they had reached a dead-end. They realised that their confrontation with the state had weakened the country and spread rancour and hatred among Egyptians. The years of conflict had resulted in thousands of deaths and the imprisonment of more than thirty thousand Islamists. When senior religious scholars and Islamist intellectuals raised their voices to condemn the violence, and expose the frailty of the religious justifications that sought to legitimate its use, it became clear that the institutional violence of the state had won the battle. In 1997, the imprisoned leaders announced an initiative to end the violence.

At this point, Rifa'i Taha, one of the leaders of the Islamic Group who had fled abroad, rejected the initiative and instead organised a bloody operation that decisively discredited those advocating violence. On 17 October 1997, a cell from the Islamic Group kidnapped a large group of tourists in the city of Luxor. The operation ended with the deaths of all the jihadists and over seventy tourists. The incident shook Egyptians and deepened the isolation of the armed jihadists. In the coming months, the initiative to cease violence was upheld and the authorities gradually began to release thousands of prisoners who had not faced trial or had served their sentences. After a short time, the imprisoned leaders also began to revise their positions on violence. However, the abating of armed conflict in Syria and Egypt did not necessarily mean an end to violence elsewhere. In Algeria, which moved overnight from ballot boxes to civil war, blood still flowed profusely.

❦❦❦

The situation in Algeria in the 1990s is one of the strangest and most horrific cases of conflict between Islamists and state authorities. Just before Algeria was overwhelmed by waves of violence, it was experiencing a very real democratic transition that could potentially have served as a model for other nations and states in the region. However, the Algerian state and ruling class refused to accept a peaceful transition to democracy, and to prevent the Islamists from attaining power through the ballot box, they pushed the country into a bloody civil war that lasted more than a decade.

A massive popular uprising in October 1988 heralded a new phase of Algerian history. The direct cause of the uprising was massive inflation and the state's flagrant disregard for the deteriorating quality of life for the majority of its citizens. However, the roots of the uprising lay much deeper than this.[8]

While Algeria of the 1980s had reached a critical point of socio-economic decline that was aggravated by the sharp collapse in oil prices and the ever-growing national debt, this deep socio-economic crisis combined with the Islamic revival happening in the region, and several other factors specific to Algeria, contributed to the emergence of an Islamist movement in the country. In fact, the ruling National Liberation Front had faced concrete Islamist opposition since Algeria's independence in 1962. The majority of Algerians were of the view that they had fought the long war of liberation against French occupation for the sake of an Arab-Islamic Algeria.

However, the elite who took control of the new state were Franco-philes, and the strengthening of Arab–Islamic identity was not among their priorities. In confronting the Islamist opposition groups, Algeria's first president after independence, Ahmad bin Bella, placed Shaykh al-Bashir al-Ibrahimi, the president of the Jam'iyat al-'Ulama (Society of Islamic Scholars) under house arrest. By contrast, Bin Bella's successor, Houari Boumedienne, the second president of the republic, strove to contain the Islamist influence by attempting to find a balance between Arabist and socialist policies. To please the Islamists, Boumedienne pursued a broad-based policy to Arabise education. At the same time, he entrenched socialist policies that encompassed a programme of agrarian reforms and industrial development. One of the ways in which Boumedienne implemented his socialist policies was to appoint members of the Algerian left to key posts in his administration.

When al-Shadhili Bin Jadid took over the presidency in 1978, Boumedienne's agrarian and industrial revolution had to be abandoned. The agrarian reforms had not revitalised the agricultural sector and state-owned industries had proven themselves incapable of meeting the needs of the country. However, Bin Jadid's policies of relative liberalisation led to further economic decline.

In a country where those under the age of thirty constituted more than 60 per cent of the population, unemployment figures reached unprecedented levels. Algeria was being divided from within, with those who were allied to the Francophone elite controlling all the key state institutions. Millions of students and unemployed youth began organising via institutes that promoted the Arabic language, but while young people gathered in the streets and in the mosques, civil and military bureaucrats continued to squander public wealth and funds.

In November 1982, a group of religious scholars and Islamist leaders, led by Shaykh 'Abd al-Latif Sultani, the most prominent Islamist in the country, called on Bin Jadid to reform the government and the country. When Sultani passed away in April 1984, the Islamists revealed the extent of their support for his views: his funeral was attended by close to half a million people. When the uprising broke out in 1988, it became clear that the Islamists were playing an active role in controlling the masses on the streets and confronting the security forces.

On the eve of the uprising, the Rabitah al-Da'wah (Propagation League) was formed, and several religious scholars and active Islamists joined the organisation. Among these were one of Algeria's most prominent religious scholars Shaykh Ahmad Sahnun, the young 'Ali Belhaj and a former member of the Liberation Front and a freedom fighter in Algeria's war of liberation, 'Abbasi Madani. Since the League was not a political party, and its leadership did not agree with one another, Madani and Belhaj decided to set up the Islamic Salvation Front (FIS) in March 1989. The party was Islamist in orientation and it encompassed several different groups.[9] Over the next few months, several other Islamist parties emerged.

The 1988 uprising had taken place amid major global changes, epitomised by the rapid collapse of the communist bloc and the mushrooming of popular movements in the former Soviet states. In this context, Bin Jadid realised that it would be difficult to continue ruling Algeria as it had been ruled since independence. In July 1989, a constitutional amendment was approved that allowed for political pluralism and a transition to democracy.

No one expected the Islamist movement to gain the confidence of more than 30 per cent of Algeria's voters. However, the municipal elections held in July 1990 took everyone by surprise. The Islamic Salvation Front alone won 55 per cent of the vote, allowing them to occupy 856 of the 1541 seats in one municipality for example.[10] Popular support for FIS was highest in the capital Algiers, as well as in Oran and Constantine, where the party won as much as 70 per cent of the vote.

These municipal election results illustrated the collapse of support for the ruling National Liberation Front, which had led the war of liberation and had been in power since independence. In the months that followed, the Islamists were able to consolidate their popularity by their fair and competent administration of the municipalities. The ruling elite then enlisted the help of Mawlud Hamrush,[11] one of Algeria's shrewdest politicians and gave him the task of saving the state from the FIS. Hamrush announced plans to increase the number of seats in parliament and redraw the electoral wards. It was clear that the aim of the Hamrush government was to prevent the FIS from winning the national parliamentary elections. The FIS leaders sensed danger, not only in relation to Hamrush's proposed amendments, but also due to the possibility of elections being postponed or cancelled.

On 25 May 1991, the FIS leader 'Abbasi Madani called for a general strike and a mass meeting in Martyrs' Square in the centre of Algiers. The meeting began with a small crowd, but slowly the number of protestors began increasing, reaching a peak as the security forces and the army moved to occupy the surrounding streets. Several clashes broke out between security officers and protestors in which some protesters were killed and others injured.

The protestors then called for Bin Jadid's resignation and for the national election to take place immediately. Several days later, the government declared a state of emergency and postponed the election. The strike had proved to be a rash provocation of the ruling elite. However, its suspension on 8 June after a vague agreement between the FIS leadership and the new prime minister, Ahmad Ghazali, revealed the FIS's indecisiveness and inexperience.

A period of calm followed that allowed the government and the army to catch their breath. They then arrested Madani and Belhaj, and charged them with conspiring against the state. Unrest and instability prevailed again, and was subdued only when parliamentary elections were held at the end of December. The FIS contested the elections under the leadership of its acting-president 'Abd al-Qadir Hashani, and proved once again that it enjoyed the confidence of the majority of Algerians. In the results from the first round of elections that were announced, the FIS won 188 of the 232 seats. It was obvious that the FIS would win the majority of seats in the National Council in the second round.

A decision was taken to hold by-elections in the undecided wards on 26 January 1992. However, on 11 January, Algeria, and the rest of the world, were caught off-guard when Bin Jadid resigned, thus forcing the upcoming elections to be cancelled. Although it was never named as such, there is no doubt that Bin Jadid's move was prompted by a military coup. Senior military officers, Khalid Nazzar, Muhammad al-'Imari, Isma'il al-'Imari and Tawfiq Midyan forced Bin Jadid to resign and took control of the country while maintaining a civilian façade. It is widely believed that the coup leaders received support from the USA and France.

To prevent the Islamists from coming to power, the military violated the law and propelled the country into a long dark vortex. In the coming years, thousands of young people made for the mountains and took up arms, returning to the culture that prevailed during the war of liberation. Some refused to be ruled by a state they saw as un-Islamic, some were protesting the lack of popular representation in government, and some were moved by extreme anger, a loss of hope and an uncertain future. Mujahidin returning from Afghanistan swelled their ranks. Instead of seeing FIS leaders such as Abbasi Madani, 'Ali Belhaj and 'Abd al-Qadir Hashani as role models to look up to, many young Algerians began learning about of the leaders of the armed groups, such as 'Abd al-Qadir Shabuti, al-Madani Marzuq and 'Antar al-Zuwabiri.

Essentially, Algeria's political climate shifted from one of democratic political activity to mass incarceration, death by torture, armed conflict, assassinations and random bombings. Not all acts of violence were committed by the Islamists. Various sources have noted that the military leaders formed private militias that were disguised as municipal guards. These militias then undertook actions that the military could claim to have no knowledge of. Villages and rural areas were divided up between those loyal to the state and those loyal to the Islamists, and both sides then began to engage in mass slaughter. Soon, no one remembered who was responsible for what. The site of the Bin Talhah and Sidi Ra'is massacres, in which 511 civilians were killed, was just a few kilometres from the military barracks. There is also widespread belief that military intelligence personnel infiltrated the armed groups and used them for their own ends. For example, groups would attack villages, causing residents to flee from their homes and the state would then gain control over the land in these areas.

In February 1992 the leaders of the coup installed Mohamed Boudiaf, a former leader of the national liberation struggle, as president. However, Boudiaf, who had been in exile in Morocco, took his role as president very seriously, and did not serve his military masters as he was required to. He was quickly assassinated and his murder remains shrouded in mystery.

When General al-Amin Zirwal took over as president in 1995, he took the initiative of making contact with various armed groups. In October 1996, the Islamic Salvation Army agreed to a ceasefire. However, real political efforts to rescue Algeria from the cesspool of violence were not effectively initiated until Abdelaziz Bouteflika was elected president in 1999.

Bouteflika announced a general amnesty and a programme of national reconciliation. A large number of rebels were won over by this and left their camps. However, small extremist groups refused to respond to Bouteflika's initiatives, so the violence was curbed but not eradicated. Nevertheless, Bouteflika regarded what had been achieved as sufficient, and upon starting his second term of office in 2004, he began to try to rein in the military. Senior leaders of the 1990s coup were forced to retire and replaced with professional military officers. In 2003, Madani and Belhaj were released after having spent twelve years in prison or under house arrest, but they were both banned from any political or party activity. Madani was later given permission to leave the country, but Belhaj stayed on in Algeria, allowed to shake hands with whoever he meets at mosque but not allowed to speak to them; at the time of writing, the FIS was still banned in Algeria.

❦❦❦

Whether in Syria, Egypt or Algeria, the Islamists have used various justifications to legitimise the use of armed struggle. At times, they have justified violence by invoking the concept of al-hakimiyyah (divine governorship), and at other times by the concept of al-jahiliyyah al-mu'asirah (the contemporary state of ignorance). Salafist notions that deem all ruling authorities apostates and makes opposition into a religious obligation have also been used. In all cases, however, the violence was a reflection of the strong polarisation within these states. Experiencing huge frustration at their tightly closed political horizons, supporters of violence have sought to legitimise their views by any means at hand.

Waves of violence ended when the various social forces were unable to match state violence, but the root problems remained unresolved in Syria, Egypt, Algeria, and many other Islamic countries. The military and structural violence of the various state authorities and their security forces provided a set of veiled answers to the bitter questions put forward by the Islamists. Thus although the Islamists were defeated and isolated, their calls for political pluralism, popular participation in state governance, and an end to corruption remained unanswered. These calls are still supported by large numbers of people in all Islamic societies.

12

Islamist resistance fighters

While several Islamist groups were resorting to violence as a means of political transformation, others were leading movements of national liberation against foreign occupation. Foreign interference is nothing new in Islamic countries. Throughout the colonial period, Islam provided a frame of reference for national liberation movements, from Indonesia to Morocco. What was new in this period was that Islam began to be an organising force, and was differentiated from other forms of nationalism by its Islamic identity and vision for the future. The Afghani mujahidin, Hizbullah in Lebanon, as well as Hamas and the Islamic Jihad in Palestine, all see themselves as unique in this way, and see opposing foreign occupation as a religious obligation. The first Islamic movement to reawaken the consciousness of Muslims in a way that echoed around the globe was the Afghani resistance movement.

❦

The Afghani crisis began in early 1978, when a communist coup led by Nur Mohammad Taraki put an end to two-and-a-half centuries of monarchy. In December 1979, a Soviet military force crossed into Afghanistan. The Soviets' declared intention was to protect communist rule in Kabul, but in truth, their goal was far greater. Advancing towards the warm southern oceans has been a central goal for Russia since the nineteenth century, and the 1970s saw the Soviets expanding their influence across the globe. The Cold War had reached its apex, with the Soviets exploiting the US defeat in Vietnam and the West's loss of influence in Iran to attempt to win a decisive strategic victory in Afghanistan. However, what the Soviets faced in Afghanistan defied all their expectations.

In the coming decade, a broad-based Islamist resistance, characterised by a high degree of determination, grew ever stronger in Afghanistan. Effectively, Afghanistan became the setting for the final great battle of the Cold War, albeit through no choice of its people. When the Russian forces withdrew from the shattered country, the Soviet Union had reached a point of such exhaustion that the entire communist bloc collapsed.[1]

For years, this large, impoverished country with its wild landscape and harsh climate was regarded by the world as a remote no-go area, caught between communism and capitalism, and between Soviet and Western forces. It was the fate of Mohammad Zahir Shah to be the last of the Afghan kings. Zahir Shah ruled Afghanistan for decades, and although he introduced some modernisation, the society remained very traditional on the whole. Tribal allegiances remained dominant outside of the capital, Kabul, with Muslim clerics from the Hanafi School, and the shaykhs of the Sufi Tariqas, exercising huge influence over people's lives and shaping their worldview.

Inside the city of Kabul, modern institutes and foundations were strong, and Islamist organisations, influenced by Egypt's Muslim Brotherhood and Pakistan's Jamaat-i-Islami were prominent. It is therefore not surprising that the seizure of power by the communists provoked some Islamist opposition, even if this was initially extremely limited.

The Islamist opposition had attracted the attention of US president Jimmy Carter's administration, and the Americans began cultivating links with them through their allies in Pakistani president Zia-ul-Haq's government. However, active American intervention in the country did not begin until after the Soviet occupation. The reason for this is simple: the Soviet occupation instantly provoked Islamic resistance from all sides – from modern Islamists, to Sufis, clerics, and even nobles who had been aligned to the monarchy.

Despite the plurality of Afghani resistance, three central organisations quickly rose to prominence. The first was al-Jam'iyyah al-Islamiyyah (the Islamic Society), led by Burhanuddin Rabbani. Before the occupation, Rabbani had studied Islamic Sciences at al-Azhar University in Egypt, and worked as a professor of Islamic law at Kabul University. The Islamic Society was active in areas populated by Afghanis of Tajik origin, and its military wing was led by a former engineering student Ahmad Shah Masoud. The second organisation was al-Hizb al-Islami (the Islamic Party), which was led by Gulbuddin Hekmatyar, and enjoyed huge support from Pakistan's military intelligence and General Zia-ul-Haq. The third organisation was al-Ittihad al-Islami (the Islamic Union), which was established by Abdul Rasul Sayyaf, who had studied Islam in Saudi Arabia.

Resistance spread out across most of the country and, in spite of the brutality with which the Soviets dealt with rebel fighters and anyone who supported them, resistance fighters were able to inflict grave losses on the occupying forces. The US administration soon realised that helping the Afghani resistance would give them a valuable opportunity to help wear down the Soviets, and avenge the defeat they had suffered in Vietnam.

During the Soviet occupation, the USA and its allies in the Islamic countries, especially the Saudi kingdom, pumped more than US$6 billion into supporting the Afghani resistance. In 1985, Ronald Reagan, hosted a delegation of Afghani leaders and Afghani mujahidin featured prominently on Western television. Meanwhile, Pakistan became a secure rear base for Afghani resistance fighters and refugees, and many other Islamic and Arab countries collected donations and hosted conferences to support and assist in the recruitment of young Islamist volunteers. Islamic and Arab relief and charitable foundations mushroomed along the border between Afghanistan and Pakistan to assist both Afghani refugees and the mujahidin. As in the early centuries of Islamic conquest, the traditions and culture of jihad and garrison life developed along the border between the two countries, and specifically in the Pakistani city of Peshawar.

This culture was strengthened by the arrival in Peshawar of 'Abdallah 'Azzam, a Jordanian of Palestinian origin who was a professor of Islamic Law, and a young Saudi university graduate, Osama Bin Laden, who hailed from an extremely wealthy family. In 1984, 'Azzam established the Maktab al-Khadamat (Services Bureau) to welcome Arab and Muslim volunteers and co-ordinate their participation in the Afghani jihad. In the same year, and in the same city, Bin Laden established the Bayt al-Ansar (House of Helpers) with a similar purpose. By the mid-1980s it was estimated that more than 150 000 fighters had joined the Afghani resistance forces; alongside these were several thousand Islamist volunteers who were not Afghans, most of whom were from Arab countries.

The decisive moment arrived in 1986, when the USA began supplying the Afghani mujahidin with anti-aircraft Stinger missiles that were easy to transport and use. The missiles put an end to Soviet superiority in skirmishes with the resistance fighters and hastened the defeat of the occupying army. In the next two years, the mujahidin shot down 269 Soviet helicopters and fighter planes. Public support in the Soviet Union began to wane in the face of these mounting losses, and the new leaders in Moscow under Mikhail Gorbachev acknowledged that the war in Afghanistan was unwinnable. In February 1989, the Soviet army of occupation withdrew from Afghanistan via the very same road that they had used when they invaded the country ten years earlier.

Within a few months, the forces of Ahmad Shah Masoud, who were aligned to the Islamic Society, took control of Kabul. However, this was not to the liking of Hekmatyar, the leader of the Islamic Party, which was supported by the country's Pashtun majority. Despite repeated attempts to bring the various mujahidin groups together to meet and negotiate, the country spiralled into a bloody civil war that continued for more than two years. More than a million Afghanis had been killed fighting off the Soviet occupation. Now hundreds began dying daily from mortar fire as contesting forces fought for control of Kabul. As the image of the mujahidin began to deteriorate in the eyes of the public, an Afghani cleric who was just starting his intellectual career attempted to save his country from chaos. Mullah Mohammad Omar was the leader of an organisation that was to become known as the Taliban.

Omar and many of his colleagues had studied Hanafi jurisprudence and Deobandi methodology; their syllabus draws its legitimacy from a seminary established in Deoband in India in the nineteenth century, which aimed to preserve the Hanafi school as it had crystallised in the Ottoman and Mughal eras. Omar and a number of his colleagues decided to form the Taliban to rid Afghanistan of civil war and end the conflicts between different mujahidin forces.

As soon as the Taliban forces made some headway, they came to the attention of Islamists in Pakistan's military intelligence organisation. These officers quickly realised that the Taliban could help them re-establish stability in Afghanistan under the authority of a government that would be friendly to Islamabad. More importantly, however, a large number of mujahidin from various organisations also offered to support the Taliban.

The Taliban began with a few hundred members, but by the time they gained control of Kandahar in 1994, they numbered in the thousands. Two years later, the Taliban won control of Kabul from Ahmad Shah Masoud's forces, and two years after that, they took control of Mazar-e Sharif, the last of Afghanistan's important northern cities. With that, more than 90 per cent of Afghani territory was under the authority of Mullah Omar and the Taliban.[2]

The Taliban established peace and security anew in most of the country. However, their views on culture and society seemed to belong to a time and place other than the present! If the Taliban drew anything from the practical legacy of the Hanafi School, it seems to have been

197

from the worst it has to offer. They prohibited all forms of modern media and communication; they prevented females from being educated or working; they prohibited male doctors from seeing female patients; and insisted that all men grow beards. Cruel punishments were meted out to anyone who disobeyed these rules.

Although the Taliban had managed to end the worst of the fighting, many of the former mujahidin opposed the new rulers, and remained active where they could. In the end, however, the Taliban were not defeated by Afghani opposition forces, they were dispersed (for a while) by a massive US invasion after 9/11. After the invasion, the US and their allies installed a puppet government in Kabul and the Taliban lost their foothold. They regrouped quickly, however, and formed a new leadership structure. Then, errors made by the Washington-installed government in Kabul, and by the invading foreign forces, pushed a wide swathe of the Afghani people closer to the Taliban. In 2007, the level of conflict in Afghanistan mirrored what it had been in the 1980s: this time, however, the foreign occupation was led by the USA and resistance to it was led by the Taliban.

❦❦❦❦❦

The Afghani resistance was in its early years when Israeli forces pushed through from occupied northern Palestine towards the Lebanese capital, Beirut, on 6 June 1982. The Israelis were attempting to crush Palestinian bases in Lebanon, and strengthen the Maronites (who were allies of Israel) in the Lebanese civil war. A few years later, Israeli defence minister Yitzhak Rabin succinctly expressed the outcome of Israeli aggression against Lebanon, saying, 'We let the Shi'a Genie out of the bottle'. On this score, Rabin was correct. From the ruins of Israel's devastating invasion of this small Arab country, Hizbullah was born.

Israeli forces occupied southern Lebanon in the first few days of the invasion, but they failed to break the will of the Palestinian fighters or their allies in the Lebanese capital, Beirut. In fact, the steadfastness of the capital drew the attention of every Arab and Muslim. The Islamic Republic of Iran was still in its prime, and although the Iraq–Iran War was at its height, the Iranian public pushed for assistance to be provided to the resistance forces in Beirut. Accordingly, few days after the start of the invasion, units from the IRGC's Muhammad is the Prophet of Allah Brigade began arriving at Damascus International Airport. Various complex regional and international considerations meant that the Iranians were not given an opportunity to participate in the fighting directly, but they gathered in the Beqaa valley's Baalbek al-Hurmul area to see how things would develop.

Despite Beirut's initial steadfastness, it became clear that Lebanon would not be able to hold out against the siege. By the beginning of September, the Palestine Liberation Organization (PLO) forces had effectively left Beirut. The Israelis, with backup from US and French troops, occupied Lebanon from the south up to the capital. The Israeli invasion did not affect Lebanon and the Palestinians alone. As the Arab country with the greatest influence in Lebanon and whose forces had helped confront the Israelis, Syria was also directly affected.

Of course, the Israeli invasion brought about a major shift in the balance of power within Lebanon. Bashir Gemayel, the Maronite leader allied to the Israelis was appointed president but was assassinated before he could take office. His older brother Amin was then appointed in his place. Lebanon signed a peace treaty with Israel on 17 May 1983, but neither Syria nor the majority of Lebanese were ready to submit.

Most of the inhabitants of South Lebanon, which was occupied by the Israelis, are Shi'a Muslims. Since the late 1970s, the Amal Movement had been their central political and military force. One of the results of the Israeli invasion that few people paid much attention to at the time was that a group of Islamists and young Islamic scholars broke away from the Amal Movement. This breakaway group were protesting the movement's dishonourable performance in response to the Israeli occupation, and the bias of their leader, Nabih Berri, who opposed the Lebanese nationalist forces. The breakaway group gathered in the Beqaa Valley, where they also came under the protection of Iran's Islamic Revolutionary Guard Corps (IRGC). In the next few months, other young Shi'a Islamists from Lebanon's Da'wah Party joined them, along with young Shiites who had joined the PLO. From all of these groups, and under Iran's Islamist patronage, Hizbullah was born.[3]

Hizbullah's development was not instantaneous, but its long gestation period was definitely achieved under fire. The young activists gathered in the Beqaa Valley were united by their belief in velayat-e-faqih (custodianship of the jurist) and their respect for Ayatollah Khomeini. They agreed with Khomeini that Israel was a danger to Islam and to all Muslims, and that America was the wellspring of all the world's evils. With support and training from the IRGC in the Beqaa, the group began to prepare themselves to take on both the Israeli occupation and the US-French presence in Lebanon.

Meanwhile, Lebanese nationalist resistance forces (which included leftist, nationalist and Islamist groups) had forced the Israelis to withdraw from Beirut and pushed them back as far as the Awali River north of the city of Sidon. As the Israelis tried to entrench themselves in the south, popular protests swept through the Shi'ite cities and villages led by activist clerics such as Shaykh Raghib Harb. On 18 April 1983, a huge explosion was detonated inside the US embassy in Beirut resulting in several casualties and severe structural damage. On 23 October, in attacks that inflicted the highest number of US military casualties in one incident since the Vietnam War, the bases of the US Marines and French paratroopers near Beirut airport were bombed simultaneously; 241 American and 58 French soldiers were killed. On 4 December an Israeli military base in the city of Tyre was bombed, killing 29 Israeli soldiers. By this time, there was no longer any doubt that Shi'a Islamists loyal to Khomeini had launched a battle against all foreign troops in Lebanon.

In January 1984, the group signed their first statement as al-Muqa-wamah al-Islamiyyah (Islamic Resistance), indicating their growing confidence and their desire to differentiate themselves from other forces fighting under the banner of nationalism. Within the next two months, only a short time after the group's arrival on the scene, US, British, Italian and French forces withdrew from Lebanon. Grasping the significance of this, Lebanese president Amin Gemayel and his allies annulled the peace treaty with the Zionist state.

By mid 1985, Israeli forces had also been forced to withdraw and abandon their attempts to hold the city of Sidon. The Israelis then announced that they were going to occupy a strip of land inside the southern border of Lebanon that stretched across a thousand square kilometres and was inhabited by a large number of Shi'a Muslims and a smaller number of Christians. The Israelis tried to pretend they had some Lebanese support for this by establishing a mercenary Lebanese militia force who were loyal to Israel inside the southern strip. However, mounting Israeli losses from attacks by the resistance clearly indicated the collapse of Israel's strategy in Lebanon.

On 16 February 1985, the martyrdom of Shaykh Raghib Harb, who had been assassinated by the Israelis the previous year, was commemorated at the Chiyah husayniyyah (a Shi'a centre for worship) in a suburb in south Beirut. During the event, al-Sayyid Ibrahim al-Amin stood before a massive crowd and read out an open letter from Hizbullah. This was the first announcement of the existence of the organisation. The letter indicated that the Islamist forces that had come together in the Beqaa Valley less than two years before had matured and were ready to announce their presence as an independent political and military force. Ever since, Hizbullah has walked a path strewn with danger and challenges that persist to this day.

The statement announcing Hizbullah's existence was written in the fiery language of revolution and resistance, and a sense of global Islamic responsibility. The statement affirmed the group's commitment to purging Lebanon of Western influence and expelling Israel from the country 'as the first steps towards wiping Israel out of existence and liberating Jerusalem'. The organisation made it clear that it regarded Israel as a threat to the future of the Muslim community, and denounced all peace agreements and attempts at negotiations between Israel and Arab countries. The statement also affirmed the need to confront the USA and its allies. Perhaps the most provocative paragraphs in the statement are the lines which define 'Islam as a system of belief and a political order, intellectually and authoritatively', and the invitation it extends 'to all to become familiar with Islam and to seek recourse in the shari'ah'.

Hizbullah's statement created the impression that it was striving to establish another Islamic Republic, this time in Lebanon. In a country inhabited by people of as many religious faiths as is the case in Lebanon, the statement provoked deep fears in many. However, the road ahead for Hizbullah was long and its terminology has since been subject to both minor and major reformulations.

From the start, Hizbullah faced several challenges. It was required to stand firm against Israeli retaliation, while also facing animosity from Lebanon's Amal Movement and Syria's mistrust. The Syrian regime regained much of its influence in Lebanon, and was not particularly comfortable with the Islamists. Hizbullah's allegiance to the Islamist leadership in Iran only increased Syria's reservations. In February 1987, these doubts exploded into an open Syrian offensive against Hizbullah forces in the Fathallah Barracks in the Basta Quarter; twenty-three Hizbullah members were killed.

Attempts by the Amal Movement to liquidate Hizbullah completely were the biggest challenge. Amal was motivated not only by its alliance with Damascus, but also by mounting fear that Hizbullah would undermine its influence over Lebanon's Shi'a population more generally. Amal's war on Hizbullah lasted from early 1988 to the end of 1990, and covered all the areas in which Hizbullah had a presence. In one extended battle, the Amal Movement kept Hizbullah forces under siege in the

Tuffah region for a hundred days. In another episode, members of Amal almost succeeded in assassinating Ibrahim al-Amin, Hizbullah's official spokesperson, as well as their future leader, Hasan Nasrallah. Like all conflict between kin, the fight was bloody and costly, and it almost led to the resistance to the Israeli occupation coming to a standstill.

This all changed in a moment with a dramatic transformation in the global context. In 1990, Syrian president Hafiz al-Asad visited Moscow, Syria's long-time ally. The visit occurred just as the Cold War had ended and the Soviet Union was on the verge of collapse. Gorbachev informed al-Asad that Moscow would no longer be able to assist Syria as it had before, and al-Asad realised that he would have to depend on Syria's own capacities and regional alliances. Al-Asad then visited Iran, paving the way for Hizbullah and Amal to come to an understanding in Lebanon and cementing Syria's longstanding alliance with Hizbullah.

Effectively, Hizbullah emerged victorious from the struggle in Lebanon. Its steadfastness, the faith of its members and its commitment to resist foreign occupation reinforced its popular support. By contrast, corruption and selfishness in the Amal Movement and its leaders contributed to its loss of popular support and the organisation crumbled. From the beginning of the 1990s, Hizbullah was clearly Lebanon's main Shi'a organisation.

By October 1989, the Lebanese civil war officially ended with the signing of the Ta'if Accord, which restructured the Lebanese state. Hizbullah initially rejected the accord, but quickly saw its impact on the situation in Lebanon and affirmed its Lebanese nationalist identity. The Lebanese government disbanded all armed militias in the country by March 1991, but made an exception for Hizbullah, describing it as a resistance movement that was not part of the civil war.

Hizbullah reciprocated by strengthening its relations with the Lebanese authorities and its central figures. With the steady improvement of the internal situation in Lebanon and growing popular support for Hizbullah, activities inside the border strip were escalated to an unprecedented level. The Israeli occupation quickly became extremely costly for the Israelis as Hizbullah maintained pressure on them, showing exceptional capability and commitment.

On 17 February 1992, the Israelis transgressed the unwritten rules of engagement by assassinating Hizbullah's secretary-general al-Sayyid 'Abbas al-Musawi and several members of his family. (Many believe that an explosion that rocked a Jewish Community Centre in Argentina's capital Buenos Aires shortly thereafter was a message from Hizbullah to the Israelis to be wary of breaking these rules of engagement.) Hizbullah then elected Hasan Nasrallah as its new secretary-general. This young and much loved Islamic scholar was popular among the group's cadres as well as its rank and file. Nasrallah was thirty-two years old at the time. He had studied in Najaf and Qom and had held several leadership positions in Hizbullah from its inception. In the years that followed, Nasrallah's charisma and unifying voice ensured his emergence as a major Arab and Islamist figure.

Meanwhile, Hizbullah's attacks continued to inflict casualties on the Israelis on an almost daily basis. The continuous bloodshed provoked sectors of Israeli society, especially the mothers of the soldiers, to call for their withdrawal from South Lebanon. Israeli prime minister Shimon Peres ordered a major attack on Lebanon in March 1996 that proved to be the turning point in the war. The Israelis named their operation 'The Grapes of Wrath', and began shelling Hizbullah positions from land, air and sea. This went on continuously for sixteen days. Hizbullah fighters responded by firing hundreds of rockets at Israel's northern settlements.

On 11 April, the Israelis bombed a UN base in Qana, where hundreds of families from the area had taken shelter. When the bombing stopped, 118 civilians were dead. The massacre provoked global outrage. Western journalists in the area and a subsequent UN report refuted Israeli claims that the UN facility was hit in error. The Israeli government finally realised that it was facing a stubborn and determined foe in Hizbullah, and that its involvement in Lebanon was untenable.

After several rounds of negotiations, in which Syria, France and the US participated, what became known as the April 1996 Accord was reached. According to the accord, the Zionist state and Hizbullah were required to restrict conflict to the border strip and desist from attacking other Lebanese or Israeli-held areas. Although the Israelis did not honour the agreement for long, the April Accord was a major victory for Hizbullah, making it clear to the world that they were a force to be reckoned with, and no longer simply a resistance movement.

In the mid-1980s Hizbullah began establishing organisations for social care, education and infrastructure development.[4] These organisations are still making major contributions to the renewal of Shi'a areas in Lebanon that had suffered prolonged neglect by the Lebanese authorities. In addition, al-Manar television network, which is run by Hizbullah, has a strong influence on public opinion in Lebanon and in the wider Arab region.

Since 1992, Hizbullah has been a significant force in parliament; in fact the election list that Hizbullah put forward in a coalition with the Amal Movement saw all its members win seats in the 2005 parliamentary elections. So, while social and parliamentary participation strengthened Hizbullah's influence, it also made the organisation more sensitive to the complexities of the Lebanese context.

In the meantime, Hizbullah's offensive against Israeli targets in the border strip continued unabated. On 5 September 1997, Hizbullah trapped an Israeli attack unit in the southern al-Ansariyyah region in a deadly ambush. Twelve Israeli soldiers were killed, and the proof this provided of Hizbullah's intelligence-gathering capacity shattered Israeli morale. Israel made two further attempts to force Hizbullah into submission and destroy the support it had among the Lebanese people before being forced to admit defeat. In June 1999 and February 2000, the Israelis targeted Lebanese infrastructure; bombing roads, bridges and power stations. Neither attack broke the resolve of Hizbullah or the Lebanese people; quite the opposite, in fact. In addition, the central

Arab states, including Egypt and Syria, lobbied for support for Lebanon, and openly expressed their support for Hizbullah's struggle.

On 24 April 2000, the Israeli forces withdrew from the border strip, abandoning militia groups who had collaborated with them during their occupation of the territory. The following day, the militias all collapsed and Hizbullah took control of the border strip. Hizbullah's forces showed a level of professionalism and restraint on the day of victory that astonished the world. Their success was a major victory for the Islamists in the Arab and Islamic world. It was also a victory for Iran, which had stood behind Hizbullah throughout the long years of its struggle, as well as for Syria's policy on Lebanon. Undoubtedly, however, Hizbullah's influence was greatest on Palestine, where the intifada began again just five months later.

Hizbullah did not lay down its arms after Israel's withdrawal from the southern strip. It continued to see itself as being in conflict with the Zionist state as long as Israel's occupation of the Lebanese Shebaa Farms region continued. In addition, many within and beyond Lebanon believed that Hizbullah had never abandoned its Islamist aims and saw itself as being closer to Iran in its strategic aims and less as a Lebanese political party.

In 2004, France and the USA collaborated in drawing up UN Security Council Resolution 1559, which called for the withdrawal of Syrian troops from Lebanon and the disarming of all non-governmental militias. The after-effects of the assassination of former Lebanese prime minister Rafic al-Hariri in February 2005 led to Syria's full withdrawal from Lebanon.

Various other political forces then began asking Hizbullah to relinquish its arms in the interests of consolidating unity in Lebanon. Nasrallah instead announced Hizbullah's commitment to holding on to its weapons with all its might. No one doubted that Hizbullah would then face facing major challenges from the Lebanese government and international forces, particularly on the issue of whether or not Hizbullah's true allegiance was to Lebanon. In mid 2006, Hizbullah won another significant victory in the war initiated by Israel against Lebanon, but this was not enough to silence opposition to the organisation, its arms, its allies, and what was seen as its failure to prioritise unity in Lebanon.

❧❧❧❧❧

If Islamist resistance in Afghanistan ended disappointingly, its success in Lebanon surpassed all expectations. For Palestine, however, there seems to be no end to the conflict. In and around Jerusalem, one of the longest and most complex conflicts in the modern world continues unabated. Islam has been ever-present in the conflict over Palestine. Jerusalem occupies an extremely important position in the Islamic faith and culture, and this has played a huge role in Arab and Islamic support for Palestine.

From the 1930s to the end of the 1950s, the Palestinian national movement was led by a religious figure, al-Haj Amin al-Husayni. Al-Husayni had strong links with the Muslim Brotherhood in Egypt and always affirmed the Islamic dimension of the Palestinian question. In the 1937 Arab–Israeli War, droves of Muslim Brotherhood volunteers from Egypt, Jordan and Syria flooded into Palestine to fight alongside the Arab armies.

Organised Brotherhood activity in the Palestinian sphere goes back to the mid-1940s. However, the Palestinian Nakbah in 1948 caused a split within Palestine's Muslim Brotherhood, between members in the West Bank (which became a part of Jordan), those in the Gaza Strip (which was initially under Egyptian administration), and those from several other regions from which Palestinians were forced to flee. For a long time, the activities of the Brotherhood in the Gaza Strip were repressed, mainly due to the Nasser administration's enmity towards it, while the Jordanian Brotherhood was generally supportive of the policies of the Jordanian authorities.

In 1957, the leaders of the Brotherhood in the Gaza Strip rejected a proposal by some of its members to take up arms against Israel.[5] The

Brotherhood's leaders argued that the circumstances were not right for such action, while the group proposing armed struggle argued that that this was the only sensible strategy. Among the most prominent members of this group were Khalil al-Wazir (Abu Jihad), Salah Khalaf (Abu Iyad), Muhammad Yusuf al-Najjar (Abu Yusuf) and Kamal 'Udwan. These men, along with Yasser Arafat and others, decided to form Fatah. Fatah presented itself as a national liberation movement with no specific ideological bent, but its early roots were dyed with an Islamist hue that remained fast for many years.

Israel occupied the West Bank and the Gaza Strip after the Arab defeat of 1967. Again, members of the Muslim Brotherhood from various Arab countries rushed to join the guerrilla forces, this time under the banner of Fatah, which initially established a base for Islamists in Jordan. In the Occupied Palestinian Territory, and in the Arab region more generally, the late 1960s marked the beginning of Islamist resurgence.

Ahmad Yasin, a refugee from the village of al-Jurah who moved to Gaza city, played a pivotal role in rebuilding the Palestinian Brotherhood's structures and opening its doors to a new generation of students and professionals. In the coming years, this primary school teacher who was afflicted by severe paralysis displayed a rare commitment and dedication to working and organising.

From the mid-1970s, Fatah and other Palestinian forces were deeply involved in the Lebanese civil war which diluted their focus on the Occupied Palestinian Territory. For their part, the Israelis hoped (for a while) that opening up some space for the Islamists might weaken the PLO in the West Bank and the Gaza Strip. This meant that when the first intifada broke out in December 1987, Islamists in the Gaza and West Bank were best placed to lead the mass movement.

The first intifada broke out under conditions of palpable Palestinian nationalist decline. For the previous two decades, people in the West Bank and Gaza Strip had endured the Israeli's heavy-handed occupation. The expulsion of the PLO from Lebanon and the resettlement of their leadership in Tunisia had drastically weakened their relationship with the people of the West Bank and Gaza.

In the years following the PLO's expulsion from Lebanon, Yasser Arafat tried to forge an alliance with Jordan. However, the Palestinian–Jordanian Agreement did not survive more than a year. Similarly, leaders at the Arab League Summit in Amman in 1987 were more concerned with the Iran–Iraq War and sidelined the Palestinian question. Palestinians in the West Bank and Gaza lost hope of any serious Arab intervention on their behalf when an Israeli settler used his vehicle to attack a group of Palestinian labourers in the crowded city of Jabari in the Gaza Strip. Palestinians in the West Bank and Gaza Strip decided to confront the occupation with their bare hands and take control of their destiny themselves, and the demonstrations protesting against this incident continued for the next six years in what became one of the most important episodes in the Palestinian struggle.

Palestinian nationalism emerged in an organised way, via an initiative introduced by Fatah under the banner of the United National Leadership of the Intifada. Khalil al-Wazir (Abu Jihad), a member of Fatah's central committee, was put in charge of this initiative. However, a widespread Islamic Awakening occurred in the Occupied Territory in the 1980s, and the Islamists proved that they too were a force to be reckoned with. Over thirteen-hundred mosques sprang up in the West Bank and Gaza; Islamist students in Palestinian universities were the most active and energetic; and most branches of the Palestinian Muslim Brotherhood in the Occupied Territory and in exile engaged in constant dialogue about the national question. Alongside the active mobilisation of the group known as the Islamic Jihad, Ahmad Yasin and a small group of Muslim Brotherhood leaders in the Gaza Strip took the initiative and established the Islamic Resistance Movement, better known as Hamas, just a few weeks after the intifada began.[6] In the following year, Hamas spread to the West Bank and, with the Muslim Brotherhood adding its support to the intifada, the Islamists became a central factor in the Palestinian national equation.

209

The first intifada ended with the signing of the first Oslo Accord between the leaders of the PLO and Israel in 1993. This vague and highly contested agreement included the establishment of a self-governing Palestinian Authority in specific areas of the West Bank and Gaza Strip.

The Islamists, who had begun to engage in armed resistance since the beginning of the 1990s, rejected the Oslo Accord, but they also avoided confronting the Palestinian Authority once this was established, continuing to focus their operations on the Israelis. The Israelis responded with an assassination campaign targeted at the Islamist leaders. In June 1995, the Israelis assassinated Mahmud al-Khawajah in Gaza City; he was the military leader of the Islamic Jihad. In October 1995, they assassinated Fathi Shiqaqi, the founder and leader of the Islamic Jihad movement. He was killed on the island of Malta, where he had stopped over after visiting Muammar Gaddafi in Libya to try to convince him to allow Palestinians to return to that country. A few months later, the Israelis killed Yahya 'Ayyash, Hamas's military leader. In retaliation, Hamas and the Islamic Jihad began a widespread bombing campaign against Israeli military and civilian targets.

The Palestinian Authority wasted no time in trying to talk to the two Islamist organisations, but instead clamped down on them heavily. Its Preventive Security Force arrested an unprecedented number of people in the Gaza Strip, and to avoid internal clashes, the Islamists suspended almost all of their military activities.

Over the next few years, the Palestinian Authority strengthened its influence in the West Bank and Gaza Strip. However, the implementation of the Oslo Accord was proceeding very slowly. The Israelis delayed the process at every opportunity, while rapidly expanding their settlements in the West Bank.

In 2000, two incidents had a tremendous impact on the Palestinian issue. In the early part of the year, the Israelis admitted their defeat at the hands of Hizbullah and withdrew from South Lebanon. A few months later, the negotiations at Camp David between Palestinian President

Yasser Arafat and Israeli Prime Minister Ehud Barak, at the invitation of US president Bill Clinton, failed miserably. At the end of September that year, the second intifada broke out in response to a provocative visit by the right-wing Israeli leader Ariel Sharon to al-Aqsa Mosque.

The second intifada was initially characterised by peaceful civil disobedience but the Israeli response was so violent and bloody that hundreds of youth and children were killed. Soon, the Palestinians took up arms once more. Again, Hamas and the Islamic Jihad stood out as the most effective Palestinian forces, both peaceful and military. In fact Hamas proved that it had become a popular force that was able to compete with Fatah, which had led the Palestinian Liberation Organisation since the late 1960s. Despite these internal realignments, the second intifada was characterised by widespread consensus among all Palestinians. Arafat supported the uprising and was subjected to a prolonged siege at his headquarters in Ramallah, while members of Fatah *and* the Palestinian Authority actively participated in the intifada.

In the second and third years of the intifada, Islamist groups carried out military operations that struck at the heart of Israel; there is also no doubt that most of these operations targeted Israeli civilians. Although many Palestinians saw this as a legitimate response to the random killing of Palestinian civilians, the attacks provoked widespread debate in Palestine and in the diaspora.

The 9/11 attacks gave Israel a golden opportunity to depict the Palestinian resistance as part of the den of terrorist forces who were bent on spreading fear and conflict worldwide.

The second intifada was tremendously costly for Palestinians generally, but especially for the Islamists, and particularly for Hamas. The Israelis killed thousands of Palestinians, trashed infrastructure in Palestinian cities, destroyed thousands of hectares of arable Palestinian land, and threw thousands of young Palestinians into Israeli prisons.

In addition, several Hamas leaders were assassinated. In March 2004, Israeli warplanes fired missiles at Hamas's founder and leader,

Ahmad Yasin who was in his wheelchair at a mosque near his home for early morning prayers. A few weeks later, the Israelis assassinated 'Abd al-'Aziz al-Rantisi, who had just replaced Yasin as Hamas's leader, and was a prominent person in his own right. Hamas, like all of the Palestinians in the West Bank and Gaza Strip, once again proved their phenomenal capacity to absorb and transcend these setbacks.

Mahmoud Abbas (Abu Mazen) took over the presidency of the PLO and the Palestinian Authority after Arafat's mysterious death in November 2004. The Islamists strove to strengthen their relationship with Abbas, despite his inclinations towards negotiations and his opposition to armed struggle. The Islamists presented Abbas with 'conducive conditions' when they agreed to suspend armed attacks on Israelis, and allow progress to be made with negotiations. The growing closeness between Hamas and Islamic Jihad on the one hand and the leadership of the Palestinian Authority on the other revealed the development of a pragmatic outlook among the Islamists. In spite of their deeply held view that that the Palestinian, Islamic and Arab right to Palestine cannot be divided, and their rejection of the legitimacy of Israel, the Palestinian Islamists began to see complete liberation as a long-term project.

As far back as October 1991, Hamas announced its general acceptance of the idea of a phased solution to the Palestinian question, based on the establishment of a state on the Palestinian land occupied in 1967. The Islamic Jihad in turn announced its acceptance of a Palestinian state, established on any land from which the Israelis withdrew, without making any concessions regarding Palestinian rights.

From the beginning of 2005, Hamas indicated its willingness to participate in municipal and parliamentary elections held by the Palestinian Authority, and their results at the municipal level showed that Hamas had as much if not a bit more popular support than Fatah. This led to increased tensions within the Palestinian community but also indicated that Palestinians were beginning to question whether it was best for Fatah to control both the PLO and the Palestinian Authority. This was even clearer when Hamas won a decisive majority in the Palestinian parliamentary elections in January 2006. By supporting Hamas in this way, Palestinians effected what amounted to a strategic coup, and affirmed that Palestinian politics was aligned with the transformations taking place in the majority of Arab and Islamic countries.[7]

However, the EU, the USA and several Arab nations responded to Hamas's election victory, and its formation of a Palestinian government, by introducing an intensely punishing blockade. In addition, an influential bloc within the Palestinian Authority persisted in trying to undermine and unseat Hamas. By middle of 2007, tensions exploded, resulting in Hamas taking full control over the Gaza Strip, while the West Bank remained under the Palestinian Authority and Mahmoud Abbas. This new phase was followed by attempts at reconciliation and the rebuilding of unity, and the US tried to initiate a new round of negotiations to try to bring about a settlement between the Palestinians and the Israelis.

❧❦❧

Islamists involved in various resistance movements have strengthened the influence of political Islam throughout the world. However, resisting foreign invasion, no matter how legitimate this resistance might be, is never enough on its own to transcend divisions and the pluralism of contemporary Islamic societies. Afghanistan, Lebanon and Palestine are all characterised by political, ethnic and sectarian diversity with the potential to devolve into destructive political divisiveness.

The Afghani mujahidin and their Taliban successors never succeeded in building national consensus and dragged their country into a civil war that was aggravated by the US occupation. Hizbullah has shown signs of taking Lebanese pluralism very seriously, but the success of its co-existence with other forces faced huge challenges and questions after the assassination of Rafic al-Hariri. As for Palestine, there is no doubt that Fatah lost much of its support after signing the Oslo Accords, and this led to the collapse of internal consensus among Palestinians. It will be very difficult for the Islamists, and specifically Hamas, to make further progress until they can secure some level of national consensus once more.

13

The Islamist military coup

*O*n the morning of 30 June 1989, residents in the Sudanese capital Khartoum awoke to find their country's history had taken a new turn, and an unknown group of military officers had seized control of the government. This was not the first military coup in Khartoum. In fact, since Sudan's independence, the country had been under military rule more often than not.

The 1989 coup wasn't really a surprise. Khartoum had been awash with rumours of an imminent military take over for at least a month. In truth, however, the coup of 1989 was of a very different variety. This was the first military coup in any Arab or Islamic country in which Islamist officers succeeded in seizing power and taking control of the state.

The leader of the coup was a middle-ranking officer named Omar Hassan al-Bashir, and he became the head of the military council that assumed control of the country. However, the de facto leader of the new administration, and the inspiration and point of reference behind the revolutionary officers was Hasan al-Turabi, a prominent contemporary Islamist thinker and the secretary-general of Sudan's al-Jabhah al-Qa-wmiyyah al-Islamiyyah (National Islamic Front). Behind the coup lies a long story about the Islamist movement and its attempts to come to terms with political and social changes in a country of many ethnicities and faiths. After the coup, another story began that has mainly been about internal crises and turmoil.

Modern Sudan was born in the shadow of British colonialism but Islam has played a central role in Sudan's political edifice since its inception. From as early as the nineteenth century, two Sufi Orders, the Mahdiyyah and the Khatmiyyah, provided cultural and political frames of reference for the majority of the country's Muslim population. However, in the twentieth century, modern education with its new intellectual and political trends, swept through Sudan just as it did many other Islamic countries. Sudan had been part of Egypt for much of the nineteenth century, so the Sudanese people had strong links with their northern neighbours. At the beginning of the twentieth century, the prominent reformist Muhammad 'Abduh visited Sudan and Mustafa al-Maraghi, one of 'Abduh's best-known students, served as head of the judiciary in Sudan for many years. It was therefore no surprise when some of Sudan's more educated Muslims led an Islamic reformist rebellion that was directed mainly at the strongly influential Sufi orders.

By the late 1940s, the ideas propagated by the Muslim Brotherhood began to take root within Sudan's newly educated classes. However, the Muslim Brotherhood, as such, did not take shape in Sudan until the late 1950s. It was in August 1954 that various Sudanese Islamist groups agreed to adopt the name Muslim Brotherhood at a gathering that became known as the 'Eid Conference.[1] Agreement was not easily reached however. At that time, Sudan was caught up in a strong wave of sentiment calling for independence from Egypt, and this affected Sudanese Islamists too. Some participants at the conference were unwilling to be linked with the Egyptian Muslim Brotherhood and chose to break away and form an independent Islamist group instead. In fact, relations between the Sudanese Islamists and the Muslim Brotherhood in Egypt remained tenuous until the end of the 1970s when matters between them were finally resolved.

Sudan achieved independence in 1956. Three forces have jockeyed for power ever since: the Ummah Party (which is linked to the Mahdiyyah Sufi Order), the Ittihadiyyah (Unionist Party) (which represents the Khatamiyyah Sufi Order) and the army.

In November 1958, Sudan's first attempt at democracy was crushed when General Ibrahim 'Abboud seized power. In general, the Muslim Brotherhood supports democracy, but on this occasion the Sudanese Brotherhood did not condemn the coup. One of the reasons for this was their hope that military rule would help to rid the country of corruption and chaos. Another reason was that everyone was aware that the army had made its move with the agreement of key political players, or at the very least, with the agreement of the Ummah Party. In any event, the Brotherhood had little influence and carried weight only among a small group of teachers in the capital.

The Brotherhood began to express some misgivings about military rule when 'Abboud shut down the media and closed all political-party offices, as well as the Omdurman Club, which was an Islamist centre. In November 1959, the leader of the Brotherhood al-Rashid al-Tahir made another coup attempt, which he had planned without the knowledge of his organisation. The coup failed, al-Tahir was sentenced to five years in prison, and the ranks of the Brotherhood were divided as they argued about the actions taken by their leader.

For the next few years the Brotherhood desisted from any political activity, and the military regime slowly began to collapse of its own accord. In 1962, fresh energy was pumped into the Brotherhood when Hasan al-Turabi returned to the country from abroad.

Turabi had been part of the Islamist student circles that spawned the Sudanese Muslim Brotherhood since the early 1950s. When he completed his legal studies at Khartoum University in 1955, he left for London where he earned a master's degree. On his return to Egypt in 1957, he was elected onto the Muslim Brotherhood's executive council. However, his influence at this stage was limited, and he soon moved to Paris to enrol for a doctorate. Since his youth, Turabi had always shone academically; he was extremely intelligent and constantly exploring new vistas.

The combination of his years of studying the Islamic Sciences with his studies in the West made him very independent and reform-minded. On his return from Paris in 1962, the first suggestion he put to the Brotherhood's constitutional council reflected the free-thinking inclinations, which he carried with him on the long road that lay ahead. In brief, Turabi called for transforming the Brotherhood from a party into an organisation similar to that which then formed the intellectual and political base of the British Labour Party. Turabi's aim was to liberate the reformist Islamist views of the Brotherhood from the shackles of party-political thinking. When his suggestion was rejected, Turabi put forward a memorandum, calling on the Brotherhood to engage in coalitions with other political forces to rid Sudan of military rule.

By 1963, the situation in the country had deteriorated dramatically. 'Abboud's regime was fighting an extremely costly and losing battle against rebels in southern Sudan. The country was overflowing with pamphlets calling for an end to military rule. A wave of university unrest, led by the student union, which was controlled by the Brotherhood, swept through some areas but was not strong enough to overthrow the regime.

In mid-1964, Turabi resolved to remain in Sudan for good and was appointed as a university professor. In September of that year, which marked the beginning of the new academic year, Turabi delivered a lecture to the university's Social Sciences Society, in which he stated that the problem of south Sudan was a constitutional one, and that military rule violated the freedoms of all Sudanese, in both the north and south. The lecture provoked widespread response in Khartoum and the regime attempted to ban discussion about the topics Turabi had raised. University students took to the streets again in a series of demonstrations, in which students who were Brotherhood members played a central role. Turabi emerged as a popular leader who participated alongside the students in the uprising, even transporting students who had been injured in clashes with the security forces to hospital in his own car.

On 30 October 1964, the military regime collapsed and power was handed over to a coalition government headed by Khatim al-Khalifah. A single minister represented the Muslim Brotherhood in the ruling coalition. At the end of November in the same year, the Brotherhood's consultative assembly elected Turabi as their general-secretary. In April 1965, the Brotherhood stood in the Sudanese elections with its young leader at the helm under the name of the Jabhah al-Mithaq al-Islami (Islamic Covenant Front). The Front, of which the Brotherhood formed the core, was an attempt by Turabi to draw more people into the Islamist circle. The Covenant Front's election manifesto had a strongly social democratic orientation. It called for the implementation of the shari'ah, the granting of civil liberties, the separation of the powers of the state, and social justice. This was a Turabi programme par excellence – integrating his Islamic commitment and the influence of European political policies.

The Covenant Front won less than 6 per cent of the vote, and just seven parliamentary seats. Most of its support came from city wards, specifically those inhabited by university graduates, illustrating its limited popular support base. Over the next few years, the Front was preoccupied with the struggle to affirm an Islamic constitution for Sudan, and trying to limit the influence of the Sudanese Communist Party at a time in which the left was in ascendance in the Arab World and elsewhere.

Meanwhile, Turabi continued trying to push the Sudanese Brotherhood into the broader political sphere, in the face of strong opposition from its more traditional members. In April 1969, the general congress was held, and a strong bloc emerged which accused Turabi of abandoning the values of Islamic education that are central to the Brotherhood. The bloc was led by Ja'far al-Shaykh Idris and Muhammad Salih 'Umar, both of whom were strongly influenced by the ideas and writings of Sayyid Qutb. Turabi managed to overcome his detractors, however, and actually strengthened his support within the Brotherhood.[2]

In May 1969, with the failure of the traditional political parties to administer the state, and the democratic process descending into chaos,

Sudan was subjected to another military coup. This time, Colonel Ja'far al-Numayri – together with a group of communist officers – seized power. Initially, the leaders of the political parties cautiously supported the coup, but quickly changed their minds when Numayri's intentions to monopolise power and establish military rule became clear.

Numayri's regime was openly hostile towards the Brotherhood, which reciprocated by accusing the new prime minister of trying to turn Sudan into a communist country. A faction within the Brotherhood then played an important role in encouraging al-Hadi al-Mahdi, the leader of the Mahdiyyah Order, to initiate an armed rebellion against the regime. In March 1970, rebels opposed to Numayri's rule staged a sit-in on Aba Island, a stronghold of the Mahdiyyah. This grossly imbalanced confrontation ended in the massacre of al-Hadi al-Mahdi and many of his supporters, as well as the death of Brotherhood leader Muhammad Salih 'Umar.

Despite the fact that Turabi had played no role in the rebellion or the sit-in at all, he was arrested and spent most of the 1970s in prison. Other members of the Brotherhood went into exile where they joined forces with the Ummah Party and the Democratic Unionist Party to form the National Front, which tried to mobilise against Numayri. The leaders of the National Front conducted most of their activities from exile.

The National Front received considerable support from Saudi Arabia and Libya, both of which were opposed to Numayri's rule. The Front was given an opportunity to set up military training camps in Libya for its members. In 1976, the National Front attempted to get rid of Numayri by a launching a military attack on the regime from outside Sudan. The attempt failed but, in the following year, the leaders of the National Front initiated talks with Numayri. At first it seemed that the three parties within the National Front had reached an agreement with Numayri, but then al-Sadiq al-Mahdi, the leader of the Ummah Party, and al-Sharif al-Hindi, the leader of the Democratic Unionist Party, withdrew from the agreement. This left only the Muslim Brotherhood, who then agreed to disband and fall in under the banner of Numayri's al-Ittihad al-Ishtiraki (Sudanese Socialist Union), thus leaving Sudan a one-party state.

The decision of the Sudanese Brotherhood and its political party to merge with the Numayri regime provoked astonishment among huge numbers of Islamists in the Arab world who saw themselves as different from the ruling regimes and saw merging with them as inconceivable. Turabi immediately defended his policies of reconciliation and integration, and the Sudanese Brotherhood soon cut their spiritual ties with the wider Muslim Brotherhood, effectively becoming more free-thinking and independent.

Nonetheless, Turabi proceeded with the reconciliation process with his eyes wide open. He set himself the goal of Islamising the regime from within, thus making the announcement of the disbandment of the Brotherhood little more than a ruse. In addition, the Sudanese Brotherhood maintained their organisational structure inside and outside the country, in case their project of Islamising the regime were to fail.

Turabi became a member of the political bureau, the highest authority within the Socialist Union party, and he served as the party's deputy secretary-general. In a famous turnaround in 1983, Numayri announced a series of laws aimed at the Islamisation of governance in Sudan, but this revolved mainly around the implementation of Islamic penal codes for the punishment of criminals. The penal code was implemented poorly. For example, poor people had their hands chopped off for stealing and, in January 1985, Mahmud Muhammad Taha, the leader of the controversial al-Hizb al-Jumhuri al-Islami (Islamic Republican Party) was executed for apostasy.

Because the Islamisation project was linked to Turabi and the Brotherhood's influence in the regime, the Brotherhood was accused of using its position to get rid of its opponents and of pushing Numayri to implement the shari'ah in irrational ways. In truth, Numayri was an autocrat who was using the Brotherhood to add a level of legitimacy to his regime. The crude ways in which he implemented the shari'ah revealed that he was only using the penal code to try to entrench forms of governance that had long been corrupt. Thus, in 1985, when Numayri sensed that the Brotherhood's influence within government might threaten his absolute authority, he clamped down on them mercilessly. A few weeks after Mahmud Taha had been executed, Turabi was arrested and thrown into prison. When the popular revolution broke out in April 1985, Numayri was on the verge of executing Turabi as well. Despite their pretence at Islamisation, Numayri and his regime had reached the end of the road. Sudan was suffering from drought and starvation, the war with the south had been reignited, and the extent of government corruption was a disgrace.

In some ways, Numayri's decision to incarcerate Turabi and attack other members of the Brotherhood did them a great service. When the popular revolution had brought down Numayri's regime, Turabi was in prison and Brotherhood members were seen as victims of the regime, even though they had recently been its allies. The Brotherhood undoubtedly grew stronger and bigger through this time. In Khartoum, Brotherhood members held important positions in the economy, especially in the Islamic banks that Numayri had allowed to operate. The Brotherhood had also become a significant force among the educated class and, due to Turabi's persistent efforts to open the public sphere to women, the organisation had become the primary arena for Sudanese women activists.

The year after Numayri's fall, Turabi launched al-Jabhah al-Islamiyyah al-Qawmiyyah (Nationalist Islamic Front). In so doing, Turabi wanted to permanently dispel the idea of exclusivity and the notion that any single Islamic organisation could be the sole or highest representative of Islam. Within a short time, he had succeeded in widening the Front to include the Sufi orders, various independent Islamists, and some tribal leaders. For the first time since independence, political Islam became a popular trend. This unique development was reflected in the results of the only elections to be held after the collapse of the Numayri regime, in which the Nationalist Islamic Front won fifty-one seats.

This made the Front one of three central forces in the 1988 parliament, allowing it to share power within a coalition government led by al-Sadiq al-Mahdi. However, at the beginning of the following year, the deteriorating position of the army in the war with the south led to the collapse of the new government. Sudan's third experience of democracy became a platform for regional and international interference, while the country deteriorated economically due to the civil war. When al-Sadiq al-Mahdi began taking steps to include the Nationalist Islamic Front in a new coalition government in March 1989, rumours began circulating in Khartoum that influential Arab countries had ordered him to exclude the Front from the new government. By June, the possibility of military collapse and of the southern rebels reaching Khartoum seemed set to become a reality. The country seemed overcome by a strong sense that the politicians had failed them and another military coup seemed imminent.

When Islamist officers succeeded in seizing power in June 1989 it was unclear to observers both inside and outside of Sudan whether or not they had any relationship with the Nationalist Islamic Front. Omar al-Bashir, the coup leader, came from a family that was well-known for its allegiance to the Khatamiyyah Sufi Order. The fact that the order is strong in Egypt led many to assume that the coup leaders had links with Cairo. The revolutionary officers quickly arrested Turabi and several other political figures. However, it has since emerged that the coup was initiated by the Nationalist Islamic Front, and that Turabi's arrest was pre-arranged to avoid tinting the new state with an Islamist hue until such time as the new rulers had secured control of the country. This political deception managed to fool Washington and most of the key Arab regimes including Egypt and Saudi Arabia. When the truth was revealed, all the major Arab regimes' trust in the Islamist revolutionaries collapsed.

It is not easy to discern Turabi's position on the coup. Throughout his life, he expressed his faith in people and his belief that they are the mainstay of Islam and the determinants of its fate. With the exception of his short reconciliation with Numayri's regime, Turabi always opposed military rule. Some say he was unenthusiastic about the idea of a military coup, and that, soon after its success, he tried to insist that the regime give up its military character. However, others say that no coup by officers linked to the Nationalist Islamic Front could have been undertaken without Turabi's blessing and involvement in its planning. His control over decision-making in the Front at that time was absolute and the loyalty of its leaders was unquestionable. Either way, members of the Front upheld military rule in Sudan and were allocated several leadership positions in government, which they continued to occupy for many years after the coup.

The coup leaders referred to their rule as 'the Salvation Revolution' by which they meant that they intended to save Sudan from chaos and corruption as well as from civil war with the south. However, the salvation project ended in disaster – for the Sudanese Islamists, for Sudan as an independent state, and for all of the various communities in Sudan. The coup leaders disbanded parliament and all the political parties, and handed legislative authority over to the Military Council. In the first few months, they maintained strong links with the leaders of the Nationalist Islamic Front, especially with Turabi's deputy, 'Ali 'Uthman Taha, who directed the new dispensation while Turabi was 'in prison' for six months. The coup leaders then turned their attention to the army, removing any officers who might be opposed to their rule. Then, while calling for a national convention to draw up a vision for peace in the south, they launched a major military offensive against southern rebel groups and put a lot of effort and resources into reorganising and strengthening the Sudanese army. In the second year of salvation rule, the Islamists, both officers and Front leaders, made it clear that they intended to hold on to power and rebuild the entire political edifice in

Sudan. Turabi was released from prison, and the regime's Islamist hue become much more evident.

In April 1990, twenty-eight officers, most of whom belonged to the Ba'th Party, were executed for attempting to overthrow the salvation government. The cruelty with which the Ba'thist coup attempt was dealt with drew widespread condemnation. The authorities then explained that they were attempting to establish a political system based on 'people's congresses' rather than a multi-party system. The congresses sought to establish a single political structure called the National Congress, which would function as the ruling party.

While the idea of 'people's congresses' was borrowed from Libya's Muammar Gaddafi, it was no secret that introducing them to Sudan was Turabi's idea. Essentially, the Nationalist Islamic Front was absorbed into and controlled all the most important aspects of the National Congress. In this way, intellectually, organisationally and in terms of the beliefs of its leaders, the Salvation government had become an Islamic government. The problem was that no other political organisations in Sudan were willing to submit to its rule, nor was it able to bring about peace in the south.

During the Kuwaiti crisis in 1990 and 1991, things became far more complicated. Sudan refused to join the Washington-allied Arab bloc against Iraq. This aroused the hostility of Washington and most of the Arab states, including Egypt and Saudi Arabia. In May 1991, Turabi hosted a huge public Arab-Islamic gathering in Khartoum, to which he invited a large number of Arab and Islamist forces who were opposed to US policies in the Middle East. The gathering gave birth to an organisation called al-Mu'tamar al-Sha'bi al-'Arabi al-Islami (Popular Arab and Islamic Congress) and Turabi was elected as its secretary-general.

From this, it was clear that Turabi was striving not only to rebuild Sudan, but also to transform it into a vanguard of a popular liberation movement in the Arab and Islamic region. Not surprisingly, regional and international hostility towards Sudan and its government escalated swiftly. In the 1990s, Sudan's neighbouring countries, from Egypt to Uganda to Kenya and Eritrea, became safe havens for groups from both northern and southern Sudan who were opposed to the Salvation government. This situation was exacerbated by ongoing human and material losses in the south.

The Salvation government tried to deal with its growing isolation in several ways. In 1992, Khartoum concluded an agreement with several southern leaders who had broken away from John Garang, in which, for the first time, the right of southerners to determine their own destiny was acknowledged. In 1994, the government handed over the international leftist terrorist known as Carlos to the French authorities so that he could be tried for crimes committed in France. In 1996, Osama Bin Laden – the most prominent Saudi dissident at the time – was asked to leave Sudan (in fact Sudan even offered to hand him over to the Saudis). However, none of these steps really helped to improve the regime's national, regional or international standing.

In public, a group of Islamist youth linked to the regime began to try to implement a paradigm of governance that would return power and wealth back to the people. Attempts were initiated to revive the endowment sector, and to transform popular congresses into centres for effective decision-making. Behind the scenes, however, the country's security apparatus was expanded more and more. In an atmosphere of utter crisis, sectors within the regime began blaming each other for the country's terrible deterioration.

Finally, an incident occurred that broke the camel's back. In June 1995, Egyptian president Hosni Mubarak narrowly escaped assassination in the Ethiopian capital of Addis Ababa. The perpetrators were Egyptians – members of al-Jama'ah al-Islamiyyah (the Islamic Group) who had fled from Egypt. However, they were reportedly assisted and supported by an official from one of Sudan's security apparatuses.

In a stormy meeting of Salvation government leaders, Turabi exposed the prominent Sudanese official who had been involved in the assassination attempt. Turabi clearly understood the embarrassing international and legal consequences of such action. He apparently exploded with anger at his colleagues and distanced himself from the operation and its planners. The Salvation Government denied any involvement in the assassination attempt but this did not prevent international condemnation of Sudan by the United Nations Security Council.

Among the Sudanese leaders, various camps emerged, with those involved in the assassination simply redirecting Egypt and the international community's accusations towards Turabi himself. From the late 1990s, Turabi began to acknowledge the burden that military rule had placed on his country and the utter failure of the regime to administer Sudan's affairs. He became more willing than ever to reach a negotiated settlement with the south and to revert to a system of political pluralism.

In 1996, Turabi was elected as the head of the National Council, which represented the legislative authority of government. For the next few years he worked hard to get the Council to enact a new constitution affirming political pluralism. In May 1999, Turabi met with the leader of the Ummah Party al-Sadiq al-Mahdi in Geneva, to try to convince him to return to Sudan and to withdraw from the opposition coalition. He then took similar steps in relation to the Khatamiyyah Order by sending a personal letter to their leader.

Certain sectors within the regime feared being marginalised by Turabi's moves to institutionalise political pluralism so they turned against their former leader. 'Ali 'Uthman Taha, Turabi's former student, emerged as the main player in a plan to get rid of his teacher. In the last months of 1999, several Islamist leaders drafted a memorandum calling for al-Bashir to take over the leadership of the Islamic Movement and for Turabi's influence to be curbed. Taha was not one of the signatories, but no one doubted that he was behind the initiative. A few weeks later, elections for the general secretariat of the ruling National Congress Party were held, but Taha and all of those who signed the memorandum failed to get elected. From this, it was clear that Turabi's support was strong within the National Council, while his former students had more influence in several state institutions and the army.

As soon as the National Council, led by Turabi, began the process of amending the constitution, al-Bashir issued a resolution disbanding the Council. A few months later, he issued a resolution to disband the general secretariat of the National Congress Party. With al-Bashir's bias in favour of the group that had broken away from Turabi out in the open, the implosion of the Salvation government was complete. Turabi joined the ranks of the opposition, with which he had much experience, but this time he stood in opposition to rulers who were his former students. In mid 2000, Turabi and his supporters announced the establishment of the Hizb al-Mu'tamar al-Sha'bi (Popular Congress Party). This sparked further divisions between former Islamist comrades, family members and lifelong friends.

The state's ruling faction appointed Ibrahim Ahmad 'Umar, a prominent Sudanese Islamist intellectual and a former comrade of Turabi, to head the National Congress Party. However, al-Bashir, 'Ali Taha, and Ibrahim 'Umar had little confidence in their ability to curtail Turabi's influence or match his political acumen. In fact, they were not even convinced that they could rely on those Islamists who had continued to work with them in state structures. The country was again riddled with tension, when Turabi surprised everyone, making one of the most pragmatic moves of his life.

On 19 February 2001, Mahbub 'Abd al-Salam, one of Turabi's aides, went to Geneva to sign a preliminary understanding with a delegation from the Sudan People's Liberation Movement (SPLM), which was led by John Garang and included Yasir 'Arman and Pagan Amum. Throughout the 1990s, Garang and Turabi had been on opposite poles in the bloody struggle for Sudan. The preliminary understanding that was signed indicated that Turabi was serious about reaching a negotiated settlement, and more importantly, that he was trying to establish an alliance between the Popular Congress and the SPLM.

Such an alliance, if it came about, would have fundamentally re-drawn Sudan's political map – a fact that al-Bashir and 'Ali Taha understood all too well. Three days after the signing of the understanding, Turabi and the entire leadership committee of the Popular Congress Party who were in Sudan at the time were arrested. The Sudanese people were flabbergasted as they watched the Islamists of the Salvation government arresting their former mentor. An Arab commentator wittily noted that history is replete with revolutions that devour their children, but that in Sudan the revolution was devouring its shaykh. Turabi was incarcerated for several months under extremely poor conditions and the ruling elite rejected all efforts by Arab and Islamic intercessors outside of Sudan to bring about some kind of reconciliation and secure his release.

With Turabi's arrest the Salvation government painted themselves into a corner, and were left with only two options: to abandon power to a coalition government that would lead Sudan back to political pluralism, or to respond to international pressure for negotiations with the south. The ruling elites chose the second option. Turabi's arrest was presented as a down payment towards improved relations with Cairo, Riyadh and Washington, and negotiations between the government and the SPLM began in earnest.

Unfortunately, just as the Geneva understanding between Turabi and Garang was about putting partisan political interests before those of the country as a whole, the negotiations between 'Ali Taha and Garang were motivated by self-interest. What the ruling regime was aiming to do was to reach an agreement with Garang that would prevent him from forming any kind of alliance with Turabi. Garang, who, up to this point, had been the regime's most wanted man, and hounded by the Islamists using all possible means, was suddenly seen as a most desirable ally by Sudan's Islamist factions.

In July 2002, the Sudanese government and the SPLM signed the Machakos Protocol under US mediation. The protocol established a framework for negotiating a comprehensive peace settlement with the south. The negotiations continued for the next two-and-a-half years under American patronage, with the direct participation of John Garang and 'Ali 'Uthman Taha, in his capacity as deputy president.

The Sudanese government not only followed Turabi's example in dealing with Garang, they also undertook similar discussions with opposition political parties in the north. A few months after the signing of the Machakos Protocol, Khartoum agreed to allow al-Sadiq al-Mahdi and another political figure, Muhammad 'Uthman al-Mirghani, to return home from exile. In October 2003, when the government was satisfied with the progress it had made in improving its regional and international relationships and resuming control over the internal political process, Turabi was released from prison.

The ruling Islamist group appeared relatively secure in Khartoum, but the situation in the rest of the country continued to deteriorate. The people in the province of Darfur province seemed to see in Khartoum's agreement with the south that resorting to force was the only way to get the government to grant their rights. In 2003 two groups in Darfur took up arms and initiated a series of guerrilla attacks on regime forces, demanding that the government recognise the rights of the province's non-Arab population. The leaders of one of these groups were Islamists and former allies of Turabi. For his part, Turabi did not hide his sympathies for the people of Darfur, and in 2004, he was accused of conspiring with the rebels of Darfur and incarcerated once more. The turmoil in Darfur was just one of the reasons for his arrest; the other was that since his previous release from prison, he had continued to express his opposition to the regime at every opportunity and they still saw him as a threat.

Finally, in January 2005, the Khartoum government and the SPLM signed a comprehensive peace agreement. On 1 July of that year, Turabi was released from prison. On 9 July, John Garang returned to Khartoum to be sworn in as the president's first deputy. Turabi's aides confirmed that his release did not come about as a result of al-Bashir's good graces, but due to pressure from Garang.

Either way, Sudan had entered a new era that bore no resemblance to what the Islamists had promised the people after the coup that brought them into power. Peace in the south was fragile, and disturbances continued in the east and west of the country. Furthermore, Khartoum lost control of Darfur to African peacekeeping forces and never regained authority over the South.

☙❦☙

Amid their first experiment with political power, Sudan's Islamists ended up divided among themselves; they limited people's freedom and committed countless political errors. In the end, they returned right back to where they had begun: negotiating with the opposition and accepting the need for political pluralism. If there is any lesson to be learned from the Sudanese experience, it is that attempts to achieve stable and legitimate rule by means of a military coup are destined for abject failure. Another lesson from the experiences of Sudan, Afghanistan and Iran is that the Islamists have not yet found a solution to the relationship of the modern state with society. In all three countries, seizing power proved far easier than managing state institutions in fair and sustainable ways, and without compromising crucial freedoms.

What is surprising about the Sudanese context, with all its turmoil, is that each time Turabi was released from prison he seems to have been more determined to continue his political work than before. In his understanding of Islam and his reading of the Qur'an and the Sunnah, Turabi was no different to other modern reformists from the Salafi movement. What set him apart was his deep faith in the role of the intellect and his belief that human beings have to take responsibility for their own fate – an understanding that is very close to the Mu'tazilite worldview. This was perhaps what motivated him to rise again and again and to continue to struggle despite all the setbacks and disappointments he experienced.

There is no doubt that Turabi made important contributions to contemporary Islamic thought.[3] He reaffirmed monotheism as the central tenet of faith for individuals and all human societies. He was also able to explain his understanding of the importance of monotheism without slipping into a polarising struggle with people of other faiths and worldviews. In addition, perhaps more than any other contemporary Islamist leader, Turabi strove to invite and include Muslim women in the public sphere.

From another perspective, Turabi made an important contribution to tearing down the veil of secrecy that once hid Islamic organisational work. He made it clear that no organisation is permanent, and that the goal of organisational work is to revitalise society with the power of religion and build unity between people. On the Arab front, he was one of the first voices to call for reconciliation between Islamists and Arab nationalists.

Some argue that Turabi's immersion in politics made him favour pragmatism over ethics. Indeed, the culture of political expediency that he instilled in his students may have been what encouraged so many of them to part ways with him when they saw him as a threat to their own interests. It is certainly the case that an apologetic tone is evident in comments he made in his later years about his involvement in the Salvation government and only time will tell whether the Sudanese people will forgive him for his role in that.

Turabi died in a hospital in Khartoum on 5 March 2016, at the age of 84. It is impossible to know whether his vision for Sudan will ever be fulfilled. Admittedly, it was a vision that seemed to become ever more elusive as the years passed but the shaykh never lost his enthusiasm or faith in the human capacity for good. As for Sudan, it seems to have a long way to go before it passes through the eye of the storm.

14

Transcontinental violence

When the American Airlines plane crashed into the Northern Tower of the World Trade Centre at 8:45 a.m. on 11 September 2001, no one who saw the explosion in the heart of New York thought the incident was anything more than a tragic accident. The first report handed to US president George Bush (Jr) suggested nothing sinister. Ten minutes later the situation changed completely as the second plane crashed into the World Trade Centre's Southern Tower. There was no longer any doubt that the USA, the most powerful country in the world at the beginning of the twenty-first century, was under attack. This view was strengthened when the Pentagon, which is the US defence ministry's headquarters, was also attacked by a civilian plane in a similar manner. A fourth plane crashed in Pennsylvania after a struggle between passengers and hijackers, and it was later established that the intended target was Capitol Hill, the home of the US Congress.

The 9/11 attacks resulted in the deaths of approximately three thousand people in New York and Washington. Most of the victims were civilians working in or visiting the World Trade Centre; some were employees of the US defence ministry. The attacks had a massive impact on the way Americans saw themselves and their relationship with the world. The attacks also had colossal effects on American foreign policy and on international relations throughout the world. The perpetrators were all Arab Muslims and members of an organisation known as al-

Qaʻida.[1] Islam and Muslims are thus at the centre of almost all of the major changes seen in the world since 9/11.

In the weeks following the attacks, the USA declared war on Afghanistan and toppled the ruling Taliban regime. A few months later, the US administration under Bush (Jr) announced that it had adopted a strategy of pre-emptive strikes against its enemies around the world. The USA also began exerting direct pressure on Arab and Islamic countries to change their educational syllabi and close down traditional centres of learning.

At the beginning of 2003, the USA invaded and occupied Iraq, thereby involving itself in a protracted and difficult war against a range of Iraqi forces. While the attacks on New York and Washington created a major outpouring of sympathy for the American people, US foreign policy thereafter has been widely condemned. In the USA, a general sense of being under siege predominates, and this is not seen as originating simply from al-Qaʻida but from Islamic culture and doctrine as a whole. Relations between Arabs and Muslims were already troubled before the US declared war on Afghanistan and Iraq, but the extremely costly American invasion and occupation provoked unprecedented levels of enmity and hatred.

The disastrous consequences of the 9/11 attacks might well have been what the planners were trying to achieve; not that they were necessarily able to predict exactly what would happen, but they probably had a sense of what direction the US response was likely to take. Detailed assessment, vision and planning went into planning the attacks. At the heart of this were two Arab Islamists: Osama bin Laden, an engineer and the son of one of Saudi Arabia's wealthiest families, and Ayman al-Zawahiri, a doctor, and son of one of Egypt's most prominent families.

Bin Laden was born in the Saudi capital, Riyadh, in 1957. His father Muhammad emigrated to Saudi Arabia in the early 1930s from the Yemeni village of al-Rabat in the Hadramout region's Dawan valley. Within a few years of his arrival in the newly established Saudi kingdom, Muhammad bin Laden was able to establish a small construction company that won the confidence of the founder of the kingdom, 'Abd al-'Aziz Al Sa'ud, and his sons.

Like many who had left Hadramout over the centuries in search of their fortunes, Muhammad bin Laden was a committed Muslim and a diligent worker. The growth of his business mirrored the development of the Saudi kingdom, and his company became one of the largest Arab construction companies in the region. Osama was Muhammad bin Laden's seventeenth son, and his mother was of Syrian descent.

Osama was still a child when Muhammad moved his large family from Riyadh to Madinah. When Osama was ten years old his father died in an aeroplane accident, and the young boy developed a strong spiritual bond with his mother. Osama grew up with strong religious values that were typical of Saudi Arabia at that time. While his father had tried to ensure that his family were exposed to the traditions and values of Islam, his children all had different interests and levels of commitment to their faith. Interestingly, the cities of the Hijaz region where Osama lived and was educated were generally more cosmopolitan than those in the conservative Najd region, home of the Wahhabi movement.

After completing his secondary education, Bin Laden enrolled at King 'Abd al-'Aziz University in Jeddah, where he studied economics and management. The notion that he was influenced during his university years by Sayyid Qutb's brother, Muhammad, is incorrect as Muhammad Qutb never taught at King 'Abd al-Aziz University. It is also unlikely that Bin Laden was an active Islamist during his university days, as his Islamist leanings seem to have emerged in about 1984.

During the 1980s, Saudi Arabia, along with several other Islamic countries, supported the Afghani mujahidin in their resistance to the Soviet occupation. The Saudi state always opposed Soviet expansion in the Islamic world, and the Saudi kingdom was also a strong ally of the USA, which was supporting the mujahidin. Osama was moved by stories told by visiting Afghanis about crimes committed by the Soviet forces and about the enmity displayed by the Russians and their allies towards Islam. In his late twenties, Osama moved to Peshawar, the Afghani jihad's rear base in Pakistan, where he joined many other young Arabs who were working there in support of the mujahidin.

It is important to note that, throughout the Cold War, Arab-Islamic culture was hostile towards the Soviet Union. Islamists saw the Soviet Union as the centre of godless communism and viewed its alliances with Arab states that were hostile to the Islamist movement with great apprehension. Therefore, when they saw that the Afghani resistance to the Soviet occupation was Islamic in its character and its objectives, they did not hesitate to mobilise in support of it. The USA and its allies also worked hard to encourage this participation.

From the beginning of the 1980s, therefore, a number of Arab Islamists had headed for Peshawar to join the mujahidin. Their ranks received a huge boost when the Palestinian Islamist 'Abdallah 'Azzam joined the Afghani jihad. 'Azzam had been a central figure in Jordan's Muslim Brotherhood and had played a leading role among the Arab Islamists who joined Fatah in the late 1960s. Ever since, and even after 'Azzam had obtained his doctorate from al-Azhar University in Cairo, the flame of jihad had burned strongly within him. It was therefore quite in keeping for him to move to Peshawar to join what seemed as if it might be the final chapter in the great Islamic jihad.

Bin Laden and 'Azzam got to know one another in Peshawar. 'Azzam was older and better known in Islamist circles, and Bin Laden soon offered him his full assistance. In 1984, 'Azzam established the Maktab al-Khadamat (Services Bureau) while Bin Laden established the Bayt al-Ansar (House of Helpers). Over the next five years, these organisations became the two main recruitment centres for Arab and non-Arab volunteers wishing to join the Afghani resistance movement.

In 1986, after several visits to Peshawar, Bin Laden settled in a small villa in the city's University Quarter. He was not yet thirty years old, but his Islamist–jihadist convictions had reached the point of no return. While 'Azzam toured the world encouraging Islamist youth to join the Afghani jihad, Bin Laden was supporting the mujahidin logistically, and even militarily at times. Slowly but surely the billionaire mujahid, with his humble, austere and distinguished manner, earned a prominent place among the Arab volunteers and the Afghani resistance movement. Various sources estimate that more than 25 000 Arab volunteers became involved in the Afghani jihad. As large as it is, this number pales beside the estimated 150 000 Afghanis who became mujahidin. In truth, the leaders of the Afghani resistance movement sometimes saw the non-Afghani volunteers as something of an annoyance, but their need for economic and political support forced them to make room for the Islamists.

In the early centuries of Islam, this region in the heart of Asia was once an Islamic frontier with fortified cities. The traditions of jihad and siege blossomed here, along with a lifestyle suited to garrison towns. After this, right up until the modern era, the area remained subject to wars and invasions, with human settlements in a continual state of flux. A few pockets of northeast Afghanistan were not Islamised until as late as the nineteenth century. For these reasons, the Arab volunteers were able to find space for themselves among the wide spectrum of organisations involved with the Afghani mujahidin.

Perhaps the most prominent battle fought by the Arab volunteers was near Jaji in April 1987, when they held their position for several weeks in the face of a Russian attack on their encampment. However, the Arab volunteers' real impact became apparent only after the Afghani jihad, when they helped kindle the flame of violence that swept through the Arab region or joined in the conflict between the Taliban and its opponents.[2]

It is highly likely that Bin Laden and 'Azzam were aware that the USA was providing significant amount of support to the Afghani mujahidin. However, speculations about a relationship developing between Bin Laden and US intelligence agencies in the 1980s are simply a myth.

For the Americans, Afghanistan was an extremely important aspect of the Cold War, but the Cold War had clear principles and rules of engagement: the Americans ensured that their support for the Afghanis went via the Pakistani government and they distanced themselves from direct engagement in Afghanistan. As for Bin Laden, he had no need for American support, material or otherwise. Bin Laden and 'Azzam probably saw the USA's involvement as an indication that Washington and the mujahidin had some common interests, no more and no less. Bin Laden was probably also aware that whatever doubts he may have had about US policy, his influence in Afghanistan did not extend to making decisions on behalf of the mujahidin.

In 1989, the Soviets withdrew from Afghanistan. At the end of that year, 'Azzam was assassinated and Bin Laden became the key figure among the Arab mujahidin. He stayed in Peshawar for several months after the Soviet withdrawal, and this was when he and his companions established al-Qa'ida. Initially, it was nothing more than a register that documented the roles and the fates of Arab mujahidin who had volunteered in Afghanistan. A few years later, the register had become an organisation, and a flag-bearer for international Islamist terror.

Some sources on this period mention Bin Laden's involvement (along with General Hamid Gul, the former head of Pakistan's military intelligence agency) in a failed plot to assassinate the Pakistani prime minister, Benazir Bhutto, but little evidence of this has been found. What is clear is that Bin Laden realised that his role in the Afghani jihad was over and he returned to Saudi Arabia. When he had left his homeland in the mid 1980s he was no more than the son of a very wealthy Saudi family. Just a few years later, he returned as a hero – a key mujahid Islamist leader. He was welcomed in mosques and at Islamic gatherings, and asked to speak about his experiences and his vision for the future. At the time, Saudi society was being shaken up by the strong mobilisation of the Islamist movement, and Bin Laden began to sense a role for himself.

His first move was to make a proposal to the Saudi authorities that he be allowed to recruit Islamist jihadists and confront the communist regime in South Yemen. Although his proposal was rejected, it indicates that his relationship with the Saudi authorities was still cordial at that time. His move also casts doubts on the theory that Bin Laden's primary inspiration came from Sayyid Qutb. Qutb believed that all ruling authorities in the Islamic world were in a state of ignorance (al-jahili-yyah), but Bin Laden saw no harm in co-operating with the Saudi authorities. In addition, Qutb believed in proselytising and did not suggest the use of arms at all, but Bin Laden believed in the use of violence.

Bin Laden's attitude towards the Saudi authorities changed dramatically during the Kuwaiti crisis and subsequent war. On 1 August 1990, in light of the deteriorating relationship between Kuwait and Iraq, Iraqi forces occupied Kuwait. A few days later the USA was able to convince King Fahd of Saudi Arabia that the Iraqi president Saddam Hussein was planning to invade his kingdom. From 7 August, Saudi Arabia was transformed into a military base for hundreds of thousands of US soldiers and their Western allies. Even after the expulsion of the Iraqis from Kuwait, tens of thousands of US troops remained stationed in military camps on Saudi soil.

Bin Laden, like many other Saudi Islamists, took the view that the US military presence violated the land of the two holy sanctuaries and the teachings of Islam. Bin Laden, therefore, began expressing his opposition to the US's military presence at seminars and public gatherings. In the face of a widening Islamist opposition, the Saudi authorities placed limits on Bin Laden's movements, preventing him from leaving the country and from addressing any public gathering.

In April 1991, however, Bin Laden was given permission to travel to Peshawar to conclude his work in Afghanistan. He had, in fact, decided to go into exile so that he could oppose the Saudi regime from abroad. In Peshawar he witnessed, first-hand, the bloody fight for power that had developed between the mujahidin and he lost his desire to remain in Afghanistan. Aware that the authorities in Sudan had announced their Islamist orientations two years before this, Bin Laden made his way to Khartoum and a warm welcome from the Sudanese Islamists. A strong relationship developed between Bin Laden and Hasan al-Turabi, the prominent Islamist thinker and a key figure in the Sudanese regime.[3]

Bin Laden then decided to settle in Khartoum and link his fate to that of Sudan's Islamist state.[4] He brought his family over and chose a humble home on a farm in one of the suburbs of Khartoum. In a short time, Arab Islamists began to gather around him, including those that had found refuge in Sudan or had made their way there to join Bin Laden. Some were Saudis who supported his views, others were former comrades from Afghanistan, while yet others were members of Egypt's al-Jama'ah al-Islamiyyah (Islamic Group) and Jama'ah al-Jihad (Jihad Group).

Bin Laden put all the money that was available to him at that time into commercial and industrial projects in Sudan, which was in dire need of economic investment. He established a company for commerce and another for production; a company for agricultural development and another for agricultural products. He also became the state's major partner in a project to build a highway between Khartoum and Port Sudan. Although he never stopped opposing the US presence in Saudi Arabia, there was at this time no indication that he had adopted any specific strategy in relation to this.

Meanwhile, some of Bin Laden's supporters helped to train Somalian tribal militias. In December 1992, they participated in bloody battles that took place between US forces and Somalis who were opposing the US presence in their country. This led to the withdrawal of US troops from Somalia. Bin Laden probably also extended a helping hand to Arab Islamist fighters who went to Bosnia to stand with Bosnian Muslims against the Serbs. These were, however, relatively spontaneous and limited initiatives.

Bin Laden's most public activity in the early 1990s was the formation of the Lajnah al-Nasihah wa al-Islah (Committee for Advice and Reform), through which he expressed his opposition to the policies of the Saudi regime. The committee established an office in London and Saudi citizen Khalid al-Fawwaz was appointed as its manager and spokesperson. On 13 November 1995, one of the Saudi National Guard buildings in Riyadh was bombed and fourteen people were killed. On 25 June the following year, a residential complex known as Khobar Towers occupied by US forces in the north-eastern town of Dhahran was bombed, leaving nineteen dead and five hundred injured. However, neither the Saudi nor the US authorities accused Bin Laden or his allies of involvement in these incidents.

Another important development in Bin Laden's Islamist relationships occurred during his stay in Sudan when he met the Egyptian Islamist and medical doctor Ayman al-Zawahiri. Al-Zawahiri was born into a prominent Egyptian family. His paternal grandfather was al-Ahmadi al-Zawahiri who was the head of al-Azhar University in the first half of the twentieth century; his maternal grandfather was 'Abd al-Wahhab 'Azzam, one of Egypt's most well-known intellectuals and literary figures and brother to 'Abd al-Rahman 'Azzam, who was the first secretary-general of the Arab League.

Ayman al-Zawahiri had joined Egypt's Jihad Group while he was a university student in Cairo, and was imprisoned in the clampdown after the assassination of Anwar Sadat. As soon as he was released, he left Egypt, making his way to Peshawar, where he helped to provide medical care to Afghani refugees and the mujahidin. With so much in common, it is not surprising that the two men forged a strong relationship, even though they had not actually met until they were both in Sudan in the 1990s.

In the 1990s, al-Jama'ah al-Islamiyyah and Jama'ah al-Jihad were leading a violent struggle against the ruling authority in Egypt. With the incarceration or killing of most members of al-Jihad at the hands of security officials, al-Zawahiri became one of the group's most important members in exile. Although al-Zawahiri did not announce this publically, he had lost confidence in violence as a means of bringing about political change in Egypt or anywhere else. However, in his capacity as a member of al-Jihad, he was expected to defend the ideas of Muhammad 'Abd al-Salam Faraj, author of the controversial work, *al-Faridah al-Gha'ibah* (The neglected duty). Faraj's main argument was that it is futile to challenge foreign powers, including Israel, and that activists need to work towards changing the ruling regimes, even if this means taking up arms.[5] Gradually, however, Al-Zawahiri began to turn 'Abd al-Salam Faraj's ideas on their head. In his view, the strength of the ruling Arab regimes flows from the support they enjoyed from the US and other Western powers. Thus, he saw the defeat and expulsion of the US from Arab and Islamic regions as a crucial step to complete before Islamists could attempt to establish an Islamic order.

Whenever they met, al-Zawahiri and Bin Laden discussed and debated this new vision. However, the issue was probably not resolved until after Bin Laden was expelled from Sudan. Saudi Arabia and the US put pressure on Khartoum, and in May 1996, the Sudanese Islamist regime forced their guest to leave the country. In fact, the Sudanese state even offered to hand Bin Laden over to the Saudis, but neither Riyadh nor Washington wanted to have him in custody. What the Saudis wanted was to remove him from the Arab region and prevent him from instigating further resistance to their authority. As for the Americans, they did not as yet see him as their mortal enemy.

His expulsion from Khartoum embittered Bin Laden. He was forced to leave on a small aeroplane flown by a Russian, with one of his aides helping the pilot to pinpoint their destination on an ordinary map. Meanwhile, the Sudanese Islamists, in whom Bin Laden had placed so much confidence, and in whose country he had invested sizeable amounts, seized most of the assets Bin Laden had to leave behind.

In the end, the aircraft carrying Bin Laden and his companions landed in the Afghani city of Jalalabad, which was under the control of Yunus Khalis, a veteran of the Afghani jihad. The Afghanis welcomed the outcast whom they knew well and created a sanctuary for him in their region. In the mountains of Jalalabad, droves of young Arabs who had stayed in Afghanistan after the Soviet withdrawal began gathering around Bin Laden. Soon, others arrived, including al-Zawahiri and several members of Egypt's Jihad and Islamic Groups.

At that time, bands of Taliban fighters were being launched from Kandahar, in an attempt to take control of the country and to establish stability by force. During 1996, the Taliban seized control of Kabul and most of Afghanistan. The Taliban appreciated the fact that Bin Laden distanced himself from the civil strife between Afghani forces, and because they found in his group of Arab supporters much of the expertise they desperately needed to manage the affairs of state, they strengthened their relationship with him and welcomed his presence.

In November 1996, Palestinian journalist Abdel Bari Atwan became the first media personality to meet Bin Laden in his stronghold in the mountains of eastern Afghanistan near Jalalabad. He found him living an extremely austere existence, surrounded by several devoted aides. Bin Laden's language in that interview seemed much bitterer than it had been in earlier statements he had issued, and his opposition to Saudi rule and the US presence in Saudi Arabia was much stronger. There is little doubt that Bin Laden was feeling backed into a corner, and thus more inclined to all-out war.

A major shift in Bin Laden's position came in February 1998 when he issued a statement announcing the establishment of al-Jabhah al-Islamiyyah al-'Alamiyyah lil Jihad did al-Yahud wa al-Salibiyin (World Islamic Front for Jihad against Jews and Crusaders). The statement was signed by Bin Laden, al-Zawahiri, and Rifa'i Taha (a leader of the Egyptian Islamic Group who was on the run) as well as several small Pakistani, Kashmiri and Bangladeshi jihadist organisations. The statement made reference to the Islamic causes in Palestine, Kashmir and Iraq and to the American presence in Saudi Arabia. It included a call to kill Americans and their civilian or military allies in any country, naming this as 'a religious obligation incumbent upon every Muslim...until al-Aqsa Mosque is liberated and their armies depart from the lands of the Muslims'. It is unclear what US or Saudi officials made of the announcement, but subsequent events proved that Bin Laden, al-Zawahiri and the others had meant what they said.

A few months later, on 7 August, suicide bombers hit the US embassies in Kenya's capital, Nairobi, and Tanzania's capital, Dar es Salaam. The attacks left 213 people dead and 450 injured in Nairobi; 11 people were killed in Dar es Salaam. The bombers did not differentiate between Americans and non-Americans, Muslims and non-Muslims, or soldiers and civilians, thus providing clear evidence of how far Bin Laden and al-Zawahiri were prepared to go in their war against the USA.

Two weeks after the bombings US president Bill Clinton issued orders to bombard training camps that groups linked with Bin Laden were using close to the city of Khost in eastern Afghanistan, and a Sudanese site that the US believed was still associated with Bin Laden. The bombing near Khost resulted in no casualties and it was later established that the Sudanese site was a pharmaceutical factory that had no links to Bin Laden.

In December 1999, an Algerian named Muhammad Rassam was stopped at the Canadian–American border with explosives in his car. He later confessed that his objective had been to bomb targets in the city of Los Angeles. On 12 October 2000, the American Warship *Cole* was attacked in the port city of Aden in Yemen by an explosive-carrying boat, resulting in the deaths of seventeen crew. This was followed in 2001 by the 9/11 attacks on New York and Washington, which, as noted, resulted in a major overhaul in US policy, and made Bin Laden a symbol of international terrorism and a challenge to American supremacy.

Between his departure from Saudi Arabia and the 9/11 attacks, Bin Laden and those around him did not refer to themselves as al-Qa'ida. And, in the three days that Atwan spent in Bin Laden's mountain stronghold at the end of 1996, he did not once hear the word. Responsibility for the Nairobi and Dar es Salaam bombings were claimed by al-Jaysh al-Islami li Tahrir al-Amakin al-Muqaddasah (Islamic Army for the Liberation of Holy Places). However, US security agencies were searching for an objective behind the attacks that fitted in with their conception of violent organisations. They believed they had found this in al-Qa'ida, which was, in fact, no more than an outdated register of Arab volunteers in Afghanistan. Gradually, al-Qa'ida was conceived of as a global organisation made up of cells, both active and sleeper, stretching from the western coast of the USA all the way to Indonesia.

Al-Zawahiri was not the only factor behind the adoption of the strategy of comprehensive violence; the exaggeration of Bin Laden's impact on the political context in Saudi Arabia by the Saudis and their US allies, and their pursuit of him from Saudi Arabia to Sudan and then to Afghanistan also contributed to its crystallisation. Bin Laden had neither a plan nor the experience to establish a terrorist organisation.

After settling in Sudan, he established random relationships with small Islamist forces here and there. In Afghanistan, he was surrounded by a small number of former Arab volunteers and Islamists who were all fugitives from their own countries. These individuals gradually began establishing ties with radical groups in Islamic countries that they were able to make contact with. They also began inviting angry young Islamists to join them in Afghanistan.

Besides being repeatedly vilified in Clinton's speeches and in the Western media, Bin Laden did not serve these efforts in any way. Nonetheless, from the late-1990s, in the eyes of small groups of radical Islamists, Bin Laden became a global leader. Groups who were marginalised in their own countries aspired to enter into an alliance with him or fall under his leadership. Following the widespread popularisation of the name al-Qa'ida by the US and the Western media, Bin Laden considered it convenient and politically beneficial to adopt the name, and al-Qa'ida became a reality.

It is incorrect to place Bin Laden within any fixed intellectual framework, or to link his ideas to those of Sayyid Qutb or Salafi Islamism, for example. Neither of these sources provide an interpretive paradigm for Bin Laden's methodology. Although al-Zawahiri was known for his Salafi tendencies and Bin Laden grew up in a Salafi environment, Salafism has never been a clear-cut or monolithic ideology. The Salafi School has nurtured both enlightened reformists and many Islamic scholars who have remained loyal to ruling regimes (as in the case of the Saudi religious establishment), just as much as it has spawned groups that embraced violence.

The truth is that Bin Laden chose the path of international terrorism with a degree of hesitation and within an extremely charged political context. His speeches and conversations show a high degree of political expediency and do not reflect the defining features of any particular school of Islamic thought.[6] For example, if he had Salafi inclinations, his alliance with the Taliban would have to have been based purely on political expediency, as it is impossible to describe the Taliban, whose leadership are steeped in the Hanafi School of jurisprudence, as Salafis.

Most of al-Qaʻida's relationships and activities seem to have been characterised by pragmatic thinking and fairly loose organisation. Those who undertook the 9/11 attacks on New York and Washington, for example, were from very different backgrounds. In 2002, a hotel owned by Israelis in Kenya was bombed, as were several nightclubs in Bali that were generally frequented by Australian tourists. In May 2003, several tourist sites in the Moroccan city of Casablanca were bombed. In March 2004, a series of explosions occurred on trains in the Spanish capital, Madrid. All of these attacks resulted in hundreds of civilian casualties and were almost exclusively the work of small local groups that were not necessarily closely linked with Bin Laden or other al-Qaʻida leaders.

After the US invasion of Afghanistan and the subsequent collapse of the Taliban, the Americans, with their Afghani and Pakistani allies, captured many al-Qa'ida leaders and members. It soon became clear that the group was made up of a mix of angry and adventurous young Islamists. It is therefore extremely unlikely that these operations were carried out under direct orders from Bin Laden or his aides, and they illustrate the random nature of groups currently participating in international violence. What is referred to as al-Qa'ida is not a coherent organisation united by a clear set of leaders and a single intellectual frame of reference. This is perhaps what makes it so dangerous.

All of the operations attributed to al-Qa'ida and its network after 9/11 can be described as opportunistic in that they were directed at easy targets, and designed to cause a high number of civilian casualties and generate intense insecurity. The planners and implementers of these operations seldom seem concerned about how much they might be damaging Islam's image in the world, or about the fate of Muslims, especially Muslim minorities in non-Islamic countries.

☙❦☙

Iraq is the only place where al-Qa'ida and those linked to it have achieved marked successes. There, forces linked to al-Qa'ida, more properly known as Tanzim Qa'idat al-Jihad fi Bilad al-Rafidayn (Organisation of the Jihad Base in the Land of the Two Rivers) and popularly referred to as al-Qa'ida in Iraq (AQI), were established by a young Jordanian, Ahmad Fadil al-Khalayleh, better known as Abu Musab al-Zarqawi. Even his story confirms the random nature of al-Qa'ida and the role of US policy in strengthening its influence.

Zarqawi was born in 1966 into a poor family from the strong Bani Hasan tribe in the Jordanian city of Zarqa. He did not complete his secondary education and earned a reputation in his early years for bad behaviour and gangsterism. In the early 1990s, he met 'Isam al-Barqawi, who had returned to Zarqa from Kuwait after the Iraqi invasion. Al-Barqawi, who is also known as Abu Muhammad al-Maqdasi, is regarded as one of the propagators of Salafi jihadism. Salafi jihadists pass strict religious judgements on all aspects of Islamic life and often contradict verses of the Qur'an or prophetic teachings. Borrowing the concept of al-hakimiyyah al-ilahiyah (divine governorship), they deem all regimes that do not rule by Islamic law to be disbelieving. Accordingly, Al-Maqdasi therefore regarded the Saudi regime as unIslamic and elaborated on this in a book entitled *al-Kawashif al-Jaliyyah fi Kufr al-Dawlah al-Sa'udiyyah* (Clear proofs of the disbelief of the Saudi state).

Salafi jihadists distinguish themselves from the wider Islamic Salafist sphere by their strong convictions about the efficacy of violence. However, al-Maqdasi seems more balanced than many other proponents of Salafi jihadism, or at least, he seems to have become so after being imprisoned in Jordan for a long period. He has since rejected the practise of making generalised pronouncements of disbelief against Muslims, and also refused to view Shi'a Muslims as disbelievers or to propagate violence against them. Thus, while he supports the use of arms against foreign occupiers of Islamic lands, his position on the use of violence to bring down governments in Islamic countries is less clear.

After getting to know al-Maqdasi, Zarqawi committed himself to Islam and Salafi jihadism. Together with others, the two men worked to establish a secret Islamic organisation in Jordan. In March 1994, the Jordanian authorities arrested the two men along with other members of the organisation. They and their comrades were tortured at the hands of Jordanian security officials and left in solitary confinement for long periods. All those who knew Zarqawi during his years in prison affirm his leadership qualities.

The entire group was released by royal pardon after the death of Jordan's King Hussein in 1999. After their release, the group became known as al-Tawhid wa al-Jihad (Monotheism and Jihad), which is also the name of al-Maqdasi's website. However, the group soon split up and several members, including Zarqawi, left Jordan for Afghanistan.

When Zarqawi got to Afghanistan the Taliban regime was secure, and Bin Laden had reorganised the former Arab mujahidin as well as his supporters from various Arab countries. Zarqawi was warmly welcomed and given a key position at a time when Bin Laden and al-Zawahiri were looking for a way to get closer to Palestine.

However, it is believed that when Zarqawi realised that the group around Bin Laden did not share his vision of Islam, he opted to establish a separate camp for anyone that chose to join him. As was their way, Bin Laden and his followers did not sever ties with Zarqawi, but helped him establish his camp in the Herat region, close to the Iranian border, and gave him the necessary supplies. The Herat camp soon became the preferred destination for Islamist jihadists from the Levant, Iraq and Turkey; in fact some whole families chose to settle there. Arabs, far from their countries and families, built a new jihadist community that was joined by bonds of marriage and kinship.

For two years, Zarqawi and his comrades underwent military training, in various combat and sabotage techniques, and he also devoted himself to studying Islam, history and politics. As his circle of acquaintances grew, Zarqawi discovered that, in the twelfth century, his tribe, the Bani Hasan, were among those that Salah al-Din al Ayyubi had settled to the south of Jerusalem to protect the city from the crusaders. From his reading, he also learned about Nur al-Din Zengi, who united Muslim leaders against the crusades and attempted to expel the crusaders from Palestine and Syria. Zarqawi might have wanted to repeat Nur al-Din's achievements in his own life, but he did not join al-Qa'ida.

The Taliban regime collapsed at the end of 2001, and the Herat camp disbanded. Zarqawi then joined a Kurdish camp run by the Jama'ah Ansar al-Islam (Helpers of Islam) in northern Iraq. There he encountered some of his former comrades from Jordan, such as Ra'id 'Arabiyat and Nidal Kharisat, but he soon decided to head for the central Sunni Arab area, in search of the Iraqis he had become acquainted with in Afghanistan. US threats against Iraq were escalating and Zarqawi believed that

Iraq – the heart of the Arab region – was about to become the nucleus of a war with the USA.

Zarqawi then met up with Omar Hadid, a former comrade from Afghanistan and the son of a well-known Sunni Arab family. Soon they were joined by Abu Anas al-Shami, one of the most prominent jihadists they had known in Afghanistan. Just before the USA occupied Iraq in 2003, the group established its first cells. They were soon joined by droves of young Arabs who rushed to Iraq shortly before the invasion to participate in the battle against the US invaders.

The US invasion and occupation of Iraq in March 2003 stirred widespread anger in the Arab region, creating a state of crisis and psychological estrangement between the Islamic peoples and all the Western nations. On the eve of the invasion and subsequently, especially in London and Washington, Western policies were expressed in clearly imperialist terms, stripped of any explanations or anything even resembling a justification. The invasion brought back to the Arab-Islamic collective memory all that they had experienced during the colonial period. In the many statements issued by Bush (Jr) and Blair, Arabs and Muslims could find no reason for the invasion of Iraq. All they saw were massive columns of American and British tanks cutting through the desert west of the Euphrates, long-distance missiles raining down on Baghdad, and strange young soldiers from faraway lands firing heavy-ammunition machine guns from the bridges over the Tigris. Raw power, with all its boasting and arrogance, was the only justification for the invasion of Iraq. It is therefore hardly surprising that occupied Iraq became the focus of attention for prospective young Muslim volunteers across the region, from Kuwait to Morocco.

Resistance to the invaders began a few weeks after the occupation of Iraq. The first cells were made up of members of the Ba'ath Party or the Iraqi Special Forces and other security forces. Al-Tawhid wa al-Jihad quickly joined in, led by Zarqawi, as did several other Islamist forces with Iraqi roots. Al-Tawhid wa al-Jihad did not confirm their presence in Iraq until the second year of the occupation but they were blamed for the assassination of Muhammad Baqir al-Hakim, a senior Shi'a cleric and head of al-Majlis al-'A'la li al-Thawrah al-Islamiyyah fi al-'Iraq (the Supreme Council for the Islamic Revolution in Iraq) a few months after the occupation, as well as for the Ashura massacres of Shi'as in Baghdad and Karbala on 2 March 2004. The obscurity of Zarqawi's statements, and the opacity of the Iraqi situation under the occupation, often made it very difficult to prove these accusations but Zarqawi never denied targeting Shi'ite groups in Iraq, American troops, and the new security forces that were established in Iraq after the invasion. In January 2006, Zarqawi did claim responsibility for a bloody explosion targeting volunteer police officers in the Sunni city of al-Ramadi, which resulted in many deaths.

Given that Iraqis were an extremely divided nation after the invasion and during the occupation, Zarqawi's group, and other militias linked to various sectarian political forces, played a huge role in fuelling sectarian violence. Zarqawi's goal was to subvert all attempts to build the new Iraqi state, which like many Iraqis, he saw as the illegitimate outcome of an illegitimate invasion.

In October 2004, Zarqawi announced that his organisation was officially joining al-Qa'ida's network and pledged his loyalty to Bin Laden. He also announced that the group's name had been changed to Tanzim Qa'idat al-Jihad fi Bilad al-Rafidayn (Jihad Base in the Land of the Two Tributaries). This apparently occurred after Zarqawi was informed that if he did not announce his loyalty to al-Qa'ida, Bin Laden planned to establish a separate group in Iraq. In a sense, Zarqawi already saw himself as acting on behalf of al-Qa'ida, and he might have made the announcement to prevent problems arising between himself and Bin Laden.

Surprisingly, the war on al-Qa'ida, and extensive efforts by US and other forces to capture Zarqawi and his supporters in Iraq, had little effect on the strength of the organisation. Similarly, the destruction of

Fallujah, the killing of Omar Hadid in the battle for the city, and recurring American operations in the Anbar Province were unable to weaken Zarqawi's group. By 2006, the third year of the occupation, Zarqawi's AQI had become one of the most important armed groups opposing the occupation and the new Iraqi authorities. The group had strengthened their Iraqi roots and spread across central and northern Iraq. Evidence also emerged which indicated that members of the former Iraqi regime, including military officers, had assumed leadership roles in most of the groups cells inside Iraq.

AQI fed on the ever-growing Arab and Iraqi anger towards the occupation; however, it represented only one of many Iraqi resistance groups, many of which disapproved of Zarqawi's methods. In addition, reports of large numbers of Arab volunteers in the ranks of the group seem to have been exaggerated. Among the tens of thousands of prisoners incarcerated for resisting the occupation in Iraq, the number of non-Iraqis was insignificant. However, the presence or otherwise of non-Iraqi Arabs in the ranks of his organisation was not a source of concern for Zarqawi. Throughout the previous century, the borders between the Arab states had failed to weaken Arab and Islamic solidarity. The traditional condolence ceremonies held for Saudi, Syrian and Jordanian youth who were killed in Iraq became occasions for popular celebration in their countries of origin.

Amid continual and bloody conflict, and despite the destruction of its birthplace in Taliban-ruled Afghanistan, AQI grew from strength to strength. At the end of 2005, Zarqawi announced that al-Qa'ida was responsible for shelling targets in Israel from across the Lebanese border, thus confirming the organisation's firm commitment to broadening their activities outside Iraq and to attacking the Zionist state.

However, Zarqawi did face growing anger in Iraq's Anbar province where attacks against tribal and other leaders in the region were attributed to him. In June 2006, he was killed when US troops shelled one of his camps close to the city of Ba'quba. After his death, relations between AQI, several of the Iraqi tribes and various other Iraqi resistance forces deteriorated rapidly.

Similarly, random acts of violence between al-Qaʻida and sectarian Shi'ite militias led to the formation of armed groups in the Sunni areas who allied themselves with the US forces in an attempt to defeat al-Qaʻida and Shi'ite militias. These groups became known as the Quwat al-Sahwah (Awakening Forces). During 2008, these forces created significant setbacks for al-Qaʻida in most of the areas in which it was operating.

❧❧❧

In July 2005, several explosions rocked London's underground rail network. Besides resulting in many casualties, the bombings were extremely damaging to the British economy, and raised major misgivings about the anti-terrorist strategy developed by the US administration under Bush (Jr) and strongly supported by Tony Blair. However, the damage also extended to Britain's huge Muslim community, whose roots stretch back more than half a century.

Various obscure statements were made attributing responsibility to al-Qaʻida, and the British government made it clear that they were almost certain that al-Qaʻida operatives were responsible. The view in security circles is that al-Qaʻida is now relying on a new generation of activists. These individuals have no experience in Afghanistan, profess no strong religious commitments, and do not mingle with well-known Islamists. The London bombings clearly showed that, to wreak hideous destruction anywhere they choose, and not only in the lives of those who are killed, injured or bereaved, but also in the relationships between Muslims and non-Muslims throughout the world, al-Qaʻida need only win over tiny groups of activists.

Bin Laden and al-Zawahiri attempted to launch a global war against the USA and its allies, accusing them of violating Muslim lands and rights. It was left to the USA, unquestionably the largest global power, to respond to the challenge. However, the US response was neither wise nor appropriate considering the nature and relative size of its opponents. Instead of dealing with al-Qaʻida as a security threat, the US response came across as a declaration of war against Islam as a whole – its countries, its people and its heritage. Of course, the alliance between Israel and the US only makes things worse.

The crisis between the Western powers and the Islamic world is becoming ever more complex. Al-Qaʻida will never attain victory by military or political means. In the end, the US and its allies will probably contain and destroy the threat they face. However, this will not happen without damaging relationships between countries and cultures and obstructing global peace and order. To confront the violence that has helped to spawn and continues to nourish this crisis, millions of Muslims in the Islamic world, and in Western countries, will have to stand up to it. The violence, and those that advocate it, have to be isolated from the Islamic body-politic. However, such a stand cannot be undertaken while the world is so overshadowed by the West and its policies, which ceaselessly widen the gap between itself and other peoples and their cultures. Each time this gap widens, those who advocate violence and isolation gain a little more ground.

This problem is of global proportions, and in essence it is about relations between the Islamic world and the Western powers; it must be dealt with on this basis.

15

Rise of reformist Islamists

espite the world's preoccupation with violent Islamist organ-isations, the vast majority of Islamists reject violence as a means of political change, and engage with politics just like citizens of many other contemporary societies. As we enter the twenty-first centu-ry, most Islamists support democracy, political pluralism and the peace-ful rotation of power. They see the state (from an Islamic perspective) as a civil not a religious institution. They are calling for equal citizen-ship and human rights (rather than subject status) and for the strength-ening of civil society in ways that limit state power.

The major trends in political Islam are reformist, and those who align themselves with these trends are striving to strengthen the posi-tion of Islamic values in political life peacefully and gradually, rather than by means of coups or revolutions. Since they first rose to promi-nence in the 1920s, the Islamists have made much progress in formulat-ing their vision and articulating their political views. In a large number of Islamic countries, where despotism, one-party rule and poor admin-istration continue to dominate, Islamist forces seem to be the only hope for reforming political life, building good governance and states that are accountable to their people. However, it is important to realise that many of the key developments in the thinking behind political Islam were not arrived at in moments of quiet self-reflection. They were born amid bitter experiences in local and international contexts characterised by intense pressure and haste.

In the 1940s, Hasan al-Banna attempted to engage in the democratic process, but met with strong opposition from then-Egyptian prime minister Mustafa Nahas. The last time the Egyptian Muslim Brotherhood participated in an election under the monarchy was indirect, when they voted in huge numbers for the Wafd Party and contributed to its great election victory in 1950. In Syria, the Muslim Brotherhood played an active role in parliamentary life in the 1950s and 1960s. In Pakistan, the Jamaat-i-Islami has been an important component of political pluralism since the 1960s. In Malaysia, despite the dominance in government of the United Malays National Organisation (UMNO), which is a partially secular popular nationalist party coalition, the Islamist Pan-Malaysian Islamic Party (PAS) has not only advocated peaceful political activity but also actively participated in parliamentary elections.

Nonetheless, it can be argued that these examples were spontaneous, and seldom arose out of a specific or carefully conceptualised awareness of the aims and objectives of political activity. In the 1980s and 1990s, however, this kind of awareness grew rapidly, motivated by a series of changes in the Islamic and global spheres.

In early 1989, the Islamic revolution in Iran created strong support for Islamist forces and for the idea of political change within an Islamic framework. However, from another perspective, it also presented Islamists with a major challenge. Tainted by violence and dissent, the Iranian experience forced Islamists to consider some very pressing questions about how it might be repeated in other countries.

In November 1989, came the collapse of the Berlin Wall, bringing with it a series of global changes; the communist bloc fell apart along with the challenges that Marxism and socialism had presented to the liberal capitalism of the West and to Islam. Change swept through most of the former communist countries, making democracy, political pluralism and human rights the 'holy grail' of a new global ideology and central points of reference for the dominant political value system.

It was only natural that Islamist movements were influenced by this global shift and for them to strive to answer the questions it posed. The eruption of violence in Egypt and Algeria in the 1980s and 1990s, followed by the emergence of al-Qa'ida on the international stage, also both had a major influence on this process. It soon became necessary for reformist Islamist groups to affirm their intellectual and political opposition to the use of violence in the name of Islam. This gave rise to an exceptionally rich debate within the Islamic sphere that led to important revisions of the Islamic intellectual heritage and to innovative new readings of modern history in Islamic countries. Whereas many observers tried to exploit the difficulties and divisions that overshadowed military Islamist rule in Sudan to cast doubt on the entire Islamist movement, most Islamists saw the Sudanese experience as an opportunity to affirm their reformist orientation while rejecting military coups as a means of achieving their aims.

From another perspective, popular anger and resentment increased dramatically in most Islamic countries during the 1980s and 1990s. With the failure of liberalisation and capitalist investment programmes to create real economic growth, social inequalities increased rapidly. The collapse of the communist bloc left Islamic countries more vulnerable to US pressure, under which the boundaries of national sovereignty began to buckle. Feelings of anger and bitterness worked to the advantage of certain Islamist forces, whose popular support grew at unprecedented rates, and the escalation of mass support deepened the Islamists' feelings of responsibility and urgency.

Their first priority was to put forward a clear vision, wide enough to encompass broad sectors of society and inspire confidence and trust, while responding to the people's aspirations. Many Islamist scholars, thinkers and activists contributed to the development of a new reformist Islamist discourse, some of whom were not even aware of the importance of the role that they were playing. Among the most influential of these neo-reformists in the contemporary Islamist sphere are Yusuf

al-Qaradawi, Mohammad Salim al-'Awa, Tariq al-Bishri, Fahmi Huwaydi, Rachid Ghannouchi and Munir Shafiq.[1]

❦

Shaykh Yusuf al-Qaradawi was born in 1926 in the village of Saft
al-Turab near the city of al-Mahalla in Egypt's Delta region. In 1954,
he graduated from al-Azhar University, the centre of Islamic Sciences
in Egypt and the Arab East. At the start of his career as a Muslim scholar, Qaradawi was known to be close to reformists who were pushing
for the renewal of al-Azhar University in the early 1960s, converting it
into a massive institution that teaches a diversity of Islamic and modern
sciences.

According to Qaradawi, Mahmud Shaltut (who was head of al-Azhar
in the 1960s) and Muhammad al-Bahi (head of the university's cultural
section and one of its key intellectuals) encouraged him to write his first
book. *Al-Halal wa al-Haram fi al-Islam* was first published in 1959.
Since then, the book has been translated into several languages and
over thirteen editions of the book exist. The English title is *The Lawful
and the Prohibited in Islam,* and the book remains one of Qaradawi's
most influential works.

Qaradawi did not pursue his career in Egypt for very long after graduating from al-Azhar. His affiliation to the Muslim Brotherhood made
him a target of the Nasser regime, and after repeated incarcerations, he
left for Doha, the capital of Qatar, in 1961. He returned to Egypt in the
early 1970s, and earned a doctorate from al-Azhar for his extensive
work on fiqh al-zakat (the jurisprudence of religious almsgiving). In
1973, Qaradawi established the Shari'ah College at Qatar University
and stayed on as dean of the college until 1990. At the time of writing,
he was head of the university's Markaz Buhuth al-Sunnah wa al-Sirah
(Centre for Seerah and Sunnah Research). Qaradawi is one of the most
important and eminent of contemporary Sunni Muslim scholars; his

influence is vast, and he is affiliated with several Islamic jurisprudential and scientific societies.

Mohammad Salim al-'Awa is an internationally renowned lawyer and writer. Born in Alexandria in 1942, al-'Awa earned his first degree from the Law College of Alexandria University in 1963. In 1972, he was granted a doctorate in comparative law from London University's School of Oriental and African Studies. In Egypt, the shaykh of al-Azhar, Muhammad Mustafa Shalabi (also a prominent jurist) was one of al-'Awa's teachers. In London, al-'Awa studied under two well-known Orientalists, JND Anderson and NJ Coulson. He then taught law in Nigeria, Saudi Arabia and Egypt, before finally settling in a private law practice in Cairo. Al-'Awa has published more than ten books on specialist legal topics and issues pertaining to contemporary Islamic thought. His book *On the Political System of the Islamic State* remains highly influential.

Tariq al-Bishri is a former judge, writer and historian of tremendous influence. He is from an Egyptian family characterised by deep Islamic traditions. In the early twentieth century, his grandfather, Salim al-Bishri, was twice appointed as head of al-Azhar University. Tariq was born in Cairo in 1933 and attained a law degree from Cairo University in 1953. A year after he graduated, he was appointed to Egypt's State Council, the highest legal body charged with settling disputes pertaining to the Egyptian state. He retired from the council in 1998, after becoming the first deputy to the president of the council and president of the section on legal opinion and legislation. He was also a member of the academic council of the Law College at Cairo's Ain Shams University, a member of the Higher Council of Islamic Affairs at al-Azhar University, and a member of the history committee affiliated to the government's Supreme Council of Culture within the Ministry of Culture. Al-Bishri's studies of modern Egyptian political, social and legal history have made him one of Egypt's most prominent and widely read historians.

Fahmi Huwaydi is a well-known Arab Islamist journalist and writer. He was born in Cairo in 1937 and graduated from Cairo University's

College of Law in 1961. During the mass arrests of Muslim Brother-hood members in Egypt in 1954, Huwaydi was just seventeen years old and was the youngest person taken into custody. Perhaps due to his age, he was not detained for long. In 1958, Huwaydi joined *al-Ah-ram* (a newspaper publishing company) as a young researcher. In the early 1970s he established and supervised the editing of the 'Religious Thought' page in their daily paper. The page played an important role in contemporary Egypt's Islamic Awakening, but this created several problems for Huwaydi. In the late 1970s and early 1980s, Huwaydi went to Kuwait to work for *al-Arabi* magazine, and then to London to work for *Arabia* magazine. However, he then returned to his position at *al-Ahram*, becoming one of its most influential writers. In fact, his weekly articles are still published in several Arabic newspapers outside of Egypt. By mid 2014, Huwaydi had published twenty books and hun-dreds of articles, all related to the ongoing debates about contemporary Islam.

Munir Shafiq was born in Jerusalem in 1936 and his membership of the Jordanian Communist Party caused him to be imprisoned for many years. In the late 1960s, Shafiq joined Fatah, which was then the central force in Palestinian nationalism, and he became one of the Palestinian resistance movement's key theorists. In the 1970s, as head of the Pal-estinian Planning Centre, which fell under the Palestine Liberation Or-ganization (PLO), Shafiq opposed the reconciliatory approach adopted by his organisation. Over the years, his intellectual persuasion shifted from Marxism to Arab nationalism, and he decisively embraced Islam at the beginning of the 1980s. Shafiq has written extensively, and par-ticularly since the publication of his book *al-Islam fi Ma'rakat al-Ha-darah* (Islam in the struggle over civilisation), his writings have been widely circulated among young Arabs and Islamist activists. Shafiq is one of the most prominent defenders of the potency of traditional forces in Islamic societies, and his writings are among the most biting cri-tiques of the divisions within and between the Arab states.

Shaykh Rachid Ghannouchi is the founder and leader of Tunisia's Ennahda Party. Besides being a religious scholar, he is also a writer and orator of great repute. Ghannouchi was born in al-Hammah village in the South of Tunisia in 1941. After completing his studies at al-Zaytuna Institute in the city of Qabis, he enrolled at the University of Damascus in Syria where he earned a degree in philosophy. Despite some early Nasserist leanings, Ghannouchi was an Islamist by the time he left Damascus. In the late 1960s, Ghannouchi spent some time at the Sorbonne in Paris, but was forced to return to Tunisia for personal reasons.

Back in Tunisia in the 1970s, Ghannouchi worked as a philosophy teacher and, with a group of his friends, he engaged in a range of activities inspired by his Islamist views. This led to the establishment of the Harakah al-Ittijaha al-Islami (Islamic Tendency Movement) at the beginning of the 1980s, and by the end of the decade this became known as Ennahda. Ghannouchi was imprisoned several times by the Tunisian government, and lived in Britain as a political refugee from 1991 to 2011. By mid 2014, Ghannouchi had published over ten books, most of which dealt with issues related to Islam, freedom and citizenship. He is one of the most prominent and influential Islamist thinkers and strongly defends political pluralism and democracy.

❦

These representatives of contemporary Islam were all born between 1926 and 1942. These were years in which the influence of the great Islamist reformists was increasingly apparent in the media, the arts, and in Islamic centres of learning. Traditional Islam went into decline, and the students of Muhammad 'Abduh, such as Mustafa al-Maraghi and Mustafa 'Abd al-Raziq began to rise within the leadership structures of al-Azhar University. During this period, these leaders increasingly called for ijtihad (renewed intellectual effort) and the need to acknowledge and respond to the impact of the modern era. Most of these Islamist thinkers saw themselves as reformist Salafis, following in the footsteps of Muhammad 'Abduh and Rashid Rida. Together with a large number of other great thinkers and Islamist scholars, these spokespersons for contemporary Islam helped construct a framework for a new Islamic Reformist School.

One of the most important intellectual concessions made by neo-reformists was to acknowledge the reality and legitimacy of the modern nation-state in the lands of Islam. Almost all of them called for co-operation and co-ordination between all Muslims, and not one placed any real hope in the notion of reviving the caliphate.

The concept of a 'national group,' put forward by Ṭariq al-Bishri decades ago, has become a pivotal concept in contemporary Islamic thought. For al-Bishri, religious identity formed the basis of political cohesion until the end of the nineteenth century. He argued that after the 1919 Egyptian revolution, political groupings became nationalist in character, founded on a bond of allegiance to their own nation and to the attainment of freedom and independence from foreign control. He noted that this is how members of society become citizens – empowered and equal in terms of both rights and responsibilities.

Fahmi Huwaydi gave further expression to this in the title of one of his books, *Muwatinun la Dhimmiyun* (Citizens not subjects), affirming that the concept of a dhimmi (a free non-Muslim subject of any state), no matter how this was previously understood, is now no more than a historical concept, and that citizenship is, in effect, the socio-political framework in modern Islamic countries.[2] This encompasses the reformist view of the question of political change in Muslim countries. All reformist Muslims reject the use of violence as a means of political change. They base this rejection on Sunni jurisprudential consensus that links violence with al-fitnah (political dissent). Similarly, none of the Muslim Reformists call for political coups. However, almost all see the need for reform, and argue that Islam should have a place and a crucial role as a general reference point in Islamic societies.

Al-Bishri, for example, stated that Egypt's problems are unrelated to state legislation since the majority of laws concord with the principles of Islam or, at least, do not contradict them. The problems lie with how legislation and state policy is implemented and in the relationship between society and the state.

Implicit in neo-reformist discourse is a desire for reconciliation between Islamists and the modern state – a desire inspired by historical Islamic experience of the relationship between Islam and the state. The neo-reformists see Islamic countries as being in need of an intellectual, scientific and economic awakening. However, they also believe that the dismemberment of the Arab and Islamic countries have given rise to entities that are too small to be capable of bearing the burdens of such an awakening.

Where the neo-reformists differ, however, is on the primacy of unity, the form it should take and what level is desirable. While some argue for *internal reform* before gradual steps are taken towards co-ordination and co-operation, others believe that a sufficient degree of *unity* is a necessary precondition to bringing about awakening and independence.

The neo-reformists have also called for the rebuilding of relationships between Islamic societies and the global community, and especially with Western countries, although they differ on how much of a priority this is. While some see independence and liberation from dependency as the highest priority, others take the view that Islam is already an indivisible part of contemporary global culture, and call for Islam to be acknowledged and recognised as contributing to prevailing human values.

The neo-reformists have called for the establishment of political pluralism and democracy, where the will of the people is respected and states are accountable to their citizens. However, they differ over the intellectual foundations of this pluralist democratic system. Al-'Awa, who wrote about the Islamic political system, sees the state from an Islamic perspective as an entity whose form changes over time, and affirmed the prevailing pluralist democratic paradigm.[3] Ghannouchi, on the other hand, who devoted his life to democratic transformation in Tunisia, took the view that freedom and human dignity are the most inspirational objectives of the shari'ah. He argued that in the contemporary era, these cannot be achieved politically outside of a pluralist democratic framework.[4] The neo-reformists thus affirmed that the ummah is the repository and protector of Islam's legitimacy. This means that a democratic choice that expresses the will of the people is necessarily an Islamic choice no matter what its nature. Similarly, democratic Islamic discourse received a huge boost when Qaradawi stated that no truly Islamic political programme can be anything other than democratic.

In this way, after decades of obscurity within the discourse of political Islam, the neo-reformists managed to bring some clarity to Islamic political thought. Even though they have not yet been successful in reconciling the Islamist movement with any modern state, they have managed to bring about a rapprochement between the majority of Islamists and politics. Of course, neo-reformist discourse has not engaged all the questions confronting contemporary Islamic societies, but it has helped bring about crucial transformations in the approach of political Islam while also associating with, and lending legitimacy to, other agents of change.

In Jordan for example, the Muslim Brotherhood has maintained cordial relations with the state since its foundation in the 1940s, even though tensions have arisen now and then. During the 1950s and 1960s, the Jordanian Brotherhood occasionally participated in parliamentary elections, albeit hesitantly and without clear objectives. However, neither the Jordanian Brotherhood, nor Jordan's Islamists more generally, could then have been considered part of a broad-based popular movement. The Islamists became a mass popular movement in the 1980s, and only after overwhelming successes in university-based student-union elections and thereafter in the trade union movement. This development occurred when the Jordanian political sphere was preparing for change. After the uprisings in the first quarter of 1989, which were sparked by the country's burgeoning economic crisis, King Hussein appointed al-Sharif Zayd bin Shakir as prime minister, giving him the responsibility of transforming the country into a parliamentary democracy. This was the first time that Jordanian Islamists found themselves facing a decision about whether or not to participate in a democratic process that had real intellectual consequences, in that their participation would influence the shaping of the Islamist political discourse in the country.

In the 1989 elections, the Muslim Brotherhood won twenty of the eighty seats in the Jordanian parliament, and independent Islamists won another thirteen seats. The results caught many observers by surprise and clearly demonstrated growing popular support for the Islamists. However, the Brotherhood's participation in the elections took place in the shadow of an internal struggle that ended with the defeat of the more conservative wing, who were led by prominent members such as Muhammad Abu Faris, Hummam Sa'id and Ibrahim Khuraysat. Nevertheless, with the First Gulf War fostering a growing regional crisis, the Islamists participated in Mudir Badran's government for the first half of 1991, carrying the burden of maintaining the country's stability along with other political parties.

In 1992, the Brotherhood decided to establish the Jabhah al-'Amal al-Islami (Islamic Action Front) as a broad-based political party encompassing Brotherhood and non-Brotherhood members. Ishaq al-Farhan, an academic and former government minister, was chosen as the Front's secretary-general. *Al-Sabil*, a national newspaper with a wide circulation, informally became the Front's mouthpiece. In the following year, the government amended the country's electoral law, aiming to weaken the Islamists' position. Meanwhile, within the Islamic Action Front, al-Farhan was leading a struggle against the conservative wing, which ultimately led to the conservatives opting to leave the party.

When the next parliamentary elections were held, the percentage of votes won by the Islamists increased, but the number of seats they won declined, with sixteen seats being won by the Islamic Action Front and six seats by independent Islamists. Clearly, the path of democratic political activity was not going to be free of obstacles. In the years that followed, tensions between the Jordanian government and the Islamists increased. The signing of the Wadi Araba Peace Treaty between Jordan and the Zionist state in 1994 exacerbated these tensions. Subsequently, and in a context of constant state harassment, the Islamic Action Front opted to boycott the 1997 elections.

The Front remains politically active, and leads a disciplined and popular opposition. In spite of the growing chasm between itself and the government, the party participated in the 2003 elections. The number of parliamentary seats in the Jordanian parliament had been increased to 110, and the Front contested just thirty seats. Given the increasing disparities between the Islamists and the government on the Palestinian question, those loyal to the government launched a campaign against the Islamists under the slogan 'Jordan first'. This did not prevent the Islamists from winning seventeen of the thirty seats that they contested. However, the election of the conservative Hummam Sa'id as superintendent-general of Jordan's Muslim Brotherhood in 2008, provided further evidence that state repression tends to give rise to extremist responses.

❦

The democratic experiences of Islamists in Yemen reflect that country's unique socio-political conditions. In the early 1970s, after a prolonged civil war, Islamists in Yemen, and especially the country's branch of the Muslim Brotherhood, played an active role in the transitional period, helping to create a basis for stability in the country. Islamists also participated actively in drafting the country's constitution of 1970.

When 'Ali 'Abdullah Saleh came to power via military coup, the Brotherhood allied itself with the new government and, in 1982, participated in a general popular congress. In fact, almost half of the members of the permanent committee of the congress, which later became the ruling party, were members of the Brotherhood. In 1989, the Islamists supported efforts to create unity between North and South Yemen, but opposed the constitutional project of the unified state, in which they saw a strong secular bias. As a result, the Yemeni Muslim Brotherhood began to be marginalised within the ruling party.

In 1990, al-Tajjamu' al-Yamani li al-Islah (Yemeni Congregation for Reform Party), popularly referred to as al-Islah, was established and 'Abdallah al-Ahmar, the leader of the powerful Hashid tribe, was named as its leader. Al-Islah represented the convergence of Brotherhood members, who were largely middle class and had a modern educational background, with tribal Yemenis, who were represented by the leader of one of its most important tribes. This gave the party a firm social base and strong ties with Yemeni society.

From its inception, al-Islah played the role of an official opposition party. However this was carefully calculated so that their activities were interwoven with actual governance. In the 1993 elections, the ruling Popular Congress Party won 121 seats in parliament, and al-Islah took second place with 62 seats. Al-Hizb al-Ishtiraki (the Socialist Party), which was the Popular Congress's southern counterpart in the unification of Yemen, won 56 seats.

Although the two allied ruling parties – the Popular Congress and the Socialist Party – received a comfortable majority in parliament, they decided, for their own reasons, to invite al-Islah to participate in the Cabinet. Al-Islah agreed and was given five ministerial portfolios in the twenty-six-member Cabinet. In the 1994 cessation war, that entrenched unity in Yemen, Al-Islah supported 'Ali 'Abdullah Saleh and was then given a third of the Cabinet's ministerial portfolios.

However, by 1997, the relationship between al-Islah and the Popular Congress had deteriorated, and in the 1997 elections, government agencies worked hard to give the Popular Congress an overwhelming victory. The Socialist Party dropped out of the election, leaving the Popular

Congress with 230 of the 301 parliamentary seats and al-Islah with just 53 seats. Thus Yemen entered the next era of the Popular Congress under Saleh, with little effective participation from al-Islah or the Socialist Party.

Although the Yemeni government attempted to answer to escalating calls for reform in the Arab region by showing off Yemen's democratic face, the results of the 2003 parliamentary elections saw the Popular Congress entrenching its power. The Congress won 227 of the 280 seats, and although al-Islah managed to double the number of votes it had received in the previous election, they secured just 47 seats – six fewer than the party had won in the previous elections. The Socialist Party secured just seven seats.

⊛⊛⊛⊛

The notion that a state has a higher purpose, beneath which political parties compete (as Islamist parties in Jordan and Yemen have done), has found acceptance in Morocco as well.

In 1996, a group of young Islamists in the Harakah al-Islah wa al-Tajdid (Reform and Renewal Movement) together with 'Abd al-Karim al-Khatib, leader of the nationalist Hizb al-Harakah al-Sha'biyyah al-Dusturiyyah (Popular Constitutional Movement Party), agreed to form an Islamist party called al-'Adalah wa al-Tanmiyah (Justice and Development Party), popularly referred to by its French abbreviation, PJD. Al-Khatib was a traditional leader, and known for his strong links with the monarchy, so his involvement as the head of the new party helped to allay some of the concerns the ruling elite had about the Islamists.

Over the next few years, the PJD affirmed their commitment to democracy as well as their acceptance of the monarchy, which they saw as helping to guarantee stability and unity in Morocco. In addition, at a time when Islamist organisations in many other countries were being influenced by Salafi reformist tendencies, the PJD established a strong pact with Morocco's traditional religious establishment, which is a bastion of the Maliki School and Sunni Sufism.

The PJD has participated in Moroccan parliamentary elections since its establishment. However, like democratic Islamists in several other Islamic countries, they have not competed for all the seats, thereby avoiding provoking the fears of other political forces in the way that outright competition might do. Nonetheless, in September 2002, the PJD won 38 of the total of 325 parliamentary seats, which made them the main opposition party in the Moroccan parliament.

What complicates matters in Morocco is that the organisation al-'Adl wa al-Ihsan (Justice and Virtue), which enjoys broad-based popular support, has decided to remain outside the sphere of democratic political competition. In addition, in the heated Moroccan parliamentary elections of 2007, the PJD did not do as well as they had expected.

☙❦❧

What were seen in Jordan, Yemen and Morocco as important shifts in political life and activity was already almost an established pattern in several other countries. In Malaysia, the Pan-Malaysian Islamist Party (PAS) has been competing for political authority and control in various regional states since the 1960s. PAS has ruled the Kelantan state successfully for many years, despite its humble performance in the country's national general elections. In 2008, an alliance that includes PAS, led by Anwar Ibrahim, a former minister in the ruling UMNO party's coalition government, achieved very good results in the 2008 national parliamentary elections as well as in the regional state elections.

In Pakistan, despite the tensions and coups that have occurred since independence, Pakistani Islamists have become an established feature of political and parliamentary life. In 2008, they made significant contributions towards the country's transformation into a democratic dispensation.

In Syria, towards the end of August 2002, the Muslim Brotherhood convened a national congress in London that was attended by the representatives of several Syrian opposition political parties. The congress issued an extremely important document entitled 'The National Covenant of Syria', which diagnosed the reasons for oppression and the absence of freedom then being experienced in Syria, and called for dialogue between all democratic forces. The covenant affirmed Syria's Arab-Islamic identity, and the need to seek inspiration from global examples in the spheres of human rights and freedoms. The document also called for the construction of a modern state in Syria, and for Arab unity in the face of the Zionist project. The publishing of the covenant was a clear indication of the Syrian Muslim Brotherhood's willingness to return to the outstanding work they did in the 1950s, of their aim to establish a national consensus founded on fixed national principles and interests and of the pressing need for reform.

A clearly visible phenomenon since the mid 1980s, and the gradual growth in the strength and popularity of the Islamist movement, is that countries that have included Islamists in their political processes have been far more stable. By 2010, the Islamists had not overthrown democracy nor torn down any of these modern states. Moreover, the rise of support for the Islamists was strongly linked to the democratic transformation of several Islamic countries.

Because democratisation is being blocked, and faces great difficulties, the integration of the Islamists into political life is not always easily achieved. In Tunisia, for example, the Islamist movement has been reformist and democratic since it first appeared in the public sphere, but the Islamists are confronting a state that refuses to recognise their right to political participation. Rachid Ghannouchi, and several of his comrades in Tunisia were imprisoned for three years after they announced the formation of the Islamic Orientation Movement in 1981. In 1987, the government under President Bourguiba once again imprisoned numerous leaders and cadres of the Islamic Orientation Movement. Bourguiba's later execution of Islamist leaders led to a palace coup that gave the presidency to Ben 'Ali.

As a sign of good faith, the Islamists changed their name to the Ennahda Party, and affirmed the constitutional foundations of the Tunisian state, including its controversial statute of personal law. However, their unofficial participation in the 1989 elections, in which the undisclosed results showed that their support was much stronger than the state had anticipated, heralded disaster for them. Ben 'Ali and his government refused to grant the Ennahda Party a licence, and a year after the elections, it was announced that the government had uncovered an Islamist conspiracy to overthrow the state. In the coming months, the security forces arrested hundreds of Tunisian Islamists. Some were tried in military courts and subjected to extremely harsh judgements, while hundreds of others fled into exile in Europe or other Arab countries.

There is strong consensus that Ennahda is among the most committed of all the Islamist organisations to the principles of democracy, political pluralism and civil activism. Nonetheless, the Tunisian government has refused to normalise the country's political life or recognise the right of Islamists to exist and organise.

Tunisia's story has since been repeated in one way or another in Libya, Syria, Mauritania and several other Islamic countries. However, the crisis in the relationship between reformist Islamists and the state seems most complex in Egypt and Saudi Arabia, two of the world's most important Arab and Islamic countries, both of which are extremely influential in terms of their intellectual and political climates.

16

Crisis of reformist Islamists

$\int$audi Arabia and Egypt are among the most important Arab and Islamic countries, historically, geographically, and in terms of the roles they have played and the influence they exercise. In the last hundred years or so, both countries have been exposed to internal challenges that have led to armed confrontations between the state and Islamist forces. None of these challenges have posed a real threat to state security in either country. The success of consecutive Egyptian and Saudi regimes in dealing with armed opposition groups does not mean that they have responded to the Islamist question. In truth, most Egyptian and Saudi Islamists are reformists, who oppose and condemn violence while seeking the reconstruction of the state in ways that encourage authentic popular participation and transparent governance. It would undoubtedly be in the public interest, and help to isolate those forces that support violence, if the Egyptian and Saudi governments were to give reformist Islamists the space to express their views. However, both governments seem to have major anxieties about this kind of open dialogue.

❦

Saudi Arabia experienced a period of relative internal calm during the 1980s. The Afghani situation had sapped the energies of the Islamists even though the Saudi state and its people also contributed tremendously to the Afghani cause. In addition, the huge rise in oil revenues helped to deflect attention away from internal discontent. However, in the final years of that decade, the Soviet occupation of Afghanistan ended and the oil price collapsed. The corruption that was rife within economic and state institutions could no longer be ignored, and the impact of modernisation rose to unprecedented levels. The Islamic consensus upon which the kingdom was based began to split apart.

The country's demographic indicators were another cause for alarm. By the mid 1990s, 60 per cent of the kingdom's citizens were under the age of twenty. This, combined with increased education levels, was placing tremendous pressure on the job market; the unemployment rate rose from 14 per cent in 1994 to 30 per cent in 2001.[1]

In August 1990, Iraqi forces occupied Kuwait. In a matter of days, the US government under George Bush (Senior) was able to convince the Saudi monarch that Iraq was a threat to Saudi Arabia. The Saudi state then granted permission to international forces to establish military bases within its territory; hundreds of thousands of American troops arrived along with smaller forces from other countries. On 13 August, the Higher Council of Saudi Scholars indicated their support for the regime's decision to seek assistance from foreign troops, but this did not prevent other Saudi political and civic organisations from reacting negatively to the huge US military presence, especially when the troops remained on even after Iraq had been 'liberated'.

Many Saudi Islamists, from religious scholars to professionals, opposed Iraq's occupation of Kuwait. However, they were also, and much more strongly, opposed to the US military presence in their country. Among the voices of Islamist opposition, three young religious scholars stood out, and although they were active in different regions of the vast kingdom, a strong bond of friendship united them.

The first young scholar was Salman ibn Fahd al-'Awdah, from Buraydah, the main town in the oasis of al-Qasim in the heart of the Najd region. Al-'Awdah, who is from to the Bani Khalid tribe, was born in

1955. He received his Islamic education in study circles and at various Islamic institutes, before attaining a master's degree in 1988 from the department of prophetic studies (Sunnah) at the Imam Muhammad Ibn Sa'ud University in Riyadh. A decade of political disruption, and several years spent in prison, delayed the attainment of his doctorate until 2001. Al-'Awdah's ability to combine his knowledge of hadith (Prophetic tradition) with exceptional proficiency in fiqh (Islamic jurisprudence) is seen as unique.

The second scholar is Safar ibn 'Abd al-Rahman al-Hawali, who hails from the Ghamid tribe. Al-Hawali was born in 1952 in the city of al-Bahah in the south of the Hijaz region. He also received both a formal and an informal Islamic education, eventually attaining a doctorate in 'ulum al-'aqidah (doctrinal science) from Umm al-Qura University in 1985. Al-Hawali progressed within the university until he was made head of its doctrine department. Like his two friends, al-Hawali combines his academic focus with a broad interest in the changing political and intellectual trends in the Arab Middle East and globally.

The last of the trio is Nasir ibn Sulayman al-'Umar, who was born in Riyadh in 1952. Al-'Umar studied in the faculty of Islamic law at Riyadh's Imam Muhammad Ibn Sa'ud University, attaining his doctorate there, and specialising in tafsir (Qur'anic interpretation). Although less well known outside of the Saudi kingdom than the other two, Al-'Umar has been involved in Islamic political activity since his first years at university.

Together, the three scholars, along with several others from their generation, represent a new phenomenon in Saudi life and in the Islamic political sphere as a whole.[2] Unlike many Islamic leaders in the Arab region who have modern professional backgrounds, these individuals are religious specialists. They are not part of any break-away or rebel grouping, but have grown and been nurtured at the heart of the Saudi Islamic institutions, and have strong bonds with mainstream religious scholars in the kingdom.

None of the three are striving for political power or authority, but instead see themselves as heralds or messengers, and as another set of links in a long chain of Islamic reform. Their objective, like that of reformist scholars across the centuries, is to attain justice, serve the truth and protect the values of Islam. The idea of 'renewing the faith' is one of the most important concepts that moves them. By this they mean attaining consciousness of current reality and its requirements, while also seeking inspiration from the primary objectives of the shari'ah.

All three are devoted to the Sunni reformist traditions in their total rejection of violence and their belief that their role is about al-amr bil-ma'ruf wa al-nahi 'an al-munkar (commanding what is right and forbidding what is wrong). They are fully aware that the crises facing Islamic societies can be confronted only by reconciling fundamental Islamic values with the requirements of the modern world.

Nonetheless, the moderation that characterises al-'Awdah, al-Hawali, al-'Umar and similar like-minded reformists, has not protected them from the clutches of the Saudi state's security apparatuses. When the Gulf War began on 2 August 1990, they found themselves at the centre of a massive mobilisation in Saudi Arabia. On 19 August 1990, just days after the arrival of US troops, al-Hawali delivered a public lecture entitled 'And you will remember what I am saying to you', in which he denounced Iraq's Ba'thist regime and its invasion of Kuwait, but also made clear his opposition to US support. Just nine days later, on 28 August, al-'Awdah delivered a lecture entitled, 'Reasons for the Collapse of States', in which he elaborated on the ideas of the medieval Islamic historian Ibn Khaldun and expressed his admiration for Western democracy, with its entrenchment of freedom of speech and the responsibility that the state has towards its people. The implications of the speech were by no means lost on any of his listeners.

Subsequently, recordings of lectures given by al-'Awdah, al-Hawali and al-'Umar were copied, and hundreds of thousands of copies were distributed. The general Saudi public began referring to the three as al-Mashayikh (the Shakyhs). They, in turn, strove to affirm the legitimacy of their teachings by affirming their allegiance to the religious establishment.

In a meeting with 'Abd al-'Aziz bin Baz, then Mufti of Saudi Arabia and head of the Council of Senior Scholars, al-'Awdah proposed the convening of a monthly meeting for a select group of scholars to discuss issues pertaining to Islam and the country. Bin Baz agreed and the first meeting was convened in March 1991. The meetings continued for the next three years and stopped only when the three shaykhs were arrested. There is no doubt that the meetings served as an incubator for many Islamist initiatives that took place in Saudi Arabia in the first half of the 1990s.

In the lunar month of Shawwal 1411 (May 1991), a group of Islamist activists including Sa'd al-Faqih, Muhsin al-'Iwaji, 'Abd al-Wahhab al-Tariri, 'Abd al-'Aziz al-Qasim and Ahmad al-Tuwayjiri, drafted a letter to King Fahd. Signed by some of the most senior religious scholars in the country, including Shaykh 'Abd al-'Aziz bin Baz and Shaykh Muhammad Salih bin 'Uthaymin, in addition to many other scholars, professors and public figures, the document became known as the 'Scholars' Letter' or the 'Shawwal Letter'.

The letter made several requests of the king, including: the establishment of a majlis al-shura (consultative council), the revision of state laws so that they complement the shari'ah, the affirmation of a just policy regarding the spending of public funds, the prohibition of monopolies, judicial independence, and protection for the rights of individuals and society. The letter also asked that religious institutions and propagation activities be strengthened, that competent people with good reputations be selected to work in state apparatuses, the government affirm its responsibilities of towards the people, the media to reflect the country's Islamic identity and for various undertakings regarding military reforms. In addition, the letter demanded that any external alliances made by the state should accord with the country's interests and not contradict the principles of Islam.

In making these demands, the signatories took a step that was unprecedented since the clash between the founder of the kingdom, 'Abd al-'Aziz Al Sa'ud and the Ikhwan in the 1920s.[3] The letter was a call for the comprehensive reformation of the Saudi state and a review of its relationship with society. In many ways, the letter clarified why the monarchy was experiencing a crisis of legitimacy, even though the state was originally established upon an Islamic foundation.

Tensions between the government and the religious leaders increased over the next few months. Senior princes from the ruling family tried to convince Bin Baz to withdraw his signature from the letter, but the shaykh refused. Al-'Awdah, al-Hawali and al-'Umar continued to focus on demands for reform in their sermons and public lectures.

Given the absence of any culture of political opposition, the reformists tried to find the most effective means to convey their message. There was no Islamic political organisation to drive the reformist movement, so mobilisation occurred in typical Saudi fashion, by means of small gatherings and personal communications between scholars, professionals and opinion makers. Because what was being discussed did not question the existence of the state or the legitimacy of its rule as such, the reformists again expressed their views via a written document that came to be known as the Mudhakkirat al-Nasihah (Memorandum of good advice). In all probability, those who drafted the document were a small group of professionals and academics such as 'Abdallah al-Hamid, Muhsin al-'Iwaji, Sa'd al-Faqih and 'Abd al-'Aziz al-Qasim. The memorandum was shared widely, and after several drafts, over a hundred religious scholars, academics and public figures signed the document, and it also had the support of Shaykh 'Abdallah bin Jibrin, Shaykh Salman al-'Awdah and Shaykh Safar al-Hawali.[4] The 'Memorandum of Good Advice' was presented to the office of King Fahd in July 1992.

The document had ten chapters and dealt with most of the issues in the 'Scholars Letter', including matters pertaining to religious scholars, propagation, the judiciary and financial, military, political and foreign administration. However, this memorandum contained much more detail, clarity and prescription, and included, for the first time, an appeal for the establishment of a human rights committee based on Islamic Law, to be known as the Lajnah al-Huquq al-Shar'iyyah (Committee of Legitimate Rights).

The memorandum was distributed widely inside the Kingdom and abroad, sparking widespread media interest, but this time, the support of the Council of Senior Scholars and Bin Baz, was not forthcoming. In fact, in September 1992, the Council of Senior Scholars convened a meeting headed by Bin Baz that ended by issuing a statement condemning the memorandum. The council did not express opposition to any specific issues, but expressed dismay that the document had not been privately handed to the King but had instead been so widely and openly distributed. According to the traditions of the Saudi religious establishment, any advice directed at the monarchy should be done privately and in secret; open discussion was seen as likely to spread dissension and division.

Thus, although the 'Memorandum of Good Advice' raised the issue of reform in the Saudi kingdom both within Saudi society and internationally, it brought the consensus between the reformists and the Council of Senior Scholars to an end. Several reformist scholars responded to the statement made by the Council of Senior Scholars in a letter entitled Radd al-Islahiyyin ('Response of the Reformists'), which expressed their views on this parting of ways.

At the beginning of May 1993, reformist groups escalated their efforts by announcing the formation of the Lajnah al-Difa' 'an al-Huquq al-Shar'iyyah (Committee for the Defence of Legitimate Rights, which comprised of six members, namely: 'Abdallah bin Jibrin, 'Abdallah ibn Sulayman al-Mas'ari, Sulayman al-Rashudi, 'Abdallah bin Hamud al-Tuwayjiri, Hamad al-Sulayfih and 'Abdallah al-Hamid. Not since the founding of the Saudi kingdom in 1932 had any civic advocacy groups or political parties ever been established. The announcement of the committee's formation was an attempt to force the regime to acknowledge the reality that critical groups existed, but their gambit failed and the state refused to allow them to operate.

Strangely, while the reformist Islamists were taking this stand in defence of the people and in favour of reform, several Saudi liberals began defending the state. A verbal attack on the reformist movement was led by Gazi al-Qusaybi, a former minister and ambassador and one of the kingdom's most prominent liberals, and provoked several responses from the Islamists. An exceptionally lively intellectual and cultural exchange followed, but this served only to increase tensions.

In September 1993, the interior minister Prince Nayef bin 'Abd al-'Aziz wrote to Bin Baz complaining about 'the transgressions' of the reformist shaykhs. Bin Baz responded by promising to investigate. At the same time, Salman al-'Awdah, Safar Al-Hawali and Nasir al-'Umar were summoned to the interior ministry for a meeting with the deputy-minister. Soon thereafter, a decree was passed banning the three shaykhs from any public speaking. The three men obeyed this ruling but continued to receive people for private gatherings, and went on issuing statements expressing their views on political developments, including condemning the violence in Algeria and South Yemen's attempt to break away from the North.

In March 1994, the medical doctor Sa'd al-Faqih and the university professor Muhammad al-Mas'ari secretly slipped out of Saudi Arabia and made their way to London, where they sought political asylum. Believing that activity abroad was now the best way to support the cause of reform in their homeland, they played central roles in establishing the Committee for the Defense of Legitimate Rights.

On their arrival in London, al-Faqih and al-Mas'ari exploited every possible channel of modern communication to influence public opinion inside the Saudi kingdom. The Committee escalated its critiques of the regime in its statements and advisories until it became clear that the Committee's messages from London were not being responded to by the public at home. Nor was the regime in any mood to come to an understanding with the reformists, either in the country, or abroad.

The Saudi interior ministry believed that the three shaykhs were at the centre of reformist opposition, and intensified their efforts to limit their movements and keep them under surveillance. In September 1994, al-'Awdah sensed his imminent arrest and called for a gathering of 'solidarity with the oppressed' at the mosque in the city of Buraydah where he lived. Before the gathering could take place, al-'Awdah was arrested in the early morning of Tuesday 13 September in an operation carried out by hundreds of security officers who surrounded the entire quarter in which his house was located.

As soon as the news spread of his arrest, spontaneous marches broke out in al-Qasim region as the shaykh's supporters headed for the local government offices to protest against his arrest. Three days later security officers went to arrest al-Hawali in Jeddah, where the shaykh insisted that the police officers first join him for supper. In early October, al-'Umar was taken into custody as well.

According to Amnesty International, many Islamist activists were arrested in Saudi Arabia at this time. The Saudi interior ministry justified the arrest of the three shaykhs by claiming that they had transgressed a resolution by the Council of Senior Scholars but never specified exactly which resolution they were referring to. On 2 October, the Saudi ambassador in Washington, Prince Bandar ibn Sultan, made a statement to the BBC that the shaykhs were using Islam as a cover for other activities. Clearly, the regime was striving to use the position taken by the Council of Senior Scholars to justify its actions.

The regime promised that it had launched an investigation into the activities of the arrested shaykhs and would announce the results in due course, but no findings were ever released. Initially, the detainees were incarcerated in poor conditions, but eventually these improved, and the three shaykhs were able to use their long days in prison to read and pray.

Beyond the prison, political tensions in the kingdom continued to edge towards violence. In May 1995, the premises of the National

Guard in Riyadh were bombed, and in June 1996, an explosion took place in Khobar, targeting the US military barracks in the city. With the outbreak of violence, the security forces tightened their grip, and it seemed that the option of reforming the system had been firmly closed. Many were frightened by the violence and its impact on the cohesiveness and stability of the country, and some reformists were no longer prepared to stand by their views.

In 1997, Shaykh Bin Baz died, and two years thereafter, Shaykh Bin 'Uthaymin also passed away. The loss of these two great scholars undermined the influence and authority the Council of Senior Scholars, especially in relation to its role as a bridge between the state and the religious establishment.

In early 1996, differences that had arisen between Sa'd al-Faqih and Muhammad al-Mas'ari, who were managing the activities of the Committee for the Defence of Legitimate Rights from the UK, reached the point of no return. The activities of the committee were suspended and the two activists parted ways. Al-Faqih continued to oppose the Saudi government by joining al-Harakah al-Islamiyyah li al-Islah (Islamic Movement for Reform). With his followers, he attempted to strip the Saudi regime of all authority and called for complete regime change. This weakened his influence substantially. Al-Mas'ari, on the other hand, became involved with marginal British Islamist groups and no longer took a specific interest in Saudi affairs.

In June 1999, five years after taking the three shaykhs into custody, the Saudi authorities released al-'Awdah, al-Hawali and al-'Umar without charging them or bringing them to trial. By then, though, the challenge presented by the reformist movement had dissipated, and most of the reformists had moved off in different directions. Osama bin Laden and groups linked to al-Qa'ida had become much more of a threat.

Al-'Awdah, al-Hawali and al-'Umar then began a new phase of activity, characterised by a retreat from the confrontational political aspect of their earlier work. Their critics argue that they chose to toe the line despite the fact that the state had implemented no real reforms, either structural or otherwise. For their part, the shaykhs and their supporters argued that circumstances had changed and therefore required a different response. They also said that they had realised while they were in prison that their previous activities had been limited in the sense that they had influenced Islamist circles only. They argued that it was necessary to engage with as broad a cross-section of Saudi society as possible, including members of sects who had always felt threatened by Islamists, reformist or otherwise.

From the perspective of the three shaykhs, politics is about cultivating what is in the public interest and warding off what is not. They acknowledge that it is in everyone's interest to avoid a clash with the rulers of the kingdom at a time when their country is being exposed to violence perpetrated in the name of Islam, and (since 9/11) to increasing pressure from the West. In addition, they argue that state repression had softened to some extent. Reformists were again able to enjoy freedom of movement and expression. Since 2001, the three shaykhs have been allowed to deliver public sermons. Saudi Arabia today has a 'fundamental law' and a consultative council. It is true that neither the law nor the council fulfil all of the reformists' demands, but they are a start that can be built upon. In addition, US forces withdrew from Saudi Arabia in April 2003, thus one of the most sensitive of the reformists' demands was met.

In July 2001, al-'Awdah launched a website with the telling name of *Islam Today*; both al-Hawali and al-'Umar followed suit, each launching their own websites. The sites are visited daily by thousands of internet users and have become centres for those seeking both legal and Islamic guidance. In April 2003, on the eve of the American invasion of Iraq, the three friends helped launch a global campaign against US aggression. Two years later, the campaign held its first congress in Doha. In mid 2005, they participated in a conference organised to promote internal Saudi dialogue, which is a new development in Saudi life, and since September 2005, al-'Awdah has hosted a religious affairs pro-gramme broadcast by the Saudi satellite channel, MBC.

It seems that both the Saudi state and the reformist opposition fig-ures backed down from their previous positions and revised their views. By the end of the 1990s, both sides were in a cul-de-sac. In a context in which political gatherings and mobilisation were exceptional and unusual, the reformists were unable to create sufficient mass support for their demands. At the same time, the state was unable to complete-ly reject the reformists' demands because these were clearly balanced, rational and legitimate. For a while, the stalemate was exacerbated by the violence perpetrated by al-Qa'ida, and by the regional and global changes that this ushered in. However, both sides eventually had to acknowledge that Islam and the Saudi state cannot be separated, and that reform had to be based upon the values and concepts of Islam. The main issue then became how, when, and under what conditions the de-mands of the Islamists might converge with the readiness of the state to transform. Like every modern state, Saudi Arabia is subject to various struggles for control and power; it is not easy to imagine the current regime abandoning its post anytime soon.

❦

In Egypt, the crisis in the Islamist movement manifested itself slightly differently. After the release of the Muslim Brotherhood members who were incarcerated in the 1970s, the Egyptian state rejected all efforts to normalise relations with the Islamist movement or to incorporate it into Egypt's body politic.

In the years following the 1973 October War, Anwar Sadat became so self-confident that he believed no political opposition could serious-ly challenge his rule. Sadat saw the Muslim Brotherhood, and the entire Islamist movement, as a group of pious believers who would quickly be absorbed into the masses as he gathered them around himself. He saw himself as the guarantor and embodiment of Egyptian nationalism, Islam and the faith of the Egyptian people. In his view, any policies that did not emanate from him personally were automatically illegitimate. Even after 1976, when political pluralism was introduced to the country for the first time since the establishment of the republic, Sadat saw himself as an absolute authority who stood above party politics, like a pivot around which all political tendencies would revolve.

In reality, the Islamist trend was bursting onto the scene via all possible means. Several extremist Islamist groups emerged in Egypt in the 1970s (including takfiri groups who denounced other Muslims as unbelievers), and jihadists (who called for the removal of the regime by force).

The Muslim Brotherhood distanced itself from all extremist and pro-violence groups with admirable discipline and conviction. It was clear that the Brotherhood supporters yearned not only for the revival of a longstanding historical legacy, but also that they represented the majority of Egyptians who prefer to express their Islamist views in peaceful, moderate and rational ways.

'Umar al-Tilmisani, the Brotherhood's third al-murshid al-'am (general guide), never concealed his liberal views. The fourth murshid, Muhammad Hamid Abu al-Nasr, was also extremely explicit about his perspective, stating that parliamentary systems honestly express the will of a nation, and called for Egyptians to have the freedom to join political parties, even those that might contradict Islamic beliefs, such as communist or secular parties.

In 1976, as a first slow and calculated step towards political pluralism, Sadat granted permission for the formation of three political platforms within al-Ittihad al-Ishtiraki (the Socialist Union), which was then the only party licensed to operate in Egypt. The Muslim Brotherhood sensed that this might allow them to operate legitimately again as an Islamist political force. Therefore, in March of that year, the Brotherhood brought an application before the Egyptian court seeking to invalidate the banning order that had been in place since 1954. The court rejected their application in a judgement that was perhaps predictable. After two decades of struggle between the Brotherhood and the regime, it was unlikely that the state would grant the Brotherhood full legitimacy on its first attempt. However, Sadat's regime did not actively constrain the Brotherhood during this time, allowing them to engage in propagation and to build an effective public presence. The Brotherhood began to re-publish their monthly magazine, *al-Da'wah*, which became the group's central mouthpiece. The premises of the magazine, in Cairo's al-Tawfiqqiyah Quarter, became the Brotherhood's unofficial headquarters.

In 1977, Sadat issued new legislation on the formation of political parties and the Brotherhood, once again, tried to have their legal status reinstated by the courts. This application was also denied but this did not prevent the Brotherhood from extending its organisational base to the country's universities. Despite facing tough competition from new more radical Islamist groups, Brotherhood members soon dominated the university student unions.

Egypt's universities gradually became a source of anxiety for Sadat as they were transformed into centres of opposition, and protested loudly about his policies of seeking peace and reconciliation with the Zionist state. In September 1981, just weeks before his assassination, Sadat launched an intense campaign against his political opponents, arresting hundreds of public figures, among whom were several Brotherhood personalities including its leader, 'Umar al-Tilmisani. This was the first, and last time, that Sadat seriously engaged the Muslim Brotherhood as a political organisation. A few weeks later, he was dead.

Hosni Mubarak was made president and, during the early years of his rule, he helped to cultivate an atmosphere of tolerance and political liberalism, attempting to vanquish the sharp polarisation that Egypt had been subjected to during the final years of Sadat's rule.

By 1984, the Muslim Brotherhood felt confident enough to contest the parliamentary elections. The elections were organised on a list system, rather than around individual candidates, and because the Brotherhood was still an illegal organisation, it was forced to enter into an alliance with the Wafd Party, which had a liberal orientation, and to contest the elections under its umbrella. The Wafd Party's leader, veteran politician Fu'ad Siraj al-Din, aspired to have the Wafd Party rule Republican Egypt as it had under the monarchy, and saw the Brotherhood as an excellent ally.[5] The election results were disappointing to many of the opposition groups, however, and the Brotherhood was able to win just seven seats in the Assembly. As they took those seats for the first time, very few people seemed to notice that this was the first time since the establishment of the organisation that the voices of its representatives were being heard in the Egyptian parliament.

Over the next two years, members of the Brotherhood discussed the idea of forming a political party under another name, but the idea was quashed when the Brotherhood's leadership realised that the regime had no intention of granting it status as a legitimate political party, no matter what it called itself.

In 1987, Egypt held new parliamentary elections that observers hailed as the most free and fair in the history of the republican era. This time, the Muslim Brotherhood joined a tripartite alliance with the Hizb al-'Amal (Labour Party), which had begun to adopt an Islamist perspective, and the smaller Hizb al-Ahrar al-Libirali (Free Liberals Party). The alliance won 60 seats, 36 of which were attributed to the Muslim Brotherhood.[6]

The strength of the opposition representatives' turned the national assembly into a thorn in the regime's side at a time when economic conditions in Egypt were very difficult. Noting that Israel's withdrawal from the Sinai had been completed, opposition groups pointed out that there was therefore no real danger facing the country. The opposition, therefore, demanded the repeal of the state of emergency and the implementation of political and electoral reforms. When the state refused to respond to these demands, the opposition parties decided to boycott the 1990 elections.

In the 1990s, a long and bitter wave of internal violence was ignited in Egypt by, on the one hand, the delusions of jihadist Islamist forces trying to bring about change through the use of violence and, on the other hand, by the exterminatory inclinations of the state security apparatuses. During the state's campaign against those Islamist forces who had taken up arms, the idea that the Muslim Brotherhood was the source of all evil took root within the regime's security establishment. In the shadow of the tensions dividing the country, the Brotherhood became a prime target of the security apparatus.

In 1992, many of the Brotherhood's leaders were incarcerated as a result of what became known as the Sal-Sabil case, in reference to a computer company that was owned by Brotherhood members and accused by the state of being a front for illegal activities, including plotting to overthrow the regime. In 1994, *al-Da'wah*, the Brotherhood's magazine and only media vehicle was shut down. In the following year, the Brotherhood was subjected to another round of arrests in which eighty-two of its members were rounded up, including 'Abd al-Mun'im Abu al-Futuh and Essam el-Arian. This time, the group was accused of planning to infiltrate trade unions, to revive a banned secret organisation and of striving to overthrow the state.[7]

What no one could argue with was that the Muslim Brotherhood were completely distanced from the groups that had turned to violence, and the organisation was, in fact, helping to prevent young people from resorting to violence. Furthermore, the Brotherhood's activities in the trade unions and student organisations were nothing new. In the 1990s, the number of professional unions allied to the Brotherhood surged. These included engineers, lawyers, pharmacists, doctors and university lecturers. The security clampdown against the Brotherhood thus ran parallel with a campaign to enact legislation that would put an end to its influence in these unions. In 1993, Special Law 100 was issued pertaining to the reorganisation of the unions and just two years later, Law 5 of 1995 was issued, with the very same purpose. The Brotherhood simply found ways to adapt to the legislation, and made a comeback by further strengthening its influence in the unions.

Between the 1970s and the 1990s, the state's view of the Brotherhood shifted. From an initial view that was based on ignorance and arrogance, the state began to see the organisation as a threat to its security. Despite severe security crackdowns, the Brotherhood constantly redeveloped and reformed itself. From the late 1980s, the Brotherhood's organisational work proceeded steadily. Those given leadership positions – including that of the murshid and others in the top leadership structure, the maktab al-irshad (guidance bureau) – were chosen via free elections held among members. The maktab al-irshad consists of fourteen members and in 1992, these were chosen from among eighty-three candidates. The murshid's term of office was also limited to four years with a maximum of two terms, rather than being a life-long position.

However, the main development within the Brotherhood's political culture occurred in 1994, when the organisation stood for parliamentary elections. Although some of its leaders clearly held liberal views, its political orientation was not very clear. More than sixty years after its establishment, few observers were entirely sure of the Brotherhood's political views, and a range of questions came up. Did the organisation aspire to be a political force in a pluralist political environment, or did it see itself as somehow 'above' political parties? Was the organisation primarily religious or political? What was their true position regarding political and intellectual pluralism in Muslim society? What were their views on non-Muslims and women in communities governed by the Islamic frame of reference that they advocated?

By the middle of 1994, the Muslim Brotherhood issued two extremely important documents: the first outlined their political vision; the second explained their position on women.[8] If the Brotherhood's early development in the 1930s depended on the writings of Hasan al-Banna, its second phase (from the end of the incarceration period in the early 1970s to the early 1990s) can be summed up in its commitment to absolutely peaceful activism. The third phase in the evolution of the Brotherhood's political thinking was signalled by the development of these two documents.

In the documents, the Brotherhood affirmed their belief in the compatibility of their vision of nizam al-shura al-Islami (an Islamic system of consultation and achieving consensus) with democracy in its modern form, and with the notion of the ummah as the source of authority. The Brotherhood also affirmed that the ummah requires a written constitution. The documents also clarified the organisation's position on the protection of public and private freedoms, the responsibility of rulers and how they can be held accountable before a freely elected parliamentary assembly that enjoys legislative and oversight powers. In a decisive settlement of the longstanding debate on the nature of shura, the Brotherhood noted that resolutions of an elected assembly place rulers under obligation. The Brotherhood also expressed its acceptance of party pluralism and the peaceful rotation of power among groups and parties by means of regular popular elections. This comprehensive political vision does not differ from most modern political visions of the state except in its affirmation that the constitution be based on the principles and objectives of the shari'ah.

On the question of women, the Brotherhood affirmed women's right to work and participate in legislative and oversight assemblies, as well as their right to join political parties and hold public office, with the exception of the position of state president.

These developments in the Brotherhood's political thinking did not help the organisation much during the 1990s, especially with regard to winning back the right to exist and engage in political work in Egypt. The state continued to see the Brotherhood as a security threat, even while it was contesting elections. The Brotherhood contested the 1995 elections, nominating more than 140 candidates. However, the regime's open interference in the process left the Brotherhood with only a single seat in parliament, and the ruling National Party with over 95 per cent of the seats. In the 2000 elections, the Brotherhood managed to extract 17 seats, but the state remained stubbornly opposed to granting the Brotherhood the right to legally exist.

In 1996, a group of young former Brotherhood members tried to establish a liberal Islamist party, but were no more successful than the Brotherhood itself. The group were made up of Muslim and Christian professionals and intellectuals, headed by an engineer, Abu'l 'Ala Madi. They applied to register a new political party called Hizb al-Wasat (Centre Party). Their aim was to try and find a way out of the impasse created by the regime's refusal to licence the Muslim Brotherhood, and address the fact that Egypt's broad-based Islamist movement still had no recourse to legitimate party-political activity. Strangely, the Centre Party's project was rejected by both the Brotherhood and the regime. The Brotherhood rejected the idea of a party acting in place of itself, while the regime saw the group as a façade for the Brotherhood. The regime responded to the licensing request by arresting Madi, and two others, accusing them of forming a party to act as a proxy for a banned organisation.[9] The official Parties Committee then also rejected the Centre Party's licence application.

After a lengthy legal process, the group made a new application in 1998 under the name Hizb al-Wasat al-Misri (Egyptian Centre Party). This one was also rejected. In 2004, the group put forward a third application under the name Hizb al-Wasat al-Jadid (New Centre Party). This time, the party was indeed new in that its political programme was less Islamic and more liberal, but it too was rejected. The Centre Party then went on to legally challenge their third rejection at various legislative and governmental levels.

The situation in the country did not become any easier after the events of 9/11, and they have since improved only marginally. Apart from invading Afghanistan and Iraq, George Bush (Jr)'s administration pressured the Arab regimes to liberalise politically. The belief in Washington was that political oppression gave rise to violence and that one of the means to destroy al-Qa'ida was to accelerate democratic transformation.

The pressure from Washington came at a time of widespread political mobilisation in Egypt. Within the ruling National Party, Jamal Mubarak, the president's son and likely successor, was trying to rebuild support for the party through its policy committee, which made a series of promises to introduce gradual political reform.

Meanwhile, in 2004, a group of activists from several opposition groups joined forces to establish al-Harakah al-Misriyyah min ajli al-Tagyir (the Egyptian Movement for Change), which became known as the Kefaya Movement (Kefaya means 'enough' in Arabic). Via a series of gatherings and protest marches, Kefaya demanded the suspension of the state of emergency and democratic transformation, beginning with the freedom to form political parties and presidential elections in which more than one candidate stands for election.

In 2005, the Muslim Brotherhood launched a series of public protest meetings in Cairo and other Egyptian cities. What stood out was that the Brotherhood gatherings made nationalist demands that echoed the calls being made by other political groups and did not focus exclusively on their own agenda. The state responded to the meetings with another round of arrests in which hundreds of Brotherhood members were incarcerated, including well-known media personality and Brotherhood leader, Essam El-Arian.

The protests had two important consequences. First, the US administration stopped putting pressure on Cairo when they realised that democratic transformation in Egypt would strengthen the influence of the Islamist movement. Second, Egyptians claimed the right, albeit de facto, to hold gatherings and protest marches without asking for permission from the state.

The regime tried to contain the ongoing political mobilisation by making a constitutional amendment. In fact, the president surprised Egyptians by calling for Article 76 of the constitution, which pertained to the election of the president, to be amended. Since the establishment of the republic, the president had been chosen by parliament and this was followed by a popular referendum that had no effect on parliament's choice. Mubarak's proposal was to allow the president to be elected directly by the people from among several candidates. The constitution was indeed amended but, as things turned out, the change served to further stymie the aspirations of the Egyptian electorate.

Article 76 was replaced with a long and exasperating clause that put so many preconditions in place that virtually the only candidates who could qualify to stand for president would be leaders of the ruling party. The National Party had an absolute majority in the assembly, so the amendment was easily passed. When presidential elections were subsequently convened on 7 September 2005, Mubarak did indeed face two opponents, neither of whom presented any serious challenge to his re-election. As soon as the presidential elections were over, preparations began for parliamentary elections scheduled for November of the same year. After years of open interference by the government in previous elections, Egyptians waited to see how serious the regime really was about its promises of political reform.

The parliamentary elections were held in three phases stretching out over the entire month. The elections concluded with the Muslim Brotherhood attaining 88 seats, which was a little less than a fifth of the total of 454 seats in the Assembly (including the 10 parliamentarians who are not elected but appointed by the president). Other opposition forces attained 14 seats. This meant that the ruling National Party maintained their absolute majority with 325 seats, exceeding the sensitive two-thirds barrier necessary for any constitutional amendment.

The election process was not as transparent as it should have been, but it was an improvement on the previous elections. The one certainty was that the face of the Egyptian People's Assembly had changed, and together with it, the country's political landscape. There was no longer any doubt, among opposition forces or in government circles, that the

Muslim Brotherhood was a force capable of matching the ruling National Party and its government. Everyone now waited to see what the longer-term consequences of the elections would be.

The Muslim Brotherhood had survived for decades, defending its identity as an Islamist group and a political group. It now faced the challenge of proving itself to be an inclusive nationalist force, capable of addressing the concerns of the whole Egyptian nation and speaking on its behalf. The state faced a challenge of a different kind: that is, finding a solution for the novel and rather uncomfortable reality in which the central opposition force in government was technically illegitimate and operating despite a banning order.

Like the Saudi situation, although in a different climate and with different stipulations, the 2005 elections drew the Muslim Brotherhood and the Egyptian state closer to one another. However, the road ahead seems long and strewn with obstacles. Egyptians need to achieve consensus on the overarching principles and interests of their country, as a necessary precondition to building a rotational democratic system. Before this, however, the ruling elite has to realise that monopolising power is harming the basis and objectives of their own sovereignty.

17

The limits of the reformist victory

The third day of November 2002 was special in the history of Turkey. After a tumultuous election, the victory of the Justice and Development Party (or the AKP, as it is known by its Turkish acronym) was announced. The party had been established only two years before and already enjoyed a comfortable parliamentary majority. The extent of their victory surpassed all the indications from opinion polls as well as the expectations of observers of Turkish politics, while also signifying the astonishing collapse of Turkey's traditional political parties.

Eight decades after the establishment of the republic, a group of young Islamists – most of whom were no older than fifty – had managed to gain a sweeping victory in the general elections. These were the republic's own children; they had been nurtured in its education institutions and immersed in its culture and values, only to come into power in the name of the very same values that the republic had tried so hard to efface from Turkey's collective memory. With the AKP's victory, it was no longer possible to ignore the death-by-election of the Turkish state's longstanding, vehement war against Islam, a war that had been modern Turkey's defining characteristic since its inception.

After some procrastination and several attempts by the elite to stall the formation of the new government, Abdullah Gül, the second most highly placed leader in the AKP, formed the party's first Cabinet. The party's leader, Recep Tayyip Erdoğan, had been prevented from contesting the elections or accepting the role of party's leader by a court edict linked to his previous conviction in a case relating to insulting the memory of the founder of the republic, Mustafa Kemal Atatürk. However, the AKP's control over the parliament allowed it to introduce amendments to the country's laws, and within a matter of months, Erdoğan won a by-election held for a seat that had become vacant and entered parliament. Shortly thereafter, Erdoğan became prime minister and Abdullah Gül became his very effective and active minister of foreign affairs.

Based on the logic of the past, most observers were concerned that conflict would emerge speedily between the new government and Turkey's army generals. The AKP's Islamist tendencies were well known, and the army, which had staunchly guarded the secular nature of the republic for years, was hostile to everything Islamic. However, Erdoğan and his comrades surprised everyone by managing to govern successfully and by implementing a programme of political and economic reforms unseen in Turkey for more than half a century. This raised many questions about the secrets of the AKP's achievements, and as to whether Turkey had finally found a path to success and a way out of the bitter identity crisis it had endured for most of the twentieth century.

In truth, the AKP is not an Islamist party, either in terms of its political programme or in the rhetoric of its leaders. The problem of a non-Islamist party being led by Islamists reflects the contradiction that a secular, anti-Islamic republic emerged from the heart of the Ottoman Empire, which was the longest surviving Islamic order in world history. It also reflects the changing and unstable character of the forces of political Islam.

The Republic of Turkey came into being through the efforts of Mustafa Kemal (thereafter known as Atatürk, father of the Turks) in March 1923. Kemal was a prominent and disciplined officer in the Ottoman Army who fought bravely against the Italian invasion of Libya, and was at the heart of the battle against the British at Gallipoli at the onset of the First World War. Kemal also led the Ottoman defence of

Palestine against the British, and was probably the last senior officer to withdraw from the Palestinian front in 1917.

However, when the Greek army – with the encouragement of the British and French – occupied western Turkey's Izmir region in early 1919, Kemal handed in his resignation and rushed to help organise Turkish resistance to the Greek invasion.[1] Within a short period Kemal was able to gather an effective force from among the Anatolian tribes, remnants of the Ottoman Army, as well as clergy and civil servants. Together, these resistance fighters waged a war of independence that played a decisive role in determining the future of Turkey.

At a time when the Sultan and his government in Istanbul had become a plaything in the hands of the British Embassy and its Navy officers who controlled the Bosphorus, the resistance fighters in Anatolia began defending the country, inflicting defeat after defeat against the Greek forces in Anatolia while simultaneously encroaching on the French forces in the south. Soon thereafter, Kemal announced his challenge to the regime in Istanbul by establishing a parliamentary-type structure called the Great National Assembly for the forces and activist groups that had gathered around him in the tiny city of Ankara. By the autumn of 1922, Kemal had defeated the Greeks in Anatolia, and become a popular national hero of the Turkish people, whose pride and honour had been shattered by their defeat in the First World War. A few weeks later, Kemal announced that his national assembly and the forces he led were the ruling authorities, and not the government in Istanbul. He then abolished the Ottoman Sultanate but left the institution of the caliphate in place. At the beginning of 1923, Turkey became a republic and Ankara was chosen as its capital, over Istanbul.

Kemal was a child of the modernisation that occurred during the Ottoman epoch; he was also a member of the military, often the first state institution to be subjected to modernisation and therefore the most modernised. Since the mid-nineteenth century, most leaders in the Ottoman Empire had understood modernisation as emulating European paradigms of state and society. Thus, when Kemal became president of the new Turkish Republic, he and his companions knew no other vision of modernisation than the Western one.

From another perspective, Kemal and his companions believed that that the Ottoman legacy had become burdensome and was inhibiting the rise and progress of the new Turkey. During his long time in office as president of the republic, Kemal worked to rid Turkey of its Ottoman history and culture. Because he did not distinguish between what was Ottoman and what was Islamic, his policies implicitly waged a war against Islam.

On 3 March 1923, Kemal abolished the caliphate, and with it, the position of shaykh al-Islam (the state's most senior religious scholar), the Islamic law courts, the ministry of endowments, Islamic schools and Islamic education syllabi. In the following year, the republic enacted its first constitution, which affirmed the sovereignty of the nation, but also that Islam was the religion of the state. Four years later, even this extremely general clause was dropped.

After a short period in which multiple parties were allowed to operate, only the ruling party – the Republican People's Party – remained. All opposition movements were suppressed, by means of force where necessary, and Kemal held the reins of power with an iron grip. All state institutions began constructing a cult of personality around Kemal as deliverer and saviour and father of the Turkish nation; more accurately, he turned into a modern dictator.

No sooner had the 1920s drawn to an end than all Sufi orders were banned and their lodges shut down. Latin letters replaced Arabic ones in the Turkish alphabet and, within a few decades, the Turks could no longer read their history and literature in its original form. European terminology was borrowed at random, and educational methodologies were overhauled. Muezzins were prohibited from sounding the call to prayer in Arabic, traditional Ottoman art and music was banned, women's headscarves were banned, and European-style hats became obligatory for men. The state took control of all charity and other Islamic organisations and enacted laws that clashed with Islamic laws and values. Very strict regulations regarding permission for citizens wanting to undertake the ḥajj were enacted and their numbers restricted.

In 1931, Mustafa Kemal announced that the ideology of the state was founded on six principles: republicanism, nationalism, populism, statism, secularism, and revolutionism, and, in 1937, these principles became a part of the national constitution. If secularism in its original European form aimed to separate the spheres of authority occupied by the state and the church, in Atatürk's state, secularism was a war on all religious institutions with the aim of ensuring the domination of a single authority: the state.

Atatürk died in 1938 and his comrade in the war for independence, Ismet Inönü, became president. The prevailing view was that the state had won its battle against religion and Ottoman culture was over but reality proved otherwise. Atatürk's programme had succeeded in the military institutions, the state bureaucracy and the legislature, but the majority of Turks, especially in the countryside and the older parts of the cities, maintained their allegiance to Islam and its legacy. The Sufi Orders remained secretly active and hundreds of thousands of copies of the epistles of Bediüzzaman Said Nursî, a Muslim scholar who opposed the policies of the state and was placed under house arrest, were still being distributed. Thus, while the official Turkish radio broadcast modern Western music, the people were listening to songs in praise of the Prophet and reciting Sufi poetry. In fact, even the Turkish Language and History Academy that was established by Atatürk transformed itself into a centre for the revival of Ottoman history when its academics realised that it was impossible to envision a Turkish nation without the Ottoman legacy.

After the end of the Second World War, Turkey opted to join the Allies, and became one of the earliest signatories to the UN Charter. In the shade cast by Western liberal democracy, Inönü and others in the Republican People's Party believed there would be little danger in allowing a limited degree of party pluralism and political liberalism. Thus, even before the Second World War broke out, the ruling elite began to sense the negative effects of the state's heavy handedness on Turkish society.

Four former members of the Republican People's Party, Adnan Menderes, Refik Koraltan, Celâl Bayar and the historian Fuat Köprülü, were given permission to establish an opposition party, which they named the Democratic Party.[2] A few months after its foundation, the new party, under the leadership of Menderes, won 61 seats in the 1946 parliament. In 1950, the Democrats swept up most of the votes, winning 420 seats in parliament, and leaving the Republican Party with just 63 seats.

Menderes' manifesto, which enabled his party to attain this great victory, was amazing yet simple at the same time. He promised the people that if he won the elections, he would restore the call to prayer back to Arabic, lift the restrictions on religious practices, allow the building of new mosques, re-license the Sufi Orders, and respect people's religious beliefs.

Menderes and his party won again in the 1954 and 1957 elections. In 1960, his opponents ran out of patience and Inönü called for military intervention. Menderes and his government were quickly overthrown in a coup led by Cemal Gürsel, an army officer. Menderes and two of his comrades were executed, charged with striving to transform Turkey into a religious state and submitting to Western influence. Menderes was initially buried on the remote island of Ada until a later government under Turgut Özal undertook to reinter his body in an appropriate location in Istanbul.

Menderes's programme was not radical in any way, but his popularity exposed the deep chasm between Atatürk's vision of the Turkish republic and the Turkish people's allegiance to their faith. Menderes's ousting brought to an end the first attempt to reconcile the Turkish people with their modern state.

After the coup, Turkey entered an era of political and economic instability. The coup leaders instituted a widespread 'cleansing' campaign
among military officers who had attained the ranks of general or colonel, and targeted anyone who had shown sympathy with Menderes. A
new constitution was enacted that strengthened the state's powers and
for the first time in Turkey, a national security council was introduced
consisting of the president of the republic, the prime minister, the commander of the defence force and leaders of the various branches of the
armed forces. Through its control of the National Security Council, the
military influenced the country's leaders and dictated state policy.

In October 1961, civilian rule was reintroduced and new elections
were held. The Republican People's Party made a comeback under Inönü, and the Democratic Party returned under the new name of the
Justice Party. Two radical new nationalist parties also entered the political sphere. In addition, several Marxist organisations became active
in the country. For several years after this no single party was able to
achieve a clear parliamentary majority and form a stable government.
Instead, state governance became a toy that the generals tossed back
and forth between Süleyman Demirel, the leader of the Justice Party,
and to Bülent Ecevit, the leader of the Republican People's Party.

In 1970, Necmettin Erbakan, a young Turkish engineer who had
been educated in Turkey and in Germany, entered politics. He announced the formation of a party with an Islamist orientation called the
National Order Party.[3] Erbakan believed in democracy as sufficiently
expressing the will and the choice of the people, but in contrast to Menderes, who was a liberal who respected Islam, Erbakan affirmed his
principled allegiance to his faith.

The military generals, who saw themselves as protecting Atatürk's
republic, made their animosity towards Erbakan clear from the beginning. In the year after the establishment of the National Order Party, the

army intervened and were able to proscribe the National Order Party and the Turkish Marxist-oriented Workers Party, preventing both from continuing their political activities. The army then also amended thirty-one articles of the constitution to ensure full state control over all civil organisations and the media, and completely banned any Islamic orientation in political activity.

Erbakan was undeterred. In 1973, he returned to politics once more as leader of the National Salvation Party. The Turkish political elite were surprised when he won 49 parliamentary seats, making him the kingmaker in a coalition government. Bülent Ecevit, the leader of the party that had won the most seats but not enough for an outright majority, was forced to enter into an alliance with Erbakan, who became a partner in government for the first time.

In 1974, the coalition government reached the height of its popularity by deciding to send the army to protect the Turkish minority in Northern Cyprus. This faded quickly though. In the universities and streets of the major cities, political violence flared up between leftist forces and right-wing nationalists. Amid widespread instability, growing corruption, and the failure of Turkish politicians to safeguard the economy, the country descended into a crushing economic crisis. By the end of the 1970s, the inflation rate was over 100 per cent.

As Turkey lost its balance and direction, the Islamic revolution achieved victory in Iran, and an Islamic transformation in the region seemed as if it might be a real possibility. It was in this context that, on 6 September 1980, Erbakan organised a million-person protest in the conservative city of Konya in support of Palestine and the defence of Jerusalem. Leaders of the army and the secular political parties were astounded at the numbers that joined the protest and Erbakan's popularity grew.

Six days later, the army, led by its commander-in-chief General Kenan Evren, announced that it was taking control of the state. The leaders of the military coup disbanded the parliament, suspended the

constitution and arrested thousands of political activists of all orientations. The aims of the coup leaders were to put an end to the political
chaos and violence that were undermining the country and to prevent
the rapidly spreading Islamist movement from making further headway.

Although democracy and rule of law had become the West's most
important ideological weapon in its struggle against the Soviet Union,
NATO's generals breathed a sigh of relief as they watched Ankara's
generals take power once more. With the Cold War at its height, Turkey
occupied a pivotal position in the West's defence strategy and no one in
any of the European capitals or in America wanted to even consider the
possibility of Turkey withdrawing from NATO or the Western camp.

However, the speed with which the army was able to assert its control in Turkey did nothing to conceal the futility of the coup within the
wider context of the republic's history. The constitution that the generals had just abolished was the same one that had been written under the
supervision of the officers who led the coup in 1960, and which was
amended under the supervision of the generals who led the 1971 coup.
The republic that Kenan Evren had sprung into action to save was the
very same one that his predecessors in the 1960s and 1970s thought
they had completely safeguarded.

In essence, this third coup revealed that the country's crisis was related to the very foundations on which the republic was based, and that
Turkey would lurch from one crisis to the next until those foundations
could be laid once more. The events that unfolded over the next two
decades confirmed this. Like all the earlier coup leaders, Evren and his
comrades 'cleansed' the military apparatuses and the state bureaucra-
cies of anyone suspected of holding Islamist or leftist views, in fact of
holding any traditional religious beliefs. Attacks on individuals with
religious inclinations became an established tradition in the military.

A new constitution was put in place, regarded as the most comprehensive, both in the history of the republic and among the world's constitutions – as if its drafters did not want to leave anything to chance or

interpretation. Then a gradual and carefully supervised return to civilian life was allowed.

Undoubtedly, the person who dominated the political sphere in the 1980s and early 1990s was Turgut Özal. This insightful economist was able to gain the confidence of the generals and inspire the Turkish people to work their way out of economic decline and loosen the grip of the military over the state.

Özal founded the Motherland Party, which swept to victory in the 1983 elections, before any of the other political parties were able to organise themselves. It was clear that the army had put their faith in Özal's ability to bring about a comfortable normalisation in political life. Soon the old politicians returned, giving new names to old parties. Süleyman Demirel made a comeback at the head of the Party of the True Path, and Bülent Ecevit returned as head of the Democratic Left Party; to these two were added the Social Democrat Party led by Erdal İnönü. Necmettin Erbakan even found a place for the Islamist movement under the banner of the Welfare Party. Özal was successful in retaining power in the next elections, held in 1987, and displayed great political acumen in managing even the generals' manipulative abilities.

Özal strongly believed in the need to limit state control over society, to strengthen civic freedoms and encourage civil society initiatives. Although his reputation and his ability to build the economic sector were solid, he strove to implement his vision across other sectors as well. That is, Özal's government not only supported the private sector, but also re-established media freedom for newspapers and other media houses of various orientations; he also allowed religious and Quranic schools to re-open and for de facto endowment foundations to be re-established.

From the late-1980s, a major Islamic revitalisation took place in Turkey, and this was reflected in private television channels, newspapers, book publishing and the return of Islamic education in schools and universities. Co-operation agreements with the EU aimed at revitalising the economy of the Anatolian region, where allegiance to Islam was still deeply entrenched, played an important part in this. The economic transition in Anatolia transformed the region's business and industrial class, whose ranks swelled with increasing numbers of business executives and industrialists with strong Islamic commitments.

In 1989, Özal resigned as prime minister to become president instead. With his exit from the political party, however, the Motherland Party lost its touch. Instability wracked Turkey once more, and was made worse by rampant corruption among the ruling class. Ordinary citizens lost confidence in the political parties and their candidates.

When the results of the 1995 elections were announced it became clear that the people had surprised the mainstream political parties once more. Erbakan's Welfare Party won 158 seats in the national assembly, making it the largest party in parliament, but not by an absolute majority. Erbakan then entered into an alliance with the Motherland Party led by Tansu Çiller, and it was agreed that he would assume the position of prime minister for two years, thereafter vacating the position for Çiller. Thus, in mid 1996, after striving to achieve this goal for a quarter of a century, Erbakan finally became prime minister.[4]

His government was successful in initiating Turkey's economic recovery. In terms of foreign affairs, Erbakan pursued Islamist policies, or more accurately, Ottoman policies: he wanted to reassert Turkey's leadership of the Islamic world and did not hesitate to state his desire to establish a larger Islamic bloc. His means of achieving this was to suggest establishing an Islamic confederation similar to the EU, comprised of eight central Islamic states.

Erbakan faced great difficulties in achieving this, but he pursued his goal stubbornly, placing his faith in the passage of time and the gradual rise of popular pressure. Turkey in the 1990s was living through an intense debate about its identity and the futility of joining the EU. Erbakan strove to prove to the Turkish people that their dignity, position and prosperity were more likely to be attained by strengthening their relations with the Islamic world, and especially their Arab neighbours.

Erbakan also considered Turkey's role from a nationalist perspective, arguing that his country's sphere of influence stretched from the Balkans to the borders of western China.

Of course, the generals were lying in wait for this ambitious Islamist leader. In the first few months after he assumed the role of prime minister, military leaders began exerting pressure on the coalition government. From the beginning of 1997, the National Security Council, which is controlled by the military, began making a series of demands. Among their key demands, the generals insisted that Erbakan shut down the Islamic schools, remove religious content from all educational syllabi, increase the number of years of compulsory secular education for children, suppress the Islamic workers' leagues and shut down the newly established jurisprudential councils. They also asked Erbakan to strengthen relations with the Zionist state.

In making these demands, the generals aimed to belittle Erbakan before his supporters and show the Islamist leader as submissive to the secular system. When Erbakan was forced to receive the Israeli foreign minister, and to offer him an official welcome at the mausoleum of Atatürk on the commemoration day of the founding of the republic, many of his supporters wondered whether he thought holding office was more important than holding on to his principles and convictions.

Ultimately, Erbakan's concessions to the generals, and his attempts to reassure the country's secularists were of no use. It was clear from the outset that the generals had provisionally accepted Erbakan, in the hope that placing him in the position of the prime minister would expose his shortcomings. When Erbakan demonstrated his resolve, by bringing about a real recovery of the Turkish economy and improving his country's relations with a large number of Islamic countries, the generals realised that they would have to get rid of him. In mid 1997, only a year after Erbakan had become prime minister, Turkey stood at a crossroads once more: Erbakan would have to resign or the military would stage another coup. To avoid pushing the country into another epoch of military rule, Erbakan resigned.

In 1998, a decree was issued, banning the Welfare Party from all political activity, and the Turkish justice system began pursuing Erbakan and several members of his party on various charges relating to transgressing the secular covenants of the state and insulting its symbols. Erbakan and his party resorted to the traditional Turkish exit strategy, and simply established a new party called the Virtue Party. By 2000, this too, was banned. It became clear that influential secular groups within the army, state bureaucracy and the justice system would do anything in their power to keep Erbakan from receiving sufficient electoral support to share power.

At this point, divisions began to surface within Erbakan's party and among his followers. It was no secret that Erbakan led his party like a sultan, insisting on wielding absolute power, and managing all party affairs, no matter how small, and even during the periods in which he was prohibited from engaging in political work. After more than three decades on the Turkish political stage, at the helm of its Islamist party, Erbakan had become more of a burden than an inspiration to his colleagues. His advanced age and the aspirations of a new generation of young Turkish Islamists played a role in splitting the Islamist party. However, the split was an intellectual one too.

In February 2000, Recep Tayyip Erdoğan, who was then a prominent leader in the Virtue Party, stated that

> it was wrong to equate the party with religion and religion with politics. We do not aim to establish an Islamic state and we are not a theocratic party. But in the case where pious people immerse themselves in political life, while abstaining from regarding religious standards as their frame of reference, we cannot speak about political Islam.[5]

307

Erdoğan's statements were made in defence of the Virtue Party, but they also alluded to his search for an exit from the debilitating hostility between Erbakan and the various secular interest groups within the state. As soon as the banning of the Virtue Party was announced in 2000, Erdoğan and a group of his comrades announced their intention to establish an independent party. In the following year the AKP was born, led by Erdoğan and Abdullah Gül.

⊙᙮⊙

Recep Tayyip Erdoğan was born in 1954 in one of Istanbul's old quarters. After Atatürk chose Ankara as the capital of the new republic, Istanbul continued to uphold the Ottoman legacy. Whereas Ankara became a stronghold of the ruling secular elite who were hostile to religion, religious traditions remained alive and active in Istanbul, in the daily practices of its families, in Sufi circles and in the many Ottoman mosques spread across the city.

Erdoğan attended an Imam Hatip high school (a vocational school for religious scholars), and then studied business administration at the Aksaray School of Economics and Commercial Sciences (now part of Marmara University) in Istanbul. In his youth, he joined the National Salvation Party, and subsequently joined every party that Erbakan established after each of his previous parties were banned. In 1985, Erdoğan was made leader of the Istanbul branch of the Welfare Party. In 1994, he won a landslide victory in Istanbul's mayoral election. During his period as mayor of Istanbul, Erdoğan revived the city to a remarkable degree, thus drawing attention to himself, and becoming one of the most popular political figures in the country. However, he was simultaneously hounded by the courts because of certain verses of poetry he once recited in a speech in the city of Diyarbakir that some perceived as insulting to Atatürk's memory.

When he established the AKP, Erdoğan announced that the new party would preserve the foundations of the republic and would refrain from participating in altercations with the Turkish armed forces, saying:

> We will pursue clear and active policies in order to reach the objective that was set by Atatürk to establish a civilised and modern society within the framework of the Islamic values that 99 per cent of the citizens of Turkey believe in.

Judging from Erdoğan's subsequent statements, some saw him as no more than an ambitious Islamist who was striving to please the army and the secular state in order to attain power. However, in truth, Erdoğan and his comrades were certain that, even though sixty years had passed since the demise of Atatürk, no Islamist party could succeed in the prevailing political climate. What Erdoğan wanted, therefore, was to establish a political consensus between the supporters of Atatürk's legacy and the Turkish majority who subscribed to prevailing Islamic values. His hope was that this consensus would allow for rational governance, put an end to the state's war on religion, and stop the conflict between the defenders of Islamic identity and the guardians of the republic's secular values. The AKP is not an Islamist party, nor is it another of Erbakan's marathon attempts to rebuild the Turkish state on Islamic foundations. The AKP is a conservative secular party that respects the beliefs and faith of the Turkish people.

This tense mix of Atatürkism and Islam, combined with the enormous popularity that Erdoğan and his comrades attained during the years in which they managed several of Turkey's municipalities. Added to this was enormous support from the Muslim Businessmen's and Industrialists Union and an army of capable young activists, who enabled the AKP to launch an exceptionally successful election campaign in 2002. The AKP won a landslide victory, while the traditional secular parties on both the left and the right lost out.

The army generals expressed deep scepticism about the AKP, but made no move to prevent the party from forming a government. The timing might have been a factor in preventing the army from taking action. Turkey had been in a crippling economic crisis since 1999, with the Turkish Lire losing 50 per cent of its value. The EU summit in Helsinki had announced the beginning of negotiations about Turkey's bid to join the union. At that point, any direct military intervention or manipulation of the election results would do nothing to alleviate the economic crisis, lighten the popular mood in Turkey or convince the EU to change its views on military rule. The leadership of the AKP and the leadership of the army therefore both had to bet on time eventually strengthening their cards.

For the next two years, the AKP government put tremendous effort into reviving the economy and lowering the inflation rate and attempting to gain membership of the EU. Erdoğan used the EU's demands to improve Turkey's human rights record and to demand a complete separation between the government and the defence force, so as to put an end to military interference in matters of state and governance. In a major step, the National Security Council with its oppressive military decision-making structures was abolished and replaced by a consultative committee linked to the office of the prime minister. Most of the committee, including its secretary-general, were civilians. In addition, for the first time in Turkey, the defence budget was made subject to the approval of parliament and to judicial oversight.

The AKP's strongest support came from a totally unexpected quarter. In the context of the US-led 'war on terror' and US insistence on changing educational syllabi and the cultural and political climate in many Islamic countries, Washington saw the secular orientation of Turkey's Islamists as a model worthy of encouraging in other Islamic countries. Erdoğan was warmly welcomed at the White House in Washington and the Turkish generals were informed that the US would oppose any military action against the AKP government.

After the US invasion of Iraq, however, the US administration under Bush (Jr) realised that maintaining good relations with Turkey under the AKP was not necessarily going to be easy. The Turkish parliament, in which the AKP enjoyed a comfortable majority, voted against allowing US forces to use Turkish territory as a base in the Middle East. This decision was eventually revised several weeks after the onset of the invasion, when Erdoğan allowed the Americans to move logistical supplies from Turkey to Iraq.

Internally, the AKP governed the country fairly and had no desire to incite the military. The generals did not abandon their scepticism about Erdoğan or his party, but the regional tensions arising out of the invasion of Iraq, and the attention of the US and the EU, provided a certain amount of protection for Erdoğan and his government. Successes at home entrenched the popularity of the party and its government.

Erdoğan and his foreign minister Abdullah Gül began to gain confidence. The Erdoğan government criticised US policies in Iraq, especially America's alliance with Kurdish nationalist parties, and expressed concern about the Iraqi Turks. Erdoğan then surprised many by directing stinging criticisms at the policies of the Israelis towards the Palestinians in the West Bank and the Gaza Strip. Although some observers pointed to tensions in the Turkish-Israeli relationship being heightened by reports of increasing Israeli activities in northern Iraq, Erdoğan's statements nonetheless brought to mind Erbakan's historical commitment to the Palestinian cause.

In the third year of its first term in office, however, a strange shift tarnished the policies of the AKP. Turkey suddenly disengaged itself from developments in Iraq and suspended its criticisms of Israelis. At the beginning of May 2005, Erdoğan and his wife attracted global attention by visiting the Zionist state. There, Erdoğan met with Israeli prime minister Ariel Sharon and announced his willingness to mediate in peace talks between the Israelis and the Palestinians. His offer received no response; Erdoğan had seen his efforts as helping to open a path through which he could assist the Palestinians. However, his visit to the Zionist state, at a time when the Palestinians were subject to the tyranny of Israeli policies, was perceived as a huge concession to the Israelis. The matter did not end there, however, and just a few weeks later Erdoğan's government hosted an official meeting between the Israelis and the Pakistanis. It seemed Turkey was attempting to play a mediatory role, not only between Israelis and Palestinians, but also between the Israelis and the Islamic countries.

These shifts in Turkey's foreign policy did not occur in a vacuum. In early 2005 pressure groups linked to the military began flexing their muscles, offering incentives to several AKP parliamentarians to resign from the party and thus weaken Erdoğan's parliamentary majority. At the same time, the US increased pressure on the Turkish government to change its policies on Iraq and Palestine, and the EU's decision regarding Turkey's application to join the union was imminent. The policy changes made by Erdoğan's government did indeed contribute to a lessening of US pressure and helped to calm tensions in the country, at least for a while. In October 2005, a conference of the European foreign ministers announced their agreement to allow Turkey to apply for EU membership and to begin the long negotiations process linked to this. It appeared as if the Islamist 'problem' in Turkey was not entirely internal; indeed, it was probably more of an external problem on the whole.

In mid 2007, Turkey went through a major constitutional crisis when the AKP nominated its foreign minister Abdullah Gül for the position of president. Because Gül's wife wore a headscarf, the military generals and the secular parties opposed his nomination. Parliamentary elections were held in which the AKP again achieved a huge victory, thereby paving the way for Gül to become president. However, a shadow fell over the country once again in 2008, when the attorney general presented a file to the constitutional court accusing the AKP, its government, and its senior leaders, of striving to Islamise public life and undermine the secular system.

Turkey's future remains unpredictable. Certainly Atatürk would never have imagined the difficulties the state he had built would face within just two decades of his demise. The AKP's attempts to find a balance between Islam and Turkish secularism, which is so utterly opposed to religion, were by no means the first, but Adnan Menderes's earlier efforts ended in bloodshed. However, Turkey is now very different from what it was in the 1950s. Not only is the Islamist trend much stronger and more pervasive, but the relationship between Turkey and Europe seems to be ever-more complex.

The love–hate relationship between the EU and Turkey, as both a secular and an Islamic country, was a strong guarantor for the entrenchment of civil rule in Turkey and seems to have clipped the talons of the military institutions. However, the wisdom, fairness and strong sense of responsibility that characterises the leaders of the AKP cannot be ignored. In fact, it can even be argued that Turkey, under the AKP, finally reconciled with itself. Undoubtedly, the future failure or success of the AKP will raise the bigger question of whether the Turkish path is valid for other countries in the Islamic world.

18

Conclusion: The Islamists and the future

For several decades now, the world has witnessed a religious revival that has manifested itself in various ways and involved different faiths and traditions – Muslim, Christian, Jewish, Hindu and Buddhist. This seems to be driven by an increasing sense of alienation in an age dominated by the incessant pursuit of wealth, power and material goods; and in which human reason has ostensibly become the primary reference point for social relations and morality. At first glance, even the Islamic Awakening seems to be a part of this global religious revival. Naturally, Muslims share a common cultural space with the rest of humanity, and they, too, experience the tyranny of reason, rampant consumerism, and unfettered military power. However, there has always been something unique about Islam – something that differentiates the needs and aspirations of Muslims, and characterises the nature of their relationship with their faith and its historical legacy.

For many centuries, Islam provided the central framework and point of reference for Muslims, shaping their lives and worldview. Moreover, this framework was not displaced as a result of conflict between the Muslim community and any religious hierarchy, as was the case with Christianity in Europe. Islam was toppled by the brute force of modernisation, backed up by the power of imperialist administrations. Muslims were not consulted and, in most cases, they opposed this change. The Islamists are not fundamentalists in the manner defined by Protestantism; they claim no special religious status that differentiates them from other Muslims; they do not claim to be a chosen elite, or to have been 'born again' on the path to the Lord; nor do their leaders claim infallibility, divine insight or inspiration. The forces of political Islam are a historical response to their complex historical context.

The rise of western Europe at the beginning of the nineteenth century was a huge challenge to the Islamic world, fomenting a deep sense of weakness and inferiority, and creating an imbalance of relations in most Islamic countries and societies. In addition, at around the same time, imperial forces swept through the Islamic world, moving swiftly from one region to the next. While Muslims eventually managed to rid themselves of direct colonisation, the West's ongoing political, economic and cultural dominance has been much more difficult to challenge.

A random drive towards modernisation was an initial response to this imbalance of power, but it subverted stable traditional Islamic institutions that existed for centuries. Modernisation undermined the Islamic educational system and the traditional institution of endowments – which had ensured communities' independence from the state for centuries, and promoted strong bonds of social solidarity. Modernisation also toppled the traditional Islamic judicial system, with its mu'assasat al-ifta' (strong consultative institution of legal inquiry). This weakened the status of the shari'ah, which is the legal, moral and ethical frame of reference for all Muslims. In addition, modernisation marginalised the 'ulama, who were among the primary protectors of the Islamic legacy and its social fabric.

These hasty transformations in the political and social foundations of society opened the way for the modern states to invade all aspects of the Islamic domain. Modern Islamic states therefore began to develop in accordance with the Western model of the nation-state. In a clear departure from Islam's traditional political model, the rulers of these modern states dominated their people and their lands, exacting absolute allegiance from their citizens.

Modern states aim to control the economies, job markets, trade and mineral resources, as well as their educational institutions at every level.

They also exercise firm control over the judiciary and are responsible for drafting and enacting new laws. In addition, modern states determine all forms of taxation and have full monopoly over the institutions of power, from the police and military to other security and intelligence apparatuses. Such modern states are not only committed to marginalising the Islamic frame of reference, but in several Islamic countries, they wage war against any Islamic institutions or political forces that remain within them.

Colonial domination and the consequent rise of nationalism ultimately divided the Islamic world into small contesting states. Few of these are capable of protecting their sovereignty or the honour of their people, and most lack the capacity to ensure real national development or progress. Thus in most instances, the shaking off of imperial domination resulted in symbolic (that is, extremely limited) forms of independence, while actually increasing the dependence of these countries on the global powers, and helping to extend the West's sphere of influence. Western forces, to give just one example, have even been 'allowed' to establish military bases in the Islamic world.

Moreover, colonial era imperial domination has burdened the Islamic world with some of the most tragic and complex dilemmas, ranging from the establishment of the Zionist state in Palestine to India's occupation of Kashmir. In fact, the Zionist state alone has played a major role in strengthening foreign influence in the Arab region and has been an impediment to reform and development on every level.

In the majority of Islamic countries, the modern state has failed to deliver prosperity, progress or development. Most Islamic countries are rentier states that subsist by selling their natural resources to foreign companies, repatriating funds earned by citizens working abroad, or applying for highly conditional and strictly rationed foreign aid. A few of the better-off countries rely on the remains of their historical heritage or on the tourist industry, which is usually detrimental to the environment. The majority of their citizens suffer from high rates of illiteracy, and lack modern educational methodologies, techniques and resources.

When compared with countries that share similar historical circumstances, such as India, China and the South East Asian states, the Islamic countries seem far worse off. Nevertheless, few countries outside the West have embraced the values of modern Western consumption as fervently as many of the Islamic countries have done. Huge malls sprawl across the suburbs of the larger cities, reintroducing a cycle of poverty and draining wealth to an extent that is reminiscent of the nineteenth century.

Since most governments in the Islamic world have proven incapable of ensuring even the basic subsistence and well-being of their citizens, and therefore completely lack legitimacy, they rely on violence to maintain stability. Few Islamic countries allow real popular political representation, enable the peaceful rotation of power, and support oversight institutions that monitor the performance of their rulers. As a result, the powers of the security forces are often inflated and the relationship between the state and society is characterised by violence and force, whether subtle or open. In many Islamic countries, governing elites maintain a tight hold over both economic and military power, exercising complete control over state resources. Many Muslims are therefore overwhelmed by a sense of powerlessness and isolation, unable to influence state legislation, policies, values or relationships and alliances with the outside world.

It is not difficult to see the gaping contradictions between Muslim history and where Muslims have ended up over the last century and a half. In the Muslim collective consciousness, the history of Islam seems to be the antithesis of everything they suffer and reject at this juncture. Their historical experience is about independence, unity, strength, growth and a global sense of purpose, while, in the present, feelings of weakness, dependence upon foreign powers, economic and social imbalance, political division and disunity, and their absence from the global stage are all too clear. A widely held perception is that this collapse and decline is a consequence of a gradual move away from Islam, its values and institutions, and that no reversal of this is possible without a reawakening of the Islamic frame of reference in matters of governance, state and society.

Perceptions of powerlessness and isolation perhaps best explain why some Islamic groups have resorted to violence, both within and beyond the Islamic world. Without understanding this wider context, and acknowledging the enormous level of violence that the global system and the modern state have perpetrated, and continue to perpetrate in the Islamic world, it is impossible to understand or challenge the use of violence as a tool of retaliation.

It is naïve to speak about violence as inherent or essential to Islam, just as it is to justify violence and terrorism in defence of any faith. Islamists who have taken up arms come from a range of intellectual backgrounds. What is common to all of them is that they found themselves in circumstances that engendered violence and they imagined that violence was the shortest or only path to redress.

In no circumstances is it reasonable to see violence that resists foreign occupation in the same light as violence that brings about political change. In the twentieth-century, several movements resisted foreign occupation and were ultimately successful in achieving national independence, but the subsequent use of violence to bring about political reform or regime change has failed in most countries. In fact, as shown in several chapters of this book, the use of violence as a political tool has tended to create deeper internal divisions within states and widen the breach between Muslim countries and the rest of the world.

It is critical to note that the vast majority of Islamists are reformists, who neither perpetrate nor advocate violence. It is incorrect to imagine a hidden Islamic conspiracy that links the Muslim Brotherhood in Egypt, the AKP in Turkey and the Islamic Party in Malaysia for example. Islamist groups differ in accordance with differences between the countries in which they have emerged. These differences are related to the different histories and conditions of each society, as well as differences in their understandings of, and responses to, their situations. It is, however, very clear that the forces of political Islam all agree on the need to re-establish an Islamic frame of reference with regard to societal values and the exercising of political power.

Understanding this frame of reference, and determining who is responsible for defining and setting its limits, is an issue on which various opinions and views are expressed. In light of the fact that Islamic societies are experiencing an epoch of rapid transformation, deep and active divisions pertain to the great challenges facing nations and their citizens. In this context, the forces of political Islam are also transforming rapidly; this is evident in their discourse, political programmes and objectives. At the onset of the twenty-first century, three central trends are clearly discernible.

The first invokes a specific historical model of Islamic experience, regardless of whether the elements of that model are real or imagined. This trend is the most conservative and some (but not all) of its proponents are inclined towards adopting a radical discourse and passing absolutist, rejectionist and condemnatory judgments; some have also resorted to violence. The second trend acknowledges Islamic political and social realities and strives to reconcile these with the general values of Islam. Its proponents are sometimes referred to as Islamic liberals. The third trend is the most widespread and influential and is referred to as wasati or centrist, and includes what was earlier referred to as neo-reformist.[1]

Those who subscribe to this third trend encompass Islamists from diverse backgrounds, including religious scholars and intellectuals, student organisations and academics, research centres and civil-society institutions. To different degrees, they are critical of the various manifestations of power, politics, economics and culture in Islamic countries, and seek inspiration from the Islamic legacy – whether written or historical experience – to inform their efforts to bring about change. They avoid violence, condemn bloody internal conflicts, and believe that ultimately the people will peacefully establish a reformist vision. However, they also believe in the right of Muslims to resist foreign occupation by every possible legitimate means.

In the early 1990s, the British sociologist Ernest Gellner noted that Islam, unlike other major religions and ideologies, has managed to stand firm in the face of modernity while also being able to assimilate its tools.[2] This achievement was undoubtedly made possible by the contributions of several generations of Islamist reformists – from the first Salafi reformists at the end of the nineteenth and the beginning of the twentieth centuries, to the neo-reformists at the end of the twentieth and the beginning of the twenty-first century.

Islamist reformism has not only inspired and led the most widespread and influential Islamist groups, it has risen with them to become the largest and most important political opposition force, as well as the most serious and credible alternative to most of the ruling regimes in the Islamic world. The spectacular rise of the forces of political Islam in the last two decades of the twentieth century was no accident, nor did it occur suddenly, or as a result of some kind of historical deviation. Rather, it emerged in response to objective changes in reality.

Besides the structural problems, and the ever-widening chasm between state institutions and the people, that beset modern Islamic countries, non-Islamist political forces in those states have been in steady decline. Decades after their emergence, it is clear that liberal and Marxist organisations lack the social base capable of sustaining their political programmes. The intelligentsia who led the Marxist parties were simply not able to win over the working class, who tend to be of an Islamist persuasion. Meanwhile, the new class of business executives and industrialists, who supposedly adhere to liberal values, have fallen under the influence of ruling regimes that exercise control by systems of reward and patronage.

With the collapse of the Soviet Union and the conclusion of the Cold War, many leftist parties lost confidence and motivation, and the web of the socialist left unravelled swiftly across almost all of the Arab and Islamic countries. Some leftists turned against their own camps and now lean towards a Western liberal or neo-liberal vision. The remaining leftist parties have dedicated themselves to fighting the Islamist movements – even sometimes becoming tools of the security apparatuses and helping spread anti-Islamist propaganda. Meanwhile, the nationalist parties now carry the heavy burden of having supported rigid nationalist regimes and their shameful abuses of power. In the Arab region specifically, Arab and pan-Arab nationalists were unable to prevent the collapse of Arab unity in favour of nation states.

The disparity between the social base and political programmes of the non-Islamist parties on the one hand, and the narrow popular support enjoyed by these parties on the other, led to critical crises in party structures and political ineffectiveness. In countries that experienced military coups, political parties of various persuasions failed to effectively overcome military rule, and party leadership structures often split due to exile, forced retirement or deployment by military dictators. In countries that preserved traditional systems of governance, and suffered from prolonged periods of despotism, political parties failed to introduce constitutional systems of governance, defend the rights of their people to participate in politics or establish institutions of political oversight.

None of these situations occurred in a political vacuum; the political sphere had systems of governance with ruling parties and even (non-Islamist) opposition parties. The Islamist movement was an additional component, which, by the 1980s, had developed a discourse that was democratic, pluralistic, peaceful and promoted solidarity. The Islamist groups used a language that people were familiar with and invoked values that are entrenched in their collective consciousness. In addition, the Islamists presented themselves as guardians of unity and national welfare, protectors of the rights of the impoverished, and as the only group capable of uprooting the rampant corruption flourishing in every nook and cranny under the ruling regimes. In other words, and with some variations in their rhetoric and chances of success, the Islamists adopted key elements of liberal thinking, nationalist ideas, leftist ideals, and the concerns of the Islamic masses. This combination is probably what gave real impetus to the spectacular rise of political Islam. However, the Islamists also bear very specific obligations and responsibilities.

The Islamists have to liberate themselves from deep-seated feelings of being oppressed and pursued, even though this has been the case for decades. It is crucial that a positive and even deeper sense of responsibility is developed. Of course, the contestation between the ruling regimes and those who oppose them is not over, and seems unlikely to end soon. However, the Islamists are a massive popular force who, in addition to leading workers unions, student organisations and civil institutions, have won many seats in parliamentary elections in their countries. This requires them to take responsibility for defending the people's demands, needs and aspirations, and rise to complete the task they set for themselves.

This task includes striving to rebuild consensus within their countries. Almost two centuries after the shock of colonial domination and the onset of modernisation in the nineteenth-century, the Islamic peoples have lost the solid consensus on which they had built their lives and organised their societies for centuries. Today, few Muslims concur – at least the political and intellectual elites among them – on political, social or cultural issues, or on how best to relate to the outside world. Similarly, they are at variance on questions of development, economics and trade.

No nation can achieve progress, stability or prosperity without a certain level of consensus about the central aspects of its existence. State institutions cannot function efficiently in its absence, and democracy and a peaceful rotation of power cannot be achieved among contenders who differ on the basics. Those Western democracies whose political systems are models worth emulating, did not build their stability on

323

internal conflict and contestation. They constantly work hard to achieve consensus between various social forces on central issues. The widening of popular support for the Islamists and the declining influence of the non-Islamists means that the forces of political Islam have a historical opportunity. They must re-establish consensus by developing a broader discourse that responds to the needs of all the different social factions and strives to ensure representation for all.

It will be very difficult for the Islamists to rise to this challenge if they see themselves as an elite group, distinct from the people. The Islamist movement represents a political trend that bases its frame of reference on the Islamic vision and experience. However, adopting an Islamic frame of reference does not make the Islamists sacrosanct nor does it make them a chosen people. As a political movement, the Islamists sometimes discern correctly and sometimes they make mistakes, and this is true no matter whether they are in power or an opposition party. Only the electorate have the right to judge the viability of their political programmes and their ability to keep their promises once voted for. If the Islamists begin to think that their Islamic beliefs grant them any kind of immunity from errors, they will end up building a new dictatorship that will destroy not only people and societies, but also the appeal of political Islam itself.

Although all the main Islamist forces call for democracy, it is not difficult to see that democracy is not the final answer to questions of state. Democracy provides a means of instrumentalising governance, but it does not address the massive (and historically unprecedented) infiltration of state institutions into all aspects of individuals' lives.

Historical Islamic experience was of a strong state that provided protection for society and secured its borders, while enjoying limited influence in other spheres of life. The state did not dominate the legislative, educational, economic and other affairs of its citizens. This resulted in the establishment of strong Islamic communities, which even the most tempestuous invasions and conflicts could not uproot.

It is not difficult to see the discomfort of people in the Islamic world, and in fact of people all over the world, at the pervasiveness and dominance of state interference in daily life. Perhaps the Islamic world alone has a legacy capable of providing a robust answer to this problem.

The Islamists also have to admit that democracy does not necessarily solve the problems of poverty or the increasing social disparities that rage across Islamic societies. This problem is becoming ever more extreme with the spread of conspicuous consumption, economic policies that support globalisation and the collapse of traditional institutions of social solidarity. Although the discourse of political Islam is ethical and encourages social solidarity, this needs to be translated into active programmes that deal directly with the question of poverty and inequality.

Furthermore, democracy provides no immunity to foreign domination. In fact, calls for democracy and human rights have too often helped to justify both subtle and blatant foreign interference in the affairs of Islamic countries. Since the events of 9/11, successive US administrations have suggested that internal reform in Islamic countries is necessary to confront extremism and violence. However, US-led reform programmes have been used to justify interference in matters of religion and education, as well as support for specific individuals and groups as they climb the ladders of authority and power. In the case of Iraq, for example, the US's freedom and democracy project resulted in the complete subversion of the nation state, the daily slaughter of people and the fragmentation of a once unified country.

There are no easy choices. Islamists may, for example, be forced to choose between installing a democracy that opens their land to foreign domination while nationalist groupings threaten to split into conflicting ethnic and sectarian factions, or protecting an unjust nationalist system and accepting a slow and gradual reform process. It is clear, however, that foreign interference in the internal affairs of Islamic societies does not deliver successful solutions or political and social stability. In fact, the exact opposite is true; such interference only increases internal divisions and contestation.

In most Islamic countries, the rise of political Islam has also led to enmity, whether apparent or subtle, between Islamists and the traditional 'ulama. The Islamists often see the 'ulama as having been co-opted by state authorities and having abandoned their primary responsibility of defending the faith and its values. The 'ulama, for their part, tend to see the Islamists as not well-enough versed in the sciences and religious disciplines to speak in the name of Islam, and suspect that they are using Islam for the sole purpose of attaining power and authority. The views of both sides carry elements of truth. However, the central point to remember is that this situation was not chosen by either side; it has been determined by specific historical conditions. It is time for the forces of political Islam to draw closer to the 'ulama as this institution remains the primary protector of the Islamic legacy and its sciences, as well as the conduit of its past.

The relationship between the Islamists and the 'ulama requires a mutual recognition of the plurality of Islamic experience, political or not. In addition to the legacy of Islamic pluralism, an unexpected plurality exists within the forces of political Islam itself. At this point, it is unclear where this will lead. However, the relationships between the various forces within political Islam are an important indicator of how they are likely to relate to other groups in Islamic society. Given the constant decline of the non-Islamist political forces, Islamic pluralism might well play an important role in rebuilding the political landscape in Islamic countries. This might also contribute to re-establishing forms of national consensus by presenting programmes of action drawn from, or at the very least, showing respect for, Islam's general frame of reference.

The Islamists also need to pay more attention to their relationships with the outside world, not only because this relates to issues of national sovereignty, but also because of the sharp tensions between the Islamic world and the Western powers. Undoubtedly, much of the tension still relates to perceptions of ancient battles dating back to the Middle Ages, and to the threat that the West represents to the independence of Islamic countries in the contemporary era. The tensions also derive from Western fears of the possible global spread of Islam, and from perceptions among Muslims that the West is striving to control their countries and loot their natural resources.

In recent decades, this contestation has turned into a comprehensive civilisational clash, sometimes based on real issues, and sometimes related to coercion and propaganda. The political and economic roots of this clash threaten to isolate the Islamic World from the global community, while simultaneously being used as a pretext for the redeployment of Western naval fleets and troops in the Islamic World.

The fact is that Muslims are an indivisible part of the modern world and are linked with their European neighbours by strong interactive and ongoing relationships, just as they have been divided by wars and conflict before. Geopolitically, Muslim countries lie at the centre of the world's strategic and economic hub. In addition, an increasing number of Muslim families are settling in Western countries on either side of the Atlantic and know no homeland other than their adopted countries. The isolation of Muslims in the modern world is impossible and should not be encouraged; those who advocate it will achieve nothing good for Muslims or the rest of the world.

If the Islamists are willing to consider these issues, they might also want to pay attention to the most important question of all, namely: what constitutes an Islamic state? What are the implications of an Islamic state in the context of the dominant paradigm of the modern state, and does this require so much strife and internal division? Is an Islamic state, in the final analysis, not a state that Muslims choose for their political assembly, regardless of its operating mechanisms? Is there no way to establish a healthy relationship, or even a relatively healthy one, between the state and religion, without one exercising complete control over the other? Did visions of the Islamic state in the 1960s and 1970s not reveal essential errors in understandings of how modern states function and in the historical model of the traditional Islamic state? Is it wrong to believe in the possibility of Islamising the modern state?

In the final analysis, the spectacular rise of the Islamist movement may never lead to smooth political transitions in Islamic countries. The ruling elites in most of these countries seem quite disinclined to hand over their power to Islamists or anyone else. It is also inconceivable that the West will, in the foreseeable future, leave the Islamic world to its own devices. This is especially true in the central Arab region, which is not only the world's major source of oil but also the most important strategic sphere for any power striving for global influence.

In addition, as the West's most important ally in the region, the Zionist state helps to focus attention on the transformations playing out within the countries of the region. Since the Islamists are the most committed to the protection of Palestinian national interests, and the most strongly opposed to the expansionist inclinations of the Zionist state, it is manifestly clear that the forces of political Islam are the cause of much more concern to the West than the ongoing corruption and despotism of the region's incumbent elites.

The multi-dimensional contestation between the Islamist movement, the ruling elites and the world's global powers is one of the central causes of instability in the Arab and Islamic world. Until the larger powers decide to leave the Islamic world to its own devices, and the ruling elites realise the need for peaceful rotations of power, the birth pangs of change in the region will be difficult and prolonged.

Notes

2   The early reformists

1   Nafi (2000: 17–37).

2   Kirk (1986: 15).

3   On al-Afghani, 'Abduh and Rida see Hourani (1962: 222–244).

3   Hasan al-Banna and the Muslim Brotherhood

1   Mitchell (1969: 1–11).

2   Al-Dar al-Salafiyyah published and distributed many important classical reformist texts.

3   Al-Banna (1986: 82).

4   'Abd al-Halim (1985, vol. 2: 22–23).

5   Al-Banna (1979: 353–370).

6   Al-Banna (1986: 299).

4   The Muslim Brotherhood and the 1952 Egyptian Revolution

1   See Chapter Three for more information about Sadat's role.

2   Muhyi al-Din (1992: 43–59).

3   Translator's note: Under the terms of the treaty, the United Kingdom was also required to withdraw all its troops from Egypt, except those deemed necessary to protect the Suez Canal and its surroundings. Ten thousand soldiers plus auxiliary personnel remained stationed in Suez. In addition, it was agreed that the United Kingdom would supply and train Egypt's army and come to its aid in case of war. The terms of the

treaty were meant to last for twenty years, that is, until 1956. Britain's ongoing presence in the Suez was opposed by many Egyptians.

4   'Abd al-Halim (1985, vol. 2: 451–469).
5   Muhyi al-Din (1992: 137); Shadi (1981: 169–189).
6   See 'Abd al-Halim (vol. 3: 331–397) and Imam (1981: 111–155).
7   Translator's note: in a cruel twist of irony, the Muslim Brotherhood was banned again in 2013, soon after Egypt's first democratically elected president, Mohamed Morsi, was ousted by a military coup.

5   Al-Nabhani and Hizb al-Tahrir
1   For al-Nabhani's biography, see Taji-Farouki (1996: 1–36).
2   On the early phase of the emergence of the Liberation Party, see al-Hasan (1989: chapter 1).
3   Cohen (1982: 220–224).
4   Hizb al-Tahrir (1963).
5   Darraj and Barut (1999, vol. 2: 87–98).

6   Al-Mawdudi and the Jamaat-i-Islami
1   For his biography, see Nasr (1996).
2   Al-Nadwi (n.d.: 285–292).
3   Esposito (1980: 142–145).
4   See, for example, 'al-Mawdudi (1979).
5   Translator's note: al-Mustafa (the Chosen One) is one of many titles given to the Prophet Muhammad.
6   Haq (1988: 322–354).

7   The revenge of the intellectual
1   Interestingly, the family of Gamal Abdel Nasser, Qutb's greatest opponent, hailed from the same district. For more of Qutb's life story, see Diyab (1988), Hammudah (1996) and Abu-Rabi (1996).
2   For a discussion of Qutb's pronouncement and its veractity, see al-Khalidi (2010: 160–161, 213–255).

3   See Qutb (1980a: 33, 41–42, 44–45, 82, 183).

4   Amin (1985: 92).

5   For more extracts from some of his letters from the USA, see Hammudah (1996: 94–95, 97–108).

6   Qutb (1980b: 4).

7   Translator's note: the Kharijites were a radical sect that emerged during the first civil strife in Islamic history after the Prophet's death. This occurred during the reign of the fourth caliph, 'Ali ibn Abi Talib. The Khawarij advocated that the conflicting parties accept arbitration on the basis of the Qur'an or that the members of both groups should be put to death.

8   'Abd al-Khaliq (1987: 108–131); Ramadan (1977: 313–323).

9   Al-Hudaybi (1977: 63–66).

8   Closing of the circle

1   See Chapter 7 for more details.

2   Abu 'Izzah (1986: 59–60, 75–88); Abu 'Amr (1987: 85–100); 'Abd al-Jawwad (1990: 30–32).

3   For an insight into the history of the student movement, see Uthman (1976).

4   'Abd al-Halim (1985, vol. 3: 223–250).

5   For the full text of the essay, see Ahmad (1991, vol. 1: al-Rafidun: 31–52).

6   For the official text of Mustafa's confession, see Ahmad (1991, vol. 1: 53–109).

9   The revolution of the jurist and the people

1. For a biography, see Moin (1999).

2. For more information about the differences between the Usulis and the Akhbaris see Bahrul-'Ulum (1977: 176–177).

3. Shita (1986: 42).

4. Shita (1986: 138).

5. Shita (1986: 126).
6. Algar (1981: 246–248).
7. The autobiography of former Iranian president, Hashemi Rafsanjani, provides an interesting version of the story of the struggle of Iranian Islamists against the shah (see Rafsanjani 2005).

10 Crisis in the kingdom of plenty

1 On the Holy Sanctuary incident, see Champion (2003: 130–140).
2 Al-'Utaybi (2004: 58, 65).
3 Al-'Utaybi (2004: 81–92).
4 Al-'Utaybi (2004: 185–223).
5 Translator's note: the Prophet Muhammad had a birthmark in a similar place, which Islamic biographers describe as the 'seal' of prophethood. Juhayman saw the presence of a similar birthmark on al-Qahtani as an indication that he was the Mahdi.
6 Al-'Utaybi (2004: 30–33).
7 Translator's note: the Kharijites were a radical sect that emerged during the first civil strife in Islamic history after the Prophet's death. This occurred during the reign of the fourth caliph, 'Ali ibn Abi Talib. The Khawarij advocated that the conflicting parties accept arbitration on the basis of the Qur'an or that the members of both groups should be put to death.
8 Al-'Utaybi (2004: 80–83).
9 Commins (2006: 80–93).
10 Al-Zubaydi (2004: 220–236).
11 Al-Rashid (2002: 120 –128).

11 The spread of violence

1 On the battle for Hama see Darraj and Barut (1999, vol. 1: 298–302) and Abd-Allah (1983: 189–198).
2 Al-Siba'i (1955: 238); see also Barut (1994: 129–139).
3 Abd-Allah (1983: 103–108).

4　Translator's note: the 1978 presidential election took the form of a referendum, where voters were asked to approve or reject the only candidate on the list – the incumbent president, Hafiz al-Asad. With voter turnout at 97 per cent, official results indicated that 99.9 per cent of voters had approved of Asad.

5　For a narrative of the assassination and what followed it, see 'Hammudah (1998). For its earlier antecedents of violence among Egyptian Islamists see: Muru (1998). On the intellectual development of the Islamic Group and the Jihadist Group (mentioned below), see al-'Awa (2006), Hanafi (1986: 69 & ff) and Mustafa (1992: 149–181).

6　For the full text of al-Faridah al-Ga'ibah, see Ahmad (1991, vol. 1: 127–149).

7　For more details, see Chapter 10.

8　Burja (1992: 273–275).

9　For more information about the Islamic Salvation Front (FIS), see Al-'Abbasi (1993: 130 & ff).

10　Shahin (1998: 136–140).

11　Translator's note: Mawlud Hamrush had served as Algeria's prime minister from September 1989 to June 1991.

12　The Islamist resistance fighters

1　For one of the best works on the Afghani jihad see Roy (1986).

2　For more on the rise of the Taliban, see Rashid (2000).

3　Saad-Ghorayeb (2002: 13–15).

4　Abu al-Nasr (2003: 127–155).

5　On the Palestinian Islamists' position on Palestine, see Nafi (1999: 51–78).

6　Abu-Amr (1994: 63–127).

7　On developments related to political Islam in the Palestinian sphere, see Tamimi (2007).

13 The Islamist military coup

1. El-Affendi (1991: 52–54).
2. On the history of the Muslim Brotherhood in Sudan until Numayri's coup in 1969, see Muhammad-Ahmad, (n.d.).
3. On al-Turabi's more recent political thinking see, al-Turabi (2003), and for a more general study of his intellectual development, see El-Affendi (1991:152–180).

14 Transcontinental violence

1 For more details, see Bergen (2001: 24–43).
2 For more details, see Chapter 12.
3 For more details see Chapter 13.
4 Randal (2004: 115–162).
5 See Chapter 11 for more on Faraj.
6 See Zidan (2003).

15 The rise of the reformist Islamists

1 See Nafi (2004).
2 Al-Bishri (1980); Huwaydi (1985).
3 Al-'Awa (1989: 240–245).
4 Ghannouchi (2007, vol. 1: 132 & ff ; vol. 2: 60 & ff).

16 Crisis of the reformist Islamists

1 Champion (2003: 193).
2 For an in-depth study of the lives and discourse of these three schol-ars, see Alshamsi (2004).
3 See Chapter 10 for more on this.
4 Dekmejian (1994); Champion (2003: 221, 224–226).
5 Al-Tilmisani (1985: 185–186).
6 Ahmad (1995: 213–231).
7 'Abd al-Fattah wa Rashwan (1996: 178–180).

8   See Al-Ra'i (2001: 127–132, 241–251).

9   'Abd al-Fattah (1998: 217–230).

17 The limits of the reformist victory

1   For one of the best biographies of Mustafa Kemal, see Mango (1999).

2   For more background, see Lewis (1961: 298–313).

3   Ahmed (1988: 750–769).

4   Yavuz (1988).

5   Gunter and Yavuz (2007).

18 Conclusion: Islamists and the future

1   See Chapter 15.

2   See Gellner (1992).

Glossary

bida' (pl. of bid'ah)	heretical innovations
fatawa (pl. of fatwa)	a legal opinion or decree pronounced by an Islamic scholar
fiqh	Islamic jurisprudence
hadith	Prophetic tradition
hajj	obligatory pilgrimage to Makkah
hajr	rural co-operatives
al-hakimiyyah	divine authority; divine governorship
husayniyyah	Shi'a centre of worship
husayniyyah irshad	private tuition centre
jahili	steeped in ignorance
al-jahiliyyah	state of ignorance
al-jahiliyyah al-mu'asirah	the contemporary state of ignorance
ijtihad	dynamic intellectual effort; renewed intellectual effort; rational interpretation
Mahdi	the Awaited Saviour
maktab al-irshad	executive council (lit. guidance bureau)
marja'	Shi'i religious authority
al-murshid al-am	leader or general guide
al-nahda	awakening
qadi	chief justice; judge in the shari'ah system
shari'ah	Islamic canonical law

shaykh	religious leader with formal and traditional training; tribal leader or elder
shura	consultation
ahl al-Sunnah	followers of the Sunni doctrinal school
takfir	excommunication: the practice of declaring sinful Muslims to be unbelievers or apostates
taqlid	blind imitation
tawhid	monotheism
ummah	global Muslim community
'ulama	religious scholars; recognized religious authorities
velayat-e-faqih	custodianship of the jurist

References

English texts

Abd-Allah, Umar F (1983). *The Islamic Struggle in Syria*. Berkeley, CA: Mizan Press.

Abdel-Malek, Anouar (1968). *Egypt: Military Society*. New York: Random House.

Abdo, Geneive (2000) *No God But God: Egypt and the Triumph of Islam*. London: Oxford University Press.

Abu-Amr, Ziad (1994). *Islamic Fundamentalism in the West Bank and Gaza*. Bloomington, IN: Indiana University Press.

Abu-Rabi, Ibrahim M (1996). *Intellectual Origins of Islamic Resurgence in the Modern Arab World*. Albany, NY: State University of New York Press.

El-Affendi, Abdelwahab (1991). *Turabi's Revolution: Islam and Power in Sudan*. London: Grey Seal.

Ahmad, Feroz (1977). *The Turkish Experiment in Democracy, 1950–1975*. London: Hurst.

Ahmad, Feroz (1988). 'Islamic reassertion in Turkey,' *Third World Quarterly*, 10: 750–769.

Ahmad, Khurshid, and Zafar Ishaq Ansari (1979). *Islamic Perspectives: Studies in Honour of Mawlana Sayyid Abul A'la Mawdudi*. Leicester: Islamic Foundation.

Al-Ahsan, Abdullah (1992) *Ummah or Nation? Identity Crisis in Contemporary Muslim Society*. Leicester: Islamic Foundation.

Akhavi, Shahrough (1980). *Religion and Politics in Contemporary Iran: Clergy-state Relations in the Pahlavi Period*. Albany, NY: State University of New York Press.

Algar, Hamid (tr.) (1981) *Islam and Revolution: Writings and Declarations of Imam Khomeini*, Berkeley, CA: Mizan Press.

Alshamsi, Mansoor Jassem (2004). 'The discourse and performance of the Saudi Sunni Islamic Reformist Leadership, 1981–2003,' PhD thesis, University of Exeter, UK.

Arjomand, Said Amir (1988) *The Turban for the Crown: The Islamic Revolution in Iran*. New York: Oxford University Press.

Atwan, Abdel Bari (2006). *The Secret History of al-Qaida*. London: Saqi.

Ayubi, Nazih (1991). *Political Islam: Religion and Politics in the Arab World*. London: Routledge.

Bergen, Peter L (2001). *Holy War: Inside the Secret World of Osama bin Laden Inc*. London: Weidenfeld and Nicolson.

Boland, BJ (1971). *The Struggle of Islam in Modern Indonesia*. The Hague: Martinus Nijhoff.

Braibanti, Ralph (1995). *The Nature and Structure of the Islamic World*. Chicago: International Strategy and Policy Institute.

Brown, Daniel (1996). *Rethinking Tradition in Modern Islamic Thought*. Cambridge: Cambridge University Press.

Burgat, Francois, and William Dowell (1993) *The Islamic Movement in North Africa*. Austin: Center for Middle Eastern Studies, University of Texas.

Champion, Daryl (2003). *The Paradoxical Kingdom*. London: Hurst.

Choudhury, GW (1990). *Islam and the Contemporary World*. London: Indus Thames.

Cizre, Umit (ed.) (2007). *Secular and Islamic Politics in Turkey: The Making of the Justice and Development Party*. London: Routledge.

Cohen, Amnon (1982) *Political Parties in the West Bank under the Jordanian Regime, 1949–1967*. Ithaca, NY: Cornell University Press.

Commins, David (2006). *The Wahhabi Mission in Saudi Arabia.* London: IB Tauris.

Davis, Joyce M (1997). *Between Jihad and Salaam: Profiles in Islam.* New York: St Martin's Press.

Dawisha, Adeed (ed.). (1983) *Islam in Foreign Policy.* Cambridge: Cambridge University Press.

Dekmejian, R Hrair (1994). 'The Rise of Political Islamism in Saudi Arabia,' *The Middle East Journal*, 48 (4): 627–643.

Dekmejian, R Hrair (1995). *Islam in Revolution: Fundamentalism in the Arab World.* Syracuse, NY: Syracuse University Press,.

Enayat, Hamid (1982). *Modern Islamic Political Thought.* London: Macmillan.

Esposito, John (1980). 'Pakistan: Quest for Islamic Identity' in John L Esposito (ed.) *Islam and Development: Religion and Sociopolitical Change.* Syracuse, NY: Syracuse University Press.

Esposito, John (ed.) (1983). *Voices of Resurgent Islam.* Oxford, Oxford University Press.

Esposito, John and John O Voll (1996). *Islam and Democracy.* New York: Oxford University Press.

Esposito, John and John O Voll (2001) *Makers of Contemporary Islam.* New York: Oxford University Press.

Feldman, Noah (2003). *After Jihad: America and the Struggle for Islamic Democracy.* New York, Farrar, Straus and Giroux.

Ferdinand, Klaus and Mehdi Mozaffari (1988). *Islam: State and Society.* London: Curzon.

Gaffney, Patrick D (1994). *The Prophet's Pulpit: Islamic Preaching in Contemporary Egypt.* Berkeley, CA: California University Press.

Fuller, Graham E (1991). *Islamic Fundamentalism in Pakistan.* Santa Monica, CA: Rand.

Fuller, Graham E (1991). *Islamic Fundamentalism in Afghanistan.* Santa Monica, CA: Rand.

Gellner, Ernest, (1992) *Postmodernism, Reason, and Religion*. London: Routledge.

Gunter, Michael and M Haqan Yavuz (2007). 'Turkish paradox: Progressive Islamists versus reactionary secularists' *Critique: Critical Middle Eastern Studies*, 16 (3): 289–301.

Haq, Farhat (1988). 'Islamic Reformism and the State: The Case of the Jamaat-i-Islami of Pakistan,' PhD thesis, Cornell University, USA.

Al-Hasan, Sa'id, (1989). The Concept of the Rules of Public Order in the Political Thought of Hizb al-Tahrir. Master's dissertation, American University in Cairo, Egypt.

Hourani, Albert (1962). *Arabic Thought in the Liberal Age, 1798–1939*. London: Oxford University Press.

Husaini, Ishak Musa (1956). *The Muslem Brethren: The Greatest of Modern Islamic Movements*. Beirut: Khayat.

Keddie, Nikki (ed.) (1983). *Religion and Politics in Iran: Shi'ism from Quietism to Revolution*. New Haven, CT: Yale University Press.

Kedourie, Elie (1992). *Politics in the Middle East*. London: Oxford University Press.

Kepel, Gilles (1985). *Muslim Extremism in Egypt: The Prophet and Pharaoh*. Berkeley: University of California Press.

Khalid, Adeeb (1998). *The Politics of Muslim Reform*. Berkeley: University of California Press.

Kirk, Russell (1986). *The Conservative Mind from Burke to Eliot*. Chicago: Regnery.

Kurzman, Charles (ed.) (1998). *Liberal Islam: A Sourcebook*. New York: Oxford University Press.

Kushner, David (1986). 'Turkish secularists and Islam' *Jerusalem Quarterly* 38: 89–106.

Lawrence, Bruce B (1990). *Defenders of God: The Fundamentalist Revolt Against the Modern Age*. London: Tauris.

Lawrence, Bruce B (1998). *Shattering the Myth: Islam Beyond Violence*. Princeton, NJ: Princeton University Press.

Lewis, Bernard (1961). *The Emergence of Modern Turkey*. London: Oxford University Press.

Lia, Brynjar (1998). *The Society of the Muslim Brothers in Egypt: The Rise of an Islamic Mass Movement*. Reading: Ithaca Press.

Mango, Andrew (1999). *Ataturk*. London: John Murray.

Mardin, Serif (1989). *Religion and Social Change in Modern Turkey: The Case of Bediuzzaman Said Nursî*. Albany, NY: State University of New York Press.

Marty, Martin E and R Scott Applepy (eds) (1991). *Fundamentalisms Observed*. Chicago, IL: Chicago University Press.

Marty, Martin E and R Scott Applepy (eds), (1993) *Fundamentalisms and Society*. Chicago, IL: Chicago University Press.

Marty, Martin E and R Scott Applepy (eds) (1993) *Fundamentalisms and the State*. Chicago, IL: Chicago University Press.

Marty, Martin E and R Scott Applepy (eds) (1994). *Accounting for Fundamentalisms*. Chicago, Chicago University Press.

Masud, Muhammad Khalid (ed.) (2000). *Travellers in Faith: Studies of the Tablighi Jama'at as a Transnational Islamic Movement of Faith Renewal*. Boston, MA: Academic.

Mitchell, Richard P (1969). *The Society of the Muslim Brothers*. London: Oxford University Press.

Moin, Baqer (1999). *Khomeini: Life of the Ayatollah*, New York: St Martin's Press.

Mortimer, Edward (1982). *Faith and Power: The Politics of Islam*. New York: Vintage.

Mottahedeh, Roy (1985). *The Mantle of the Prophet: Religion and Politics in Iran*. New York: Pantheon.

Moussalli, Ahmad (1992). *Radical Islamic Fundamentalism: The Ideological and Political Discourse of Sayyid Qutb*. Beirut: American University of Beirut.

Munson Jr, Henry (1988). *Islam and Revolution in the Middle East*. New Haven, CT: Yale University Press.

Munson Jr, Henry (1993). *Religion and Power in Morocco*. New Haven: Yale University Press.

Naby, Eden (1988). 'Islam within the Afghan Resistance' *Third World Quarterly* 10: 787–805.

Nafi, Basheer M (1997). 'Islam, the army, and Democracy in Modern Turkey' *Middle East Studies* 3 (3/4): 239–258.

Nafi, Basheer M (2000). *The Rise and Decline of the Arab-Islamic Reform Movement*. London: ICIT.

Nafi, Basheer M (2004). 'Fatwa and war: On the allegiance of the American Muslim soldiers in the aftermath of September 11' *Islamic Law and Society* 11 (1): 78–116.

Nasr, Seyyed Hossein (1987). *Traditional Islam in the Modern World*. London, Kegan Paul.

Nasr, Seyyed Vali Reza, (1994). *The Vanguard of the Islamic Revolution: The Jama'at-i Islami of Pakistan*. Berkeley, CA: University of California Press.

Nasr, Seyyed Vali Reza (1996). *Mawdudi and the Making of Islamic Revivalism*. New York: Oxford University Press.

Peters, Rudolph (1979). *Islam and Colonialism: The Doctrine of Jihad in Modern History*. The Hague: Mouton.

Piscatori, James P (1983). *Islam in the Political Process*. Cambridge: Cambridge University Press.

Rashid, Ahmad (2000). *Taliban: Militant Islam, Oil and Fundamentalism in Central Asia*. New Haven, CT: Yale University Press.

Rashid, Ahmad (2003). *Jihad: The Rise of Militant Islam in Central Asia*. New Haven, CT: Yale University Press.

Al-Rashid, Madawi (2002). *A History of Saudi Arabia*, Cambridge: Cambridge University Press.

Rahman, Khalid, Muhibul Haq Sahibzada and Mushfiq Ahmad (eds) (1999). *Jama'at-e-Islami and National and International Politics*. Islamabad: Book Traders.

Rahman, Fazlur (1982). *Islam and Modernity: Transformation of an Intellectual Tradition*. Chicago, IL: University of Chicago Press.

Rahman, Fazlur (2000). *Revival and Reform in Islam* (edited by E Moosa). Oxford: Oneworld.

Rahnema, Ali (ed.) (1994). *Pioneers of Islamic Revival*. London: Zed.

Randal, Jonathan (2004). *Osama: The Making of a Terrorist*. New York: Knopf.

Rizvi, Hasan Askari (1989). *Military and Politics in Pakistan*. India: Konak.

Roff, William R (ed.) (1987). *Islam and the Political Economy of Meaning*. Berkeley, CA: University of California Press.

Roy, Olivier (1986). *Islam and Resistance in Afghanistan*. Cambridge: Cambridge University Press.

Roy, Olivier (1994). *The Failure of Political Islam* (translated by C Volk). London: Tauris.

Ruedy, John (ed.) (1994). *Islamism and Secularism in North Africa*. New York: St Martin's Press.

Saad-Ghorayeb, Amal (2002). *Hizbullah: Politics and Religion*. London: Pluto.

Sageiv, David (1995). *Fundamentalism and Intellectuals in Egypt, 1973–1993*. London: Frank Cass.

Sayeed, Khalid Bin (1995). *Western Dominance and Political Islam: Challenge and Response*. Albany, NY: SUNY Press.

Shah-Kazemi, Reza (ed.) (1997) *Algeria: A Revolution Revisited*. London: Islamic World Report.

Shahin, Emad Eldin (1998) *Political Ascent: Contemporary Islamic Movements in North Africa*. Boulder: Westview Press.

Siddiqui, Kalim (1996). *Stages of Islamic Revolution*. London: Open Press.

Sivan, Emmanuel (1990). *Radical Islam*. New Haven: Yale University Press.

Smith, Wilfred Cantwell (1957). *Islam in Modern History*. Princeton: Princeton University Press.

Taji-Farouki, Suha (1996). *A Fundamental Quest: Hizb al-Tahrir and the Search for the Islamic Caliphate*. London: Grey Seal.

Taji-Farouki, Suha and Basheer M Nafi (eds) (2004). *Islamic Thought in the Twentieth Century*. London: Tauris.

Tamimi, Azzam (2007) *Hamas: Unwritten Chapters*. London: Hurst.

Tapper, Richards (ed.) (1991). *Islam in Modern Turkey: Religion, Politics, and Literature in a Secular State*. London: Tauris.

Taylor, Alan R (1988). *The Islamic Question in Middle East Politics*. Boulder, CO: Westview.

Vatikiotis, Michael RJ. (1994). *Indonesian Politics Under Suharto: Order, Development and Pressure for Change*. London: Routledge.

Vatikiotis, P (1987). *Islam and the State*. London: Croom Helm.

Watt, W Montgomery (1988). *Islamic Fundamentalism and Modernity*. London: Routledge.

Willis, Michael (1998). *The Islamic Challenge in Algeria*. New York: New York University Press.

Yavuz, Haqan (1988). 'Political Islam and the Welfare (Refah) Party in Turkey' *Third World Quarterly* 10: 750–769.

Zakaria, Rafiq (1989). *The Struggle Within Islam*. London: Penguin Books.

Ziring, Lawrence (1980). *Pakistan: The Enigma of Political Development*. Boulder, CO: Westview.

Zubaida, Sami (1993). *Islam: The People and the State: Political Ideas and Movements in the Middle East*. London: Tauris.

Arabic texts

Abu 'Amr, Ziyad (1987) *Usul al-Harakat al-Siyasiyyah fi Qita'a Ghazzah 1948–1967*. Acca: Dar al-Aswar.

Abu 'Izzah, 'Abdallah (1986) *Ma'a al-Harakah al-Islamiyyah fi al-Duwal al-'Arabiyyah*. Kuwait: Dar al-Qalam.

Abu al-Nasr, Fudayl (2003) *Hizballah: Haqa'iq wa Ab'ad*. Beirut: Al-Sharikah al-'Alimiyyah li al-Kitab.

Ahmad, 'Abd al-'Ati Muhammad (1995). *Al-Harakat al-Islamiyyah fi Misr wa Qadaya al-Tahawwal al-Dimuqrati.* Cairo: Markaz al-Ahram li al-Tarjumah wa al-Nashr.

Ahmad, Rifa't al-Sayyid (ed.) (1991). *Al-Nabi al-Musallah* (2 vols). London: Riyad al-Ris li al-Kutub wa al-Nashr.

Ahmad, Rifa't al-Sayyid (1998). *Al-Harakat al-Islamiyyah al-Radikaliyyah fi Misr.* Beirut: Markaz al-Dirasat al-Istratijiyyah wa al-Buhuth wa al-Tawthiq.

Amin, Samir (1985). *Azmat al-Mujtama' al-'Arabi.* Cairo: Dar al-Mustaqbal al-'Arabi.

'Ashur, Mustafa Zaki (n.d.). *Badi' al-Zaman Sa'id al-Nursi: Nazrah 'Ammah 'an Hayatihi wa Atharihi.* Berkeley, CA: Dar al-Mihrab li al-Tiba'ah wa al-Nashr.

Al-'Abbasi, Muhammad (1993). *Al-Sultah wa al-Harakah al-Islamiyyah fi al-Jaza'ir.* Cairo: Dar al-Ma'arif.

'Abd al-Fattah, Nabil, (n.d.). *Al-Mushaf wa al-Sayf: Sira' al-Din wa al-Dawlah fi Misr.* Cairo: Maktabat Madbuli.

'Abd al-Fattah, Nabil (1997). *Al-Nass wa al-Rassas: Al-Islam al-Siyasi wa al-Aqbat wa Azamat al-Dawlah al-Hadithah fi Misr.* Beirut: Dar al-Nahar.

'Abd al-Fattah, Nabil wa Diya Rashwan (eds) (1995). *Taqrir al-Halah al-Diniyyah fi Misr.* Cairo: Markaz al-Dirasat al-Istratijiyyah bi al-Ahram.

'Abd al-Fattah, Nabil wa Diya Rashwan (eds) (1996) *Taqrir al-Halah al-Diniyyah fi Misr.* Cairo: Markaz al-Dirasat al-Istratijiyyah bi al-Ahram.

'Abd al-Fattah, Nabil wa Diya Rashwan (eds) (1998). *Taqrir al-Halah al-Diniyyah fi Misr.* Cairo: Markaz al-Dirasat al-Istratijiyyah bi al-Ahram.

'Abd al-Halim, Mahmud (1985). *Al-Ikhwan al-Muslimun: Ahdath Sana'at al-Tarikh* (3 vols). Cairo: Dar al-Da'wah.

'Abd al-Jawwad, Salih (1990). 'Dirasah fi Qiyadat Fatah' *Qadaya* 4: 30–32.

'Abd al-Khaliq, Farid (1987). *Al-Ikhwan al-Muslimun fi Mizan al-Haqq*. Cairo: Dar al-Sahwah li al-Nashr wa al-Tawzi.

Al-'Awa, Salwa Mohammad (2006). *Al-Jama'ah al-Islamiyyah al-Musallahah fi Misr, 1974–2004*. Cairo: Maktabat al-Shuruq al-Dawliyyah.

Al-'Awa, Muhammad Salim (1989). *Fi al-Nizam al-Siyasi li al-Dawlah al-Islamiyyah*. Cairo: Dar al-Shuruq.

Al-'Awa, Muhammad Salim (1998). *Al-Fiqh al-Islami fi Tariq al-Tajdid*. Beirut, al-Maktab al-Islami.

Al-'Awa, Muhammad Salim (2006). *Li al-Din wa al-Watan: Fusul fi 'Alaqat al-Muslimin bi-Ghayr al-Muslimin*. Cairo: Nahdat Misr.

Barut, Muhammad Jamal (1994). *Yathrib al-Jadidah: Al-Harakat al-Islamiyyah al-Rahinah*. Beirut: Riyad al-Ris li al-Kutub wa al-Nashr.

Bahrul-'Ulum, Muhammad (1977). *Al-Ijtihad: Usuluhu wa Ahkamuhu*. Beirut: Dar al-Zahra'.

Al-Banna, Hasan (1979). *Majmu'at Rasa'il al-Imam al-Shahid*. Cairo: Al-Mu'assasah al-Islamiyyah li al-Tiba'ah wa al-Nashr.

Al-Banna, Hasan (1986). *Mudhakkirat al-Da'wah wa al-Da'iyyah*. Cairo: Dar al-Tawzi' wa al-Nashr al-Islamiyyah.

Al-Bishri, Tariq (1980). *Al-Muslimun wa al-Aqbat fi Itar al-Jama'ah al-Wataniyyah*. Cairo: Al-Hay'ah al-Misriyyah al-'Ammah li al-Kitab.

Al-Bishri, Tariq (2005). *Al-Malamih al-'Ammah li al-Fikr al-Siyasi al-Islami fi al-Tarikh al-Mu'asir*. Cairo: Dar al-Shuruq.

Burgat, Francois (1992). *Al-Islam al-Siyasi Sawt al-Junub* (translated by Lurin Zakari). Cairo: Dar al-'Alam al-Thalith.

Darraj, Faysal and Jamal Barut (eds) (1999). *Al-Ahzab wa al-Harakat al-Islamiyyah* (2 vols). Damascus: Al-Markaz al-'Arabi li al-Dirasat al-Istratijiyyah.

Diyab, Muhammad Hafiz (1988). *Sayyid Qutb: Al-Khitab wa al-Idiyulujiyyah*. Cairo: Dar al-Thaqafah al-Jadidah.

Ghanim, Ibrahim al-Bayyumi (1992). *Al-Fikr al-Islami li al-Imam Hasan al-Banna*. Cairo: Dar al-Tawzi' wa al-Nashr al-Islamiyyah.

Ghannouchi, Rachid (2000). *Al-Harakah al-Islamiyyah wa Mas'alah al-Taghyir*. London: Al-Markaz al-Magharibi li al-Buhuth wa al-Tarjumah

Ghannouchi, Rachid (2001). *Min Tajribat al-Harakah al-Islamiyyah fi Tunis*. London: Al-Markaz al-Magharibi li al-Buhuth wa al-Tarjumah.

Ghannouchi, Rachid (2007). *Al-Hurriyyat al-'Ammah fi al-Dawlah al-Islamiyyah* (2 vols). Damascus: Markaz al-Naqid al-Thaqafi.

Hammudah, 'Adil, (1996). *Sayyid Qutb: min al-Qar'yah ila al-Mashannqah*. Cairo: Dar al-Khiyal.

Hammudah, 'Adil (1998). *Igtiyal Ra'is*. Cairo: Sina li al-Nashr.

Hanafi, Hasan (1986) A*l-Harakat al-Islamiyyah fi Misr*. Cairo: Al-Mu'assasah al-Islamiyyah li al-Nashr.

Hizb al-Tahrir (1963). *Muqadimat al-Dustur aw al-Asbab al-Mujibah lahu*. n.p.: Hizb al-Tahrir Publications.

Hizb al-Tahrir (1963). *Mafahim Siyasiyah*. n.p.: Hizb al-Tahrir Publications.

Al-Hudaybi, Hasan (1977). *Du'at la Qudat*. Cairo: Dar at-Tiba'ah wa al-Nashr al-Islamiyyah.

Huwaydi, Fahmi (1985). *Muwatinun la Dhimmiyun*. Cairo: Dar al-Shuruq.

Huwaydi, Fahmi (1987). *Iran min al-Dakhil*. Cairo: Markaz al-Ahram li al-Tarjumah wa al-Nashr.

Huwaydi, Fahmi (1993). *Al-Islam wa al-Dimuqratiyyah*. Cairo: Markaz al-Ahram li al-Tarjumah wa al-Nashr.

Imam, 'Abdallah (1981). *'Abd al-Nasir wa al-Ikhwan al-Muslimun*. Cairo: Dar al-Mawqif al-'Arabi.

Kassab, Akram (2007). *Al-Manhaj al-Da'awi 'inda al-Qaradawi*. Cairo: Maktabat Wahbah.

al-Khalidi, 'Abd al-Fattah (2010). *Sayyid Qutb: Min al-Milad ila al-Istishad* (5th edition). Damascus: Dar al-Qalam.

Malkawi, Fathi (ed.) (1996). *Al-'Ata' al-Fikri li al-Shaykh Muhammad al-Ghazali*. Amman: Al-Ma'had al-'Alami li al-Fikr al-Islami.

Al-Mawdudi, Abu'l 'Ala (1979). *Minhaj al-Inqilab al-Islami*. Beirut: Mu'assasah al-Risalah.

Al-Mawdudi, Abu'l 'Ala (1983). *Al-Jihad fi Sabil Allah*. Beirut: Mu'assasah al-Risalah.

Al-Mawdudi, Abu'l 'Ala. 1989. *Nahnu wa al-Hadarah al-Gharbiyyah*. Riyadh: Dar al-Sa'udiyyah li al-Nashr wa al-Tawzi'.

Al-Mawdudi, Abu'l 'Ala (1989). *Mabadi' al-Islam*. Beirut: Al-Maktab al-Islami.

Al-Mawdudi, Abu'l 'Ala (2006). *Manhaj al-Haya'ah al-Islamiyyah*. Cairo: Dar al-Tawzi' wa al-Nashr al-Islamiyyah.

Muhammad-Ahmad, Hasan Makki (n.d.) *Harakah al-Ikhwan al-Muslimin fi al-Sudan*. Khartoum: Dar al-Fikr.

Muhyi al-Din, Khalid (1992). *Wa al-An Attakallam*. Cairo: Markaz al-Ahram li al-Tarjumah wa al-Nashr.

Mustafa, Halah (1992). *Al-Islam al-Siyasi fi Misr*. Cairo: Markaz al-Dirasat al-Siyasiyyah wa al-Istratijiyyah bi al-Ahram.

Muru, Muhammad (1998). *Jama'at al-'Unf 1958-1998: Min al-Nash'ah ila Mubadirat Waqf al-'Unf*. Cairo: Al-Mukhtar al-Islami.

Muru, Muhammad (1990). *Tanzim al-Jihad: Judhuruhu wa Asraruhu*. Cairo: Al-Sharikah al-'Arabiyyah al-Dawliyyah li al-Nashr.

Nafi, Bashir Musa (1999). 'Al-Islamiyun al-Filistiniyun wa al-Qadiyyah al-Filistiniyyah, 1950–1980' *Marsad* 1(2): 51–78.

Al-Nabhani, Taqi al-Din (1953). *Al-Shakhsiyyah al-Islamiyyah* (3 vols). Jerusalem: Hizb al-Tahrir.

Al-Nabhani, Taqi al-Din (1953). *Nizam al-Islam*. Jerusalem: Hizb al-Tahrir.

Al-Nabhani, Taqi al-Din (1967). *Al-Khilafah*. Kuwait: Al-Matba'ah al-'Asriyyah.

Al-Nadwi, Mas'ud (n.d.). *Tarikh al-Da'wah al-Islamiyyah fi al-Hind*. Damascus: Dar al-'Arabiyyah.

Al-Nafisi, 'Abdallah (ed.) (1989). *Al-Harakah al-Islamiyyah: Ru'yah Mustaqbaliyyah*. Cairo: Maktabat Madbuli.

Al-Qaradawi, Yusuf (1959). *Al-Halal wa al-Haram fi al-Islam*. Cairo: Dar Ihya' al-Kutub al-'Arabiyyah.

Al-Qaradawi, Yusuf (1997). *Min Fiqh al-Dawlah fi al-Islam*. Cairo: Dar al-Shuruq.

Al-Qaradawi, Yusuf (2007). *Al-Din wa al-Siyasah*. Cairo: Dar al-Shuruq.

Qutb, Sayyid (1980a). *Al-'Adalah al-Ijtima'iyyah fi al-Islam*. Cairo: Dar al-Shuruq.

Qutb, Sayyid, (1980b). *Ma'alim fi at-Tariq*. Beirut: Dar al-Shuruq.

Al-Ra'i, Tawfiq Yusuf (ed.) (2001). *Al-Fikr al-Siyasi 'inda al-Ikhwan al-Muslimin*. Kuwait: Maktabah al-Manar al-Islami.

Al-Rabi'u, Turki 'Ali (2006). *Al-Harakat al-Islamiyyah fi Manzur al-Khitab al-'Arabi al-Mu'asir*. Casablanca: Al-Markaz al-Thaqafi al-'Arabi.

Rafsanjani Hashemi (2005). *Hayati* (translated by Dalal 'Abbas). Beirut: Dar al-Saqi.

Ramadan, 'Abd al-'Azim (1977). *Al-Ikhwan al-Muslimun wa al-Tanzim al-Sirri*. Cairo: Mu'assasah Ruz al-Yusuf.

Al-Sayyid, Ridwan (1997). *Siyasat al-Islam al-Mu'asir*. Beirut: Dar al-Kitab al-'Arabi.

Al-Sayyid, Ridwan (2004). *Al-Sira' 'ala al-Islam*. Beirut: Dar al-Kitab al-'Arabi.

Shadi, Salah (1981). *Safahat min al-Tarikh*. Kuwait: Sharikah al-Shu'a'ah li al-Nashr.

Shafiq, Munir (1981). *Al-Islam fi Ma'rakat al-Hadarah*. Beirut: Dar al-Kalimah.

Shafiq, Munir (1983). *Al-Islam wa Tahaddiyat al-Inhitat al-Mu'asir*. London: Dar Taha li al-Nashr.

Shita, Ibrahim al-Dassuqi (1986). *Al-Thawrah al-Iraniyyah: as-Sira', al-Malhamah, al-Nasr*. Cairo: Al-Zahra' li al-'Ilam al-'Arabi.

Al-Siba'i, Mustafa (1955). *Durus fi Da'wah al-Ikhwan al-Muslimin*. Damascus: Manshurat Qism al-Tullab li al-Ikhwan al-Muslimin.

Al-Tilmisani, 'Umar (1985). *Dhikrayat La Mudhikarat*. Cairo: Dar al-Tawzi' wa al-Nashr al-Islamiyyah.

Al-Turabi, Hasan (2003). *Al-Siyasah wa al-Hukm: Al-Nizam al-Sultaniyyah bayna al-Usul wa Sunnan al-Waqi'*. London: Dar al-Saqi.

Al-Turabi, Hasan (n.d.). *Manhajiyat al-Fiqh wa al-Tashri' al-Islami*. Khartoum: Dar Iqra'.

Al-Turabi, Hasan (n.d.) *Al-Shura wa al-Dimuqratiyyah*. Khartoum: Dar Iqra'.

Al-'Ubaydi, 'Awni Judhu' (1991). *Jama'at al-Ikhwan al-Muslimin fi al-Urdun wa Filistin: 1945–1970*. Amman: n.p.

Al-'Utaybi, Juhayman (2004). *Rasa'il Juhayman al-'Utaybi* (edited by Rifa't al-Sayyid Ahmad). Cairo: Maktabat Madbuli.

'Uthman, Wa'il (1976). *Asrar al-Harakah at-Tulabiyyah*. Cairo: n.p.

Zidan, Ahmad (2003). *Bin Ladin bila Qina'*. Beirut: Al-Sharikah al-'Alimiyyah li al-Kitab.

Al-Zubaydi, Mufid (2004). *Tarikh al-Mamlakah al-'Arabiyyah al-Sa'udiyyah*. Amman: Dar 'Usamah.